STERLING
Test Prep

AP Physics 2
Review

3rd edition

www.Sterling-Prep.com

Our Commitment to the Environment

Sterling Test Prep is committed to protecting our planet's resources by supporting environmental organizations with proven track records of conservation, ecological research and education and preservation of vital natural resources. A portion of our profits is donated to help these organizations so they can continue their critical missions. These organizations include:

For over 40 years, Ocean Conservancy has been advocating for a healthy ocean by supporting sustainable solutions based on science and cleanup efforts. Among many environmental achievements, Ocean Conservancy laid the groundwork for an international moratorium on commercial whaling, played an instrumental role in protecting fur seals from overhunting and banning the international trade of sea turtles. The organization created national marine sanctuaries and served as the lead non-governmental organization in the designation of 10 of the 13 marine sanctuaries.

For 25 years, Rainforest Trust has been saving critical lands for conservation through land purchases and protected area designations. Rainforest Trust has played a central role in the creation of 73 new protected areas in 17 countries, including the Falkland Islands, Costa Rica and Peru. Nearly 8 million acres have been saved thanks to Rainforest Trust's support of in-country partners across Latin America, with over 500,000 acres of critical lands purchased outright for reserves.

Since 1980, Pacific Whale Foundation has been saving whales from extinction and protecting our oceans through science and advocacy. As an international organization, with ongoing research projects in Hawaii, Australia, and Ecuador, PWF is an active participant in global efforts to address threats to whales and other marine life. A pioneer in non-invasive whale research, PWF was an early leader in educating the public, from a scientific perspective, about whales and the need for ocean conservation.

With your purchase, you support environmental causes around the world.

Table of Contents

Table of Contents (*continued*)

Table of Contents (*continued*)

Table of Contents (*continued*)

**For best results, this book should be supplemented by
"AP Physics 2 Practice Questions" book
or online practice material
at www.Sterling-Prep.com**

To access more AP Physics 2 questions online at a
special pricing for book owners, see page 407

AP Physics 2 Exam

The AP Physics 2 Exam is 3 hours long and includes a multiple-choice section (90 minutes) and a free-response section (90 minutes). The multiple-choice section is divided into two parts, and the free-response section is divided into three parts, as shown in the table below. Student performance metrics on these four parts are compiled and weighted to determine an overall AP Exam score. Questions are answered filling in the appropriate oval on the answer sheet.

Section	Question Type	Number of Questions	Timing (minutes)	Percentage of Total Exam Score
I	Multiple-choice questions (single-select)	45	90	50%
	Multiple-choice questions (multi-select)	5		
II	Part A: Experimental-design question	1	90	50%
	Part B: Quantitative/qualitative-translation question	1		
	Part C: Short-answer questions	2		

Scientific or graphing calculators may be used by students throughout both sections of the exam. A list of approved graphing calculators can be located on the College Board website.

Calculators should not be used to store data/text or to communicate between other calculators. Proctors will monitor activity to ensure compliance during the exam.

Students are not allowed to bring their equation sheets. Rather, equation tables will be provided to students at the beginning of their exam.

Assessment of Student Learning

AP Physics 2 exam questions evaluate students' ability to:

- provide qualitative and quantitative explanations of physical phenomena based on physics principles and theories;

- mathematically and symbolically solve problems;

- design and describe experiments, analyze data and sources of error, draw conclusions based on evidence;

- develop and interpret conceptual models.

Topics Covered on AP Physics 2 Exam

- Thermodynamics: laws of thermodynamics, ideal gases, and kinetic theory

- Fluid statics and dynamics

- Electrostatics: electric force, electric field, and the electric potential

- DC circuits and RC circuits (steady-state only)

- Magnetism and electromagnetic induction

- Geometric and physical optics

- Quantum physics, atomic and nuclear physics

Types of Questions

Multiple-Choice Questions

There are two types of multiple-choice questions featured on the AP Physics 2 exam, both of which include four possible answer choices per question.

The first type, *single-select*, are questions requiring students to choose the one correct answer.

The second type, *multi-select*, require students to choose the two correct answers.

Experimental-Design Questions

These questions require students to design and describe an investigation, analyze authentic lab data and observations to identify patterns or explain physical phenomena.

Qualitative/Quantitative-Translation Questions

These questions require students to translate between quantitative and qualitative justification and reasoning.

Short-Answer Questions

These questions require a paragraph long coherent argument statement. Space is provided for students to show all their work in answering these questions.

Test-Taking Strategies

The best way to do well on AP Physics 2 is to be really good at physics. There is no way around that. Prepare for the test as much as you can, so you can answer with confidence as many questions as possible. With that being said, there are strategies you should employ when you approach a question on the exam.

The task of pacing yourself will become easier if you are aware of the number of questions you need to answer to reach the score you want to get. Always strive for the highest score, but be realistic about your level of preparation. It may be helpful if you research what counts as a good score for the colleges you are applying to. You can talk to admissions offices at colleges, research college guidebooks or specific college websites, or talk to your guidance counselor. You should find out which score would earn you a college placement credit and which score would be beneficial to your application without earning credit.

Below are some test-taking strategies to help you maximize your score. Many of these strategies you already know and they may seem like common sense. However, when a student is feeling the pressure of a timed test, these common-sense strategies might be forgotten.

Mental Attitude

If you psych yourself out, chances are you will do poorly on the test. To do well on the test, particularly physics, which calls for cool, systemic thinking, you must remain calm. If you start to panic, your mind won't be able to find the correct solutions to the questions.

Many steps can be taken before the test to increase your confidence level. Buying this book is a good start because you can begin to practice, learn the information you should know to master the topics and get used to answering physics questions. However, there are other things you should keep in mind:

Study in advance. The information will be more manageable, and you will feel more confident if you've studied at regular intervals during the weeks leading up to the test. Cramming the night before is not a successful tactic.

Be well rested. If you are up late the night before the test, chances are you will have a difficult time concentrating and focusing on the day of the test, as you will not feel fresh and alert.

Come up for air. The best way to take this three-hour-long test is not to keep your head down, concentrating intensely on the entire time. Even though you only have 1 minute and 48 seconds per question (on the multiple-choice section) and there is no time to waste, it is recommended to take a few seconds between the questions to take a deep breath and relax your muscles.

Time Management

Aside from good preparation, time management is the most important strategy that you should know how to use on any test. You have an average time of 1 minute 48 seconds for each question on the multiple choice section. Even though, you will breeze through some in less than a minute, with others you may be stuck on for three minutes.

Don't dwell on any one question for too long. You should aim to look at every question on the test. It would be unfortunate to not earn the points for a question you could have easily answered just because you did not get a chance to look at it. If you are still in the first half of the test and find yourself spending more than a minute on one question and don't see yourself getting closer to solving it, it is better to move on. It will be more productive if you come back to this question with a fresh mind at the end of the test. You do not want to lose points because you were stuck on one or a few questions and did not get a chance to work with other questions that are easy for you.

Nail the easy questions quickly. Each student has their strong and weak topics, and you might be a master on a certain type of questions that are normally considered difficult. Skip the questions you are struggling with and nail the easy ones.

Skip the unfamiliar. If you come across a question that is totally unfamiliar to you, skip it. Do not try to figure out what is going on or what they are trying to ask. At the end of the test, you can go back to these questions if you have time.

If you are encountering a question that you have no clue about, most likely you won't be able to answer it through analysis. The better strategy is to leave such questions to the end and use the guessing strategy on them at the end of the test.

Understanding the Question

It is important that you know what the question is asking before you select your answer choice. This seems obvious, but it is surprising how many students don't read a question carefully because they rush through the test and select a wrong answer choice.

A successful student will not just read the question but will take a moment to understand the question before even looking at the answer choices. This student will be able to separate the important information from distracters and will not get confused by the questions that are asking to identify a false statement (which is the correct answer).

Once you've identified what you're dealing with and what is being asked, you should be able to spend less time picking the right answer. If the question is asking for a general concept, try to answer the question before looking at the answer choices, then look at the choices. If you see a choice that matches the answer you thought of, most likely it is the correct choice.

Correct Way to Guess

Random guessing won't help you on the test, but educated guessing is the strategy you should use in certain situations if you can eliminate at least one (or even two) of the four possible choices.

If you randomly entered responses for the first 20 questions, there is a 25% chance of guessing correctly on any given question. Therefore, the odds are you would guess right on 5 questions and wrong on 15 questions. However, if for each of the 20 questions you can eliminate one answer choice because you know it to be wrong (wrong order of magnitude, wrong units, etc.), you will have a 33% chance of being right and your odds would move to 7 questions right and 13 questions wrong. Correspondingly, if you can eliminate 2 wrong answers, you can increase your odds to 50%.

Guessing is not cheating and should not be viewed that way. Rather it is a form of "partial credit" because while you might not be sure of the correct answer, you do have relevant knowledge to identify one or two choices that are wrong.

AP Physics 2 Tips

Tip 1: Know the formulas

Since 70–80% of the test requires that you know how to use the formulas, it is imperative that you memorize and understand when to use each one. It is not permitted to bring any papers with notes to the test, but you will be given a sheet with formulas allowed by the College Board.

As you work with this book, you will learn the application of all the important physical formulas and will use them in different question types.

Tip 2: Know how to manipulate the formulas

You must know how to apply the formulas in addition to merely memorizing them. Questions will be worded in ways unfamiliar to you to test whether you can manipulate equations to calculate the correct answer.

Knowing that $P = I\Delta V$ is not helpful without understanding that $\Delta V = P / I$ because it is unlikely that a question will ask to calculate the power with a given current and voltage. Rather you are likely to be asked to calculate the acceleration of an object of a given mass with force acting on it.

Tip 3: Estimating

This tip is only helpful for quantitative questions. For example, estimating can help you choose the correct answer if you have a general sense of the order of magnitude. This is especially applicable to questions where all answer choices have different orders of magnitude, and you can save time that you would have to spend on calculations.

Tip 4: Draw the question

Don't hesitate to write, draw or graph your thought process once you have read and understood the question. This can help you determine what kind of information you are dealing with. Draw the force and velocity vectors, ray/wave paths, or anything else that may be helpful. Even if a question does not require a graphic answer, drawing a graph (for example, a sketch of a particle's velocity) can allow a solution to become obvious.

Tip 5: Eliminating wrong answers

This tip utilizes the strategy of educated guessing. You can usually eliminate one or two answer choices right away in many questions. In addition, there are certain types of questions for which you can use a particular elimination method.

By using logical estimations for qualitative questions, you can eliminate the answer choices that are unreasonably high or unreasonably low.

Last helpful tip: fill in your answers carefully

This seems like a simple thing, but it is extremely important. Many test takers make mistakes when filling in answers whether it is a paper test or computer-based test. Make sure you pay attention and check off the answer choice you chose as correct.

We want to hear from you

Your feedback is important to us because we strive to provide the highest quality prep materials. Email us if you have any questions, comments or suggestions, so we can incorporate your feedback into future editions.

Customer Satisfaction Guarantee

If you have any concerns about this book, including printing issues, contact us and we will resolve any issues to your satisfaction.

info@sterling-prep.com

We reply to all emails – please check your spam folder

Thank you for choosing our products to achieve your educational goals!

Chapter 1

Thermodynamics

- **The Basics of Thermal Physics**

- **Heat, Temperature and Thermal Energy**

- **Heat Capacity and Specific Heat**

- **Heat Transfer**

- **Thermodynamic Systems**

- **The Zeroth Law of Thermodynamics**

- **First Law of Thermodynamics: Conservation of Energy**

- **Second Law of Thermodynamics: Entropy**

- **The Third Law of Thermodynamics**

- **Enthalpy**

- **Gibbs Free Energy**

- **PV diagrams**

- **The Carnot Cycle**

- **The Kinetic Theory of Gases**

- **Coefficient of Linear Expansion**

- **Phase Diagram: Pressure and Temperature**

- **Latent Heat**

The Basics of Thermal Physics

Energy is defined as the ability to do work and can be classified as either kinetic or potential energy. Kinetic energy is the energy of an object in motion; for example, a rolling ball, moving the car and dropped coin all have kinetic energy. Potential energy is defined as the potential to do work. As discussed earlier, there are many forms of potential energy, including gravitational potential energy, spring potential energy, chemical potential energy, etc. For example, the hammer in the figure below initially has gravitational potential energy. When the hand holding the hammer relaxes, the hammer begins to move downward, converting its potential energy into kinetic energy.

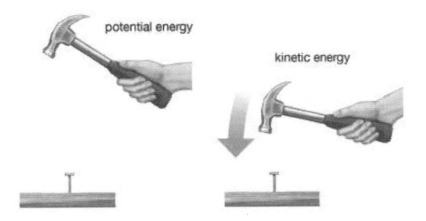

Thermal physics is the science of heat and the energy it retains. In all situations, the conservation of energy holds true, meaning there is no loss of energy. However, in most real-life examples, non-conservative forces play a role and energy is not always converted into useful work. When these forces act on an object, the energy they use by acting over a distance cannot be regained—but that does not mean the energy disappears into thin air.

If a book is pushed along a table, a force of friction is exerted on the book.

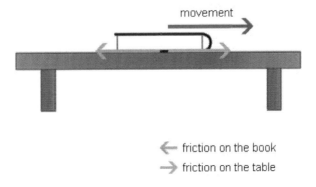

Depending on how much effort is put into pushing the book, it travels a certain distance, and then come to rest as it steadily decreases in velocity. The book comes to rest because there is a force of friction opposing its motion.

As its velocity decreases, so do its kinetic energy ($\frac{1}{2}mv^2$). Conservation of energy must hold true, so the loss in kinetic energy is energy being converted into heat. However, neither the surface of the counter nor the bottom of the book feels tangibly warm, because more energy is needed to raise the temperature to where the difference can be felt.

If the process is repeated back and forth over a period, the bottom of the book and the surface of the table begins to feel warm to the touch, because enough energy had been deposited to raise the temperature noticeably.

On a microscopic level, thermal energy is the energy related to the vibration of molecules and atoms. Every bit of matter is made of billions and trillions of small molecules, and even in solids these particles never stand perfectly still. The amount of movement an object has in its molecules relegates how much thermal energy the object holds.

The figure below displays a closed container of gas, in which the gas molecules are shown in random motion throughout the container. The thermal energy of the gas is directly related to the kinetic energy of these molecules. The more kinetic energy they have, the more thermal energy they have.

With less kinetic energy, the gas has less thermal energy.

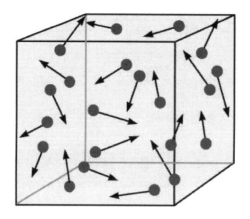

Heat, Temperature and Thermal Energy

Heat and temperature are often used interchangeably in everyday language. However, this usage is incorrect. *Heat* is a form of energy and exists independently from any medium. On the other hand, the *temperature* is a measure of energy in a specific medium and is thus dependent on the material itself. Temperature and heat are connected, but heat is the total energy due to molecular motion and temperature is the average measure of the energy stored within a certain substance. Some substances respond drastically to a change in thermal energy, and some have a subtler reaction. This all depends on the material as heat capacity, which is discussed later.

The measure of the quantity of thermal energy transmitted from one body to another is heat. An object does not "contain" heat, but it can have a certain amount of thermal energy. Heat can be measured in joules (J) but is frequently measured in calories (cal). Conveniently, *calories* relate heat to change in temperature, which is useful when solving problems in thermal physics.

The definition of a calorie is the amount of heat needed to raise the temperature of one gram of water by one degree Celsius (g/°C).

$$1\ cal = 1\ \frac{g}{°C} = 4.19\ J$$

Food Calories are not the same as heat calories. Notice one is capitalized and the other is not. This is similar to the relationship between kilograms and grams (1 Calorie = 1000 calories). Another difference to note is that while Calories measure stored energy as calories do, they measure the energy stored in the chemical bonds of food that are broken down and stored when digested.

Regardless, Calories are still a measure of energy in a substance and can be converted to their equivalents of conventional energy. For example,

Calories contained in 5 lbs. of spaghetti have enough energy to brew a pot of coffee; calories in one piece of cheesecake can power a 60W incandescent light bulb for 1.5 hours; 217 Big Macs contain enough energy to drive a vehicle for 88 miles.

In the United States, the unit of temperature is the *Fahrenheit* (°F). However, the SI unit is the *Celsius* (°C). This is an easier system to remember, as water freezes at 0°C and boils at 100 °C (instead of the 32 °F and 212 °F).

The conversion between the two scales is computed using the relationship:

$$°F = \frac{9}{5}°C + 32$$

Another unit of temperature used in scientific calculations is the *Kelvin*. This scale is used when working with gases, as usually, very low temperatures are in the question. Kelvin (K) is the measure of absolute temperature.

The coldest theoretical temperature any substance can have is *absolute zero*, and it is equal to 0 K. This is the same temperature as –273 °C!

The figure below shows three thermometers displaying equal temperatures in the three common units of temperature.

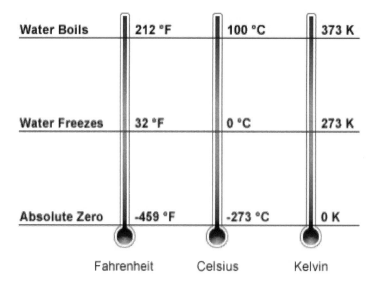

Temperature itself is the average amount of kinetic energy in the particles (molecules and atoms) that make up a material. At absolute zero, these particles will theoretically have no kinetic energy, and therefore no movement.

Kelvin and Celsius use the same step in their degree measurements, which can make many calculations easier. For example, a temperature difference is the same in Kelvin as it is in Celsius so when asked to calculate a temperature difference in either of these units you do not have to convert.

If required to convert from one to the other, the conversion can be performed by adding 273 to the Celsius temperature to determine the degrees in Kelvin:

$$K = °C + 273$$

Another important note is that absolute zero can never be attained. Scientists have achieved temperatures close to absolute zero but can never fully reach it.

For example, the lowest temperature ever recorded was in 2003, by a group of scientists from MIT. They successfully cooled sodium gas to a temperature of half-a-billionth of a degree above absolute zero, but not at absolute zero.

Notes

Heat Capacity and Specific Heat

The *heat capacity* of a substance is the ratio of the absorbed heat energy to the resulting temperature change. The SI unit for heat capacity is joule per Kelvin (J/K).

When measuring the heat capacity of a substance, a variable must be held constant, since the heat capacity of a system depends on the temperature itself, the pressure and the volume of the system. To get a constant reading, gases and liquids are normally measured at constant volume and subjected to a certain pressure.

When pressure is held constant, the process to define a heat capacity is an *isobaric process*; when the volume is held constant, it is an *isochoric process*. These are noted with either a c_p or a c_v, respectively.

A similar concept is *specific heat*. This is the measurement of heat needed to raise the temperature of a certain mass of a given substance (the heat capacity of a substance per unit of mass). Notice that the heat capacity and the specific heat of a substance are similar.

However, specific heat is the ratio of energy absorbed to the temperature rise per unit of mass of the substance, and heat capacity is the ratio of energy absorbed to the temperature rise. The specific heat is a characteristic of the substance and thus does not change.

Below is a table of the specific heats of several common substances:

Specific heats of selected materials	
Material	**C(J/kg·K)**
Aluminum	879
Concrete	850
Diamond	509
Glass	840
Helium	5,193
Water	4,181

Notes

Substances such as metals (like copper) have a low specific heat because it does not take a lot of energy to transfer the heat and excite the molecules, therefore raising the measurement of their average energy (raising their temperature). Materials that are difficult to heat, such as rubber, have a much higher specific heat because more energy is required to raise its temperature the same amount.

This is the reason for the *sea breeze effect*. The previous table shows that water has a much higher heat capacity than other common materials found on land. This means that it takes more energy to raise an ocean by 1 °C than it does to raise city sidewalks by the same amount. Thus, during the day, land warms faster than water when subjected to the same amount of thermal energy from the sun.

The hot land heats the air above it, causing it to rise and create a low-pressure system above it. The cooler water creates a high-pressure system, due to air cooling down and descending. The difference in pressures creates a flow of air from the sea to the land during the day, which is a sea breeze.

At night, the land cools faster than the water (due to its lower specific heat capacity), and the effect is reversed as air flows from land to sea.

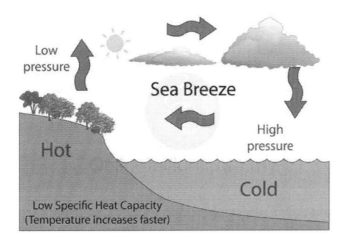

Using the specific heat of a substance (*c*), heat and temperature are related by:

$$Q = mc\Delta T$$

where *Q* is the heat transferred to the material (J), *m* is the mass of the object being heated (kg), and ΔT is the change in temperature (K).

Notes

For example, 3,200 J of heat is added to 1.0 kg of water (c = 4,190 J/kg·°C at an initial temperature of 10 °C. By rearranging the equation for specific heat, the increase in temperature can be solved for.

$$\Delta T = \frac{Q}{mc}$$

$$\Delta T = \frac{3,200 \text{ J}}{1.0 \text{ kg} \cdot 4,190 \, \frac{\text{J}}{\text{kg}} \cdot {}^{\circ}\text{C}}$$

$$\Delta T = 0.76 \, {}^{\circ}\text{C}$$

Remember when solving for ΔT, that it is the change in temperature. This value must be added to the initial temperature to find the final temperature, or subtracted from the final to find the initial.

To fully analyze a reaction, it must be contained so that all of the products can be observed. A special device called a *calorimeter* is considered ideally-insulated, such that any heat freed by the process taking place is transferred to either the other substances within the calorimeter or the calorimeter itself—but no heat is lost to the surroundings. Since no thermal energy is lost, a scientist can measure the heat of a reaction by inserting a thermometer into a calorimeter and recording the temperature before and after the reaction takes place. A device called a stirrer is used to ensure all contents of the calorimeter are well mixed and react uniformly. Below is an example of a simple calorimeter used to demonstrate the concept:

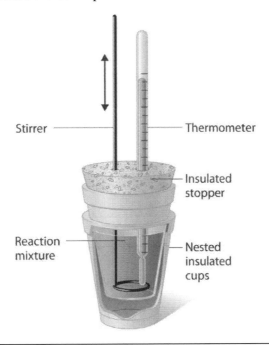

Notes

Heat Transfer

Heat can be transferred between two objects in three ways: conduction, convection or radiation.

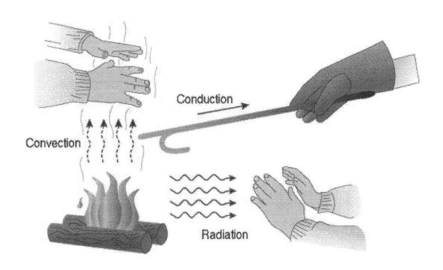

Conduction occurs when heat is transferred through direct contact. On a cold winter night, when a person wraps their hands around a cup of hot cocoa, their fingers warm up because they are in direct contact with the warm mug, which is in direct contact with the warm liquid. The same process is happening at a molecular level. The liquid in the mug contains heat energy, and the molecules of the liquid are in constant motion. These molecules then collide against the molecules in the mug, increasing their motion.

The action of the collisions gradually transfers some of the energy from the liquid molecules to the mug molecules. In the same way, the mug then transfers its heat to a persons' hands. They feel the transfer of energy as an increase in temperature; thus, their hands feel warm.

The figure below gives a visual approximation of the process of conduction through a mug:

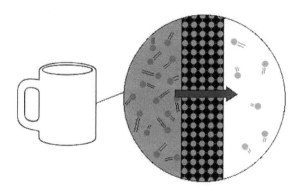

When heat is transferred by conduction, the rate of heat transfer (H) can be calculated. It is measured in joules per second, or watts (W). This describes the amount of energy (heat) conducted during a set time interval:

$$H = \frac{kA\Delta T}{t}$$

where ΔT is the temperature difference across the object (K), A is the cross-sectional area (m^2), t is the thickness of the material (m), and k is the thermal conductivity of the material (J/s·m·k). This quantity is a characteristic of the material and is usually is given in the problem.

Below is a table of common values of thermal conductivities.

Thermal Conductivities of Selected Materials	
Material	**k (J/s·m·K)**
Aluminum	237
Concrete	1
Copper	386
Glass	0.9
Stainless Steel	16.5
Water	0.6

When calculating heat conduction through an object, it is important to note that the cross-sectional area refers to the area through which the heat is being conducted. In the case of the mug example, the heat is being conducted through its outer curved surface. Therefore, the cross-sectional area is the circumference of the mug times its height. The thickness, in this case, is the thickness of the mug itself. If the mug were set down on a table and the heat conduction to the table was to be calculated, then the cross-sectional area is the area of the bottom of the mug, rather the area of the sidewalls.

Convection is the process of transferring heat through the flow of energized molecules from one place to another. This is done through the movement of fluids. Remember that gas is a fluid, as it is able to flow and change shape depending on its container.

For example, when a pot of water is placed on a stove, the water at the bottom starts to warm up first. As it warms, it rises and is replaced by cooler water. This circulation of water transfers the thermal energy from the bottom of the pot to the top and results in a closed pattern of fluid flow as *convection currents.*

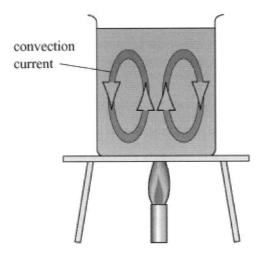

A convection oven works in a similar way, but with gas molecules instead of liquid molecules. Air is blown past a heating element to the oven chamber. When passing through the heating element, the air molecules are energized by the hot element. They are then circulated throughout the oven by the airflow provided by the fan until all of the molecules are energized to the same amount.

Although convection is similar to conduction, be sure to notice the difference.

Conduction is the flow of heat between two materials in direct contact, while convection is the flow of energized molecules. When the energized molecules settle, they then deposit their energy through conduction.

The last form of heat transfer is *radiation*. Radiation is the transfer of energy through electromagnetic waves. Radiation is emitted from all objects or surfaces with heat energy. The more energy contained, the more radiation emitted. For example, a hot piece of metal radiates heat in the form of infrared electromagnetic waves. As the metal gets hotter, it begins to radiate heat in the visual spectrum, thus making the metal appear "red hot."

Another well-known source of radiation is the Sun. It releases electromagnetic waves that travel through space, then through the atmosphere to heat up Earth. Similarly, holding one's hands next to a fire heats them through radiation. Notice that radiation is the transfer of heat through electromagnetic waves, and therefore does not require a medium; thus, it can occur in a vacuum.

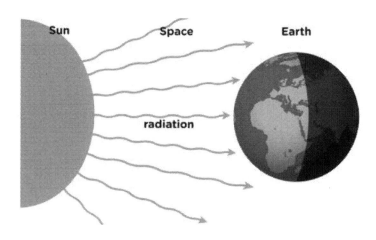

The power radiated by an object is related to its temperature and can be calculated by:

$$P = e\sigma A(T^4 - T_C^4)$$

where P is the power radiated (W), e is the emissivity of the radiator, σ is Stefan's constant equal to $5.67 \times 10^{-8} \frac{W}{m^2 K}$, where A is the area of the radiating surface (m²), T is the temperature of the radiator (K) and T_C is the temperature of the surroundings (K)

Thermodynamic Systems

A *thermodynamic system* is used to describe thermodynamic processes and is a quantity of matter around which a boundary can be drawn. Thermodynamic systems can be isolated, closed or open. An isolated system has no transfer of heat, work or matter with its surroundings. A closed system may transfer heat and work to its surroundings but never matter. An open system can transfer all three to its surroundings.

State functions, sometimes called state quantities, are a group of equations representative of the properties of a system, which depend only on the current state of the system, not on the way the current state was achieved. Thermodynamic state functions include enthalpy, entropy, and Gibbs free energy.

System	Exchanges with surrounding	Total amt. of Energy	Example	Illustration
Open	Energy & Matter	Does not remain constant	Solution kept in an open flask	
Closed	Only Energy	Does not remain constant	Solution kept in a sealed flask	
Isolated	Neither energy Nor matter	Remains constant	Sealed flask kept in a thermos flask	

Notes

The Zeroth Law of Thermodynamics

The Zeroth Law is named such because it is the logical predecessor of the First and Second Laws of Thermodynamics. The *Zeroth Law of Thermodynamics* states that if two systems are in thermal equilibrium with a third system, the two initial systems are in thermal equilibrium. This means that all three systems contain the same amount of heat energy (the same temperature) and do not exchange any heat. This is an observation and the fundamental idea behind thermodynamics.

The figure below demonstrates the Zeroth Law. If system A is in equilibrium with B, and system C is in equilibrium with B, then system A and C must be in equilibrium, and all three systems must be at the same temperature.

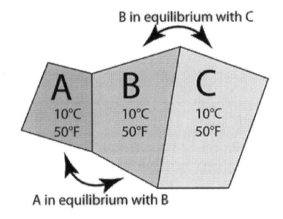

It is important to notice, however, that although no net transfer of heat occurs between systems in equilibrium, thermal energy is still technically transferring between the systems. This requires every unit of energy that is passed from any system to have the same value of energy passed back into the system.

This holds even if the two systems contain materials with different specific heats. This means that there must be a property that can be considered the same upon which heat transfer depends, and that property is temperature.

Notes

First Law of Thermodynamics: Conservation of Energy

Like matter, energy is always conserved. It can neither be created nor destroyed. The *First Law of Thermodynamics* relates closely to the *internal energy of a substance*. The internal energy refers to the microscopic energy of the disordered motion of particles. This energy cannot be seen and has no apparent effect on the motion of the object as a whole, but it does play a part in the thermodynamic properties of the substance. Internal energy is represented by the symbol (U).

For example, a glass of water does not look like it contains any kinetic or potential energy. However, on the atomic scale, its molecules are whizzing around any which way, moving at hundreds of meters per second. If the water is dumped out of the glass, its internal energy has no apparent effect on its motion.

Water

The First Law states that the internal energy of a system increases if heat is added to the system, or if work is done on the system. The difference between the amount of heat added to the system (Q) and the work done by the system (W) is equal to the total change in internal energy (ΔU):

$$\Delta U = \Delta Q - \Delta W$$

As with every energy, the unit of internal energy is the joule (J), although it is sometimes expressed using calories (cal).

By convention, work done by a system is negative, and work done on a system is positive. Occasionally, the above equation is written as $\Delta U = \Delta Q + \Delta W$, and ΔW is defined as the work done on the system. Be sure to take note of which form is being used.

Using the quantities in this equation, it can be determined what a thermodynamic system is undergoing. For example, in a chemical reaction, if ΔQ is some quantity less than zero, the reaction is losing heat.

This reaction is exothermic and contains heat as a product. If ΔQ is some quantity greater than zero, the reaction is absorbing heat from its surroundings. This is an endothermic reaction and contains heat as a reactant.

The figure below depicts both types of reactions.

On the left, the reaction is exothermic because heat is produced and released to the surroundings of the system; on the right, the reaction is endothermic because heat is absorbed from the surroundings.

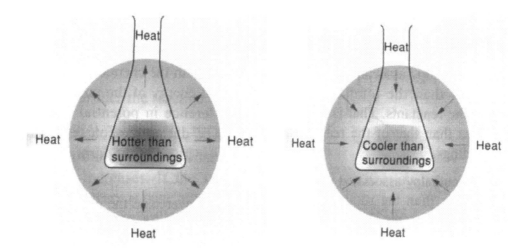

Second Law of Thermodynamics: Entropy

The *Second Law of Thermodynamics* states that in an isolated system (no transfer of heat, work, or matter), a process either increases in entropy or stays constant, but it never decreases. The only exception to this is an open system (heat, work, and matter can be transferred to surroundings), which can decrease in entropy only because it increases the entropy of its surroundings.

In terms of heat flow, the Second Law states that heat flows spontaneously from a hot object to a cold one, but it never spontaneously flows in the opposite direction. For example, a bowl of ice cream never gets colder in a warm room; it always gets warmer.

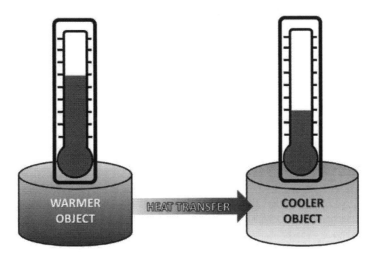

Entropy is a measure of disorder within a system. In reality, it is more a measure of multiplicity and likelihood—how likely a system will resemble the same thing twice, or how likely a reaction is to happen.

The entropy of a natural system never decreases, as it is the natural tendency of all things to move towards maximum disorder—maximum entropy.

For example, a gas expands to fill a space, because there are then more ways it can arrange its given particles—more multiplicities.

Therefore, a solid has less entropy than a liquid, which has much less entropy than a gas.

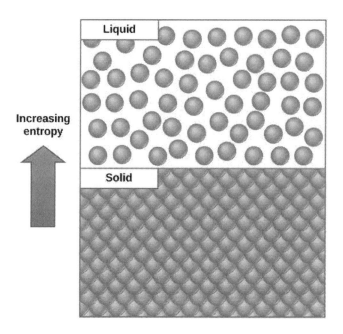

According to the Second Law of Thermodynamics, entropy is given by the equation (entropy can stay constant or increase but never decrease):

$$\Delta S \geq \frac{Q}{T}$$

where ΔS is the change in entropy of a process or reaction (J/K), Q is the heat transferred (J), and T is the temperature (K).

Understand that just because a system wants to increase in entropy does not mean that the system cannot become more orderly. It means that to do so; outside energy must be transferred into the system—it cannot do it on its own.

This is a *nonspontaneous process* because energy or work must be added for it to occur.

A *spontaneous process* is the opposite and requires no energy input to occur. For example, a valve connects a container with air and another container at a vacuum. When the valve is opened, the air flows from the container with air to the container at a vacuum.

No work or energy is needed for this to happen. Therefore the process is spontaneous; at the end of the reaction, the entropy has increased. In order for the reverse to occur, energy must be added to the system to re-pressurize the original container with air.

This is an example of a nonspontaneous reaction.

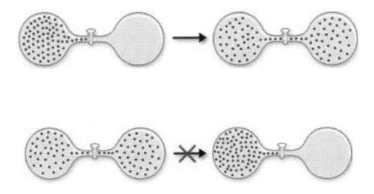

Another important idea to note is that the entropy of the universe always increases when a spontaneous process occurs.

This is expressed as:

$$\Delta S_{universe} > 0$$

Notes

The Third Law of Thermodynamics

The *Third Law of Thermodynamics* states that as the temperature of a system approaches absolute zero, the entropy approaches a constant value. Typically, this constant value is zero.

In this definition, the entropy of a system is related to the number of microstates possible. Microstates refer to all the atomic configurations possible.

This equation represents the relationship:

$$S = k \times ln\ (\Omega)$$

where S is the entropy (J/K), k is Boltzmann's constant (1.381×10^{-23} J/K), and Ω is the number of microstates.

Only one microstate is possible at absolute zero, and so Ω equals 1:

$$S = k \times ln(1) = k \times 0 = 0$$

Therefore, the entropy of a system at absolute zero is zero. However, some systems have more than one minimum energy state. That is, as their temperature approaches absolute zero, the entropy levels off at a value other than zero.

It is impossible to cool any process to absolute zero in a finite number of steps.

In the image on the left, $T = 0$ can be reached following an infinite number of steps (step lines between X_1 or X_2). However, in the image on the right, $T = 0$ is reached by a finite number of steps, each getting closer and closer to zero, but never to zero.

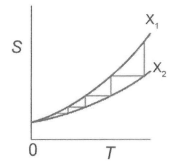 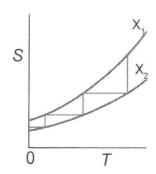

Notes

Enthalpy

The *enthalpy* of a system is the amount of heat used at constant pressure in a system or reaction and is given in SI units of Joules. It describes the energy changes of the system, and can be written as:

$$\Delta U = \Delta H - P\Delta V$$

where ΔH is the change in enthalpy of a system (J), P is the pressure (Pa), and ΔV is the change in volume (m^3).

During an isobaric process (pressure is held constant), such as that conducted in an open container, the change in enthalpy equals the amount of heat transferred during the process.

Most reactions do not give off a lot of gaseous products, and as a result, there is little work associated with the reaction. This means that the change in energy of the system is equal to the change in enthalpy:

$$\Delta E \approx \Delta H$$

Since the enthalpy is equal to the transfer of thermal energy (heat), the type of reaction, the system displays can be determined. Note, this only works at constant pressure.

An exothermic reaction has a change in enthalpy less than zero.

An endothermic reaction has a change in enthalpy greater than zero.

Since enthalpy is a state function, it represents a property of a system. It can be used to describe a reaction or an equation for a reaction.

This is stated by *Hess' Law*, which says that the change of enthalpy in a reaction is equal to the sum of the products' enthalpy, minus the sum of the reactants' enthalpy:

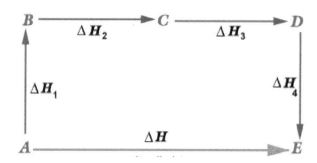

$$\Delta^H{}_{rxn} = \Sigma^H{}_{products} - \Sigma^H{}_{reactants}$$

Gibbs Free Energy

J. Willard Gibbs was an American physicist who introduced the concept of free energy to thermodynamics. The equation for free energy is given by:

$$\Delta G = \Delta H - T\Delta S$$

where G is Gibbs free energy (J).

If at a given temperature and pressure, the change in G is negative, then the reaction is spontaneous.

If G is equal to zero, the reaction is at equilibrium.

If G is positive, the reaction is nonspontaneous.

Because Gibbs free energy depends on signs, its value can be calculated quickly using rough estimates of values.

The table below gives a quick approximation for the value of the free energy, and whether the reaction is spontaneous or nonspontaneous.

ΔH	ΔS	Result
-	+	Spontaneous at all temperatures
+	+	Spontaneous at high temperatures
-	-	Spontaneous at low temperatures
+	-	Not spontaneous at any temperatures

Notes

PV Diagrams

A *PV diagram* shows the thermodynamic process by graphing pressure against volume. The work done by the system is equal to the area under the curve.

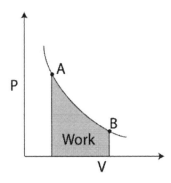

A process can be labeled with four titles: adiabatic, isothermal, isobaric and isochoric. An *isothermal reaction* keeps temperature constant ($\Delta T = 0$). This means that the change in internal energy must stay the same, as an increase in thermal energy (heat) results in an increase in temperature ($\Delta U = 0$).

The PV diagram of an isothermal process is given below:

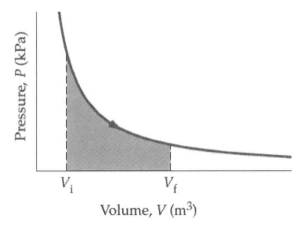

An *adiabatic process* is one in which there is no transfer of heat ($Q = 0$). This means that the change in energy is equal to the work.

This process is often confused with the isothermal process because it is sometimes assumed that no transfer of heat means no change in temperature.

However, this is not true—in isothermal instances, heat energy must be allowed into or out of the reaction to keep the temperature constant.

Unlike the isothermal reaction, an adiabatic process occurs quickly and has a PV graph much steeper than the isothermal process, but in the same shape.

Adiabatic processes include a tire pump or a sharp expulsion of breath.

Adiabatic PV diagrams are shown in reference to isothermal lines called *isotherms*.

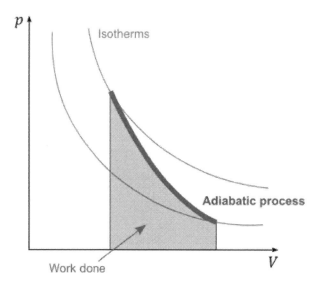

Isobaric reactions keep the pressure constant. When this occurs, the work is equal to the pressure times the change in volume ($W = P\Delta V$).

The graph of an isobaric reaction is a horizontal line. Some examples include a piston in an engine, or a flexible container open to Earth's atmosphere.

When pressure is constant, the PV graph of an isobaric process is a straight line.

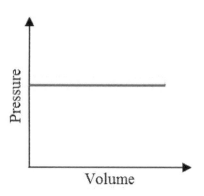

An *isochoric process* is called an isovolumetric process. This means the volume is kept constant. Since there is no movement, the work is zero, and all of the change in energy is due to the amount of heat added to the system (W = 0, ΔE = Q).

Isochoric processes include those inside a closed and rigid container or a constant volume thermometer. The graph of an isochoric reaction is a vertical line.

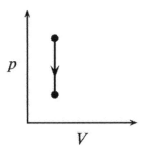

A recap of the processes, along with their relationships to the Ideal Gas Law, is displayed below:

Process	Constant	PV Diagram	Ideal Gas Law	First Law of Thermodynamics
Isobaric	Pressure	Horizontal line	V α T	$\Delta U = Q + W$
Isochoric	Volume	Vertical line	P α T	$\Delta U = Q$
Isothermal	Temperature	Curved line	PV α T	$\Delta U = 0$
Adiabatic	No heat exchanged	Curved line (jumps to different isotherm)	PV = nRT (only "nR" are constant)	$\Delta U = W$

Types of Work Cycles

In cyclic reactions, the work done is the area enclosed in the graph. These reactions are comprised of different processes, as shown below.

As in the diagram, work is done by the gas when the volume increases and the pressure decreases and is done on gas when volume decreases and the pressure increases.

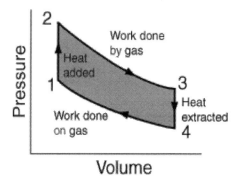

The Carnot Cycle

The *Kelvin-Planck statement* of the Second Law of Thermodynamics references heat engines. It states that it is impossible to extract an amount of heat from a "hot reservoir" (Q_2) and use all of it to do work. Some of this heat must be exhausted to a "cold reservoir" (Q_1). A perfect heat engine would use all of the energy taken from the hot reservoir to do work. This is not possible because all real heat engines lose some heat to the outside environment.

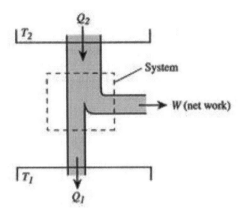

The *Carnot Cycle* represents the most efficient heat engine cycle. It is made of two isothermal processes and two adiabatic processes.

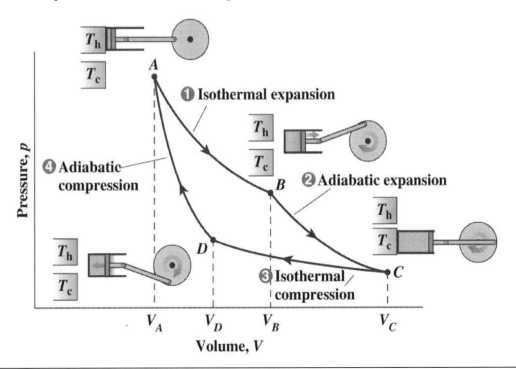

However, the Carnot cycle is an ideal situation and can never be perfectly replicated in real life.

To follow the Second Law, an equation of the *Carnot efficiency* sets a limiting value on the fraction of heat taken from the hot reservoir, which is used for work:

$$n = \frac{T_H T_C}{T_H} \times 100\%$$

where n is the Carnot efficiency, T_H is the temperature of the hot reservoir (K), and T_C is the temperature of the cold reservoir (K).

To achieve this efficiency, the entire process must be reversible, and the change in entropy must be zero. This is impossible, as no process of a real engine is reversible, and every process involves an increase in entropy because maximum entropy is the natural state of the universe.

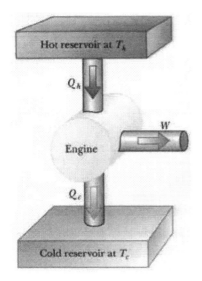

The Kinetic Theory of Gases

The Kinetic Theory of Gases relates the microscopic values of atomic kinetic energy to tangible quantities like temperature and pressure. There are four basic premises behind this theory:

1. Gases are made up of molecules. Molecules may be treated as perfect spheres of mass, and the space between each of these masses are many times greater than their diameters.

2. The motion of each molecule is random. There is no order or pattern to either their direction or magnitude of the velocity.

3. Molecules follow Newton's Laws of Motion. Each molecule moves in a straight line with a constant velocity. If they collide, the molecules exert an equal but opposite force on one another.

4. The collisions of molecules are perfectly elastic—they lose no kinetic energy.

These rules display gases as ideal substances and only approximate their behavior. However, their description is remarkably accurate.

Using these definitions, it is possible to define and derive laws for a gas's behavior.

Ideal Gas Law

The *Ideal Gas Law* is used to explain the relationship between pressure (P), volume (V), and temperature (T). The gas law is expressed as:

$$PV = nRT$$

where n is the number of moles and R is the universal gas constant with a value of 8.314 J/mol·K.

One mole is equal to 6.023×10^{23} molecules. Technically, it is the number of hydrogen atoms in one gram of hydrogen. Because atoms are so small, it is much easier to count them in moles than it is to count them individually.

The Ideal Gas Law was found by looking at the pressure exerted by a gas on a cylinder with a moving wall.

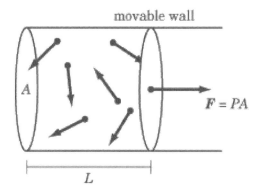

Since pressure is equal to $P = F/A$, the force that the gas exerts on the wall is equal to $F = PA$. If this force moves the wall back a length of L, then the volume of the cylinder increases by $\Delta V = LA$. By solving for A and substituting this back into the equation for force, the result is $F = P\Delta VL$. This is equal to $P\Delta V = FL$.

Previously, work been defined as force multiplied by a distance traveled. By pushing the wall at a distance of L with a force of F, the gas has done work equal to FL. When gas does work, it symbolizes a change in energy. This means that if a change in PV is equal to a change in energy, then PV itself is the total energy of the gas. In terms of the Ideal Gas Law, this means that $n\text{R}T$ is the expression for the total kinetic energy of the gas molecules as well.

The Ideal Gas Law can be related to the number of molecules (N) and the Boltzmann's constant (k). The value of k is 1.381×10^{-23} J/K:

$$PV = NkT$$

Other laws can be derived from the Ideal Gas Law, by holding a variable constant. The number of moles (n) and the gas constant (R) are already constant, so there are four more laws that can be created out of the Ideal Gas Law: Boyle's Law, Charles' Law, Combined Gas Law, and the Closed Container Law.

Boyle's Law (isothermal process)

When using *Boyle's Law*, the temperature of a gas is held constant. It states that an increase in pressure causes a decrease in volume, or that a decrease in pressure causes an increase in volume. Boyle's Law is expressed as:

$$P_1V_1 = P_2V_2$$

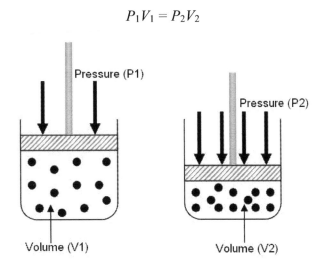

Charles' Law (isobaric process)

When gas is under constant pressure, its behavior is approximated by *Charles' Law*. In this relationship, volume and temperature are directly proportional; when the temperature increases, the volume increases; when the temperature decreases, the volume decreases. Charles' Law is expressed as:

$$\frac{V_i}{T_f} = \frac{V_i}{T_f}$$

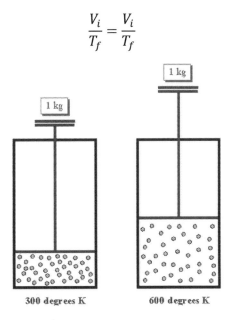

Closed Container Law (constant volume)

The *Closed Container Law* refers to situations in which the volume is constant. In such cases, pressure and temperature are directly proportional:

$$\frac{P_i}{T_i} = \frac{P_f}{T_f}$$

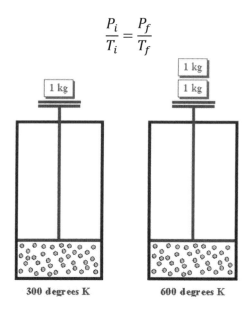

Combined Gas Law

The *Combined Gas Law* is a combination of Boyle's and Charles' Laws. It relates the pressure, volume, and temperature of a gas, and is expressed as:

$$\frac{P_i V_i}{T_i} = \frac{P_f V_f}{T_f}$$

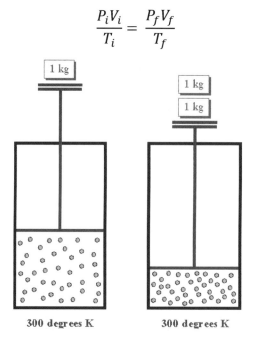

Coefficient of Linear Expansion

When a material changes temperature, it shrinks or expands, depending upon the temperature difference. As the temperature increases, the molecules within the material gain energy and vibrate at higher rates. This increases the distance between the molecules and causes the material to expand. If the material does not experience a phase change (liquid to gas), this expansion of material can be connected to the change in temperature.

The coefficient of expansion is a measurement of the expansion or contraction per unit of length of a material that occurs when the temperature is increased or decreased by 1 °C. This term is referred to as expansivity.

The *coefficient of thermal expansion* (α) is given as:

$$\alpha_{linear} = \frac{\Delta l}{l_i \cdot \Delta T}$$

where α_{linear} is the coefficient of thermal expansion (K^{-1}), Δl is the change in length (m), l_i is the initial length (m), and ΔT is the change in temperature (K).

For example, in the figure below a bar of material is at an initial temperature, and has a length denoted as *L*.

If the bar is heated such that its temperature rises, it expands linearly by some length ΔL.

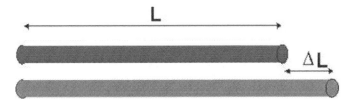

Objects can undergo area expansion and volume expansion due to the same principles.

The *coefficient of area expansion* is expressed as:

$$\alpha_{area} = \frac{\Delta A}{A_i \cdot \Delta T}$$

where α_{area} is the coefficient of thermal expansion (K^{-1}), ΔA is the change in area (m^2), A_i is the initial area (m^2) and ΔT is the change in temperature (K).

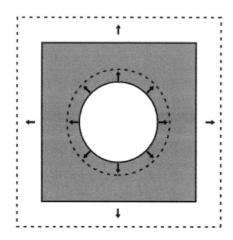

The *coefficient of volume expansion* is expressed as:

$$\alpha_{volume} = \frac{\Delta V}{V_i \times \Delta T}$$

where α_{volume} is the coefficient of thermal expansion (K^{-1}), ΔV is the change in volume (m^3), V_i is the initial volume (m^3), and ΔT is the change in temperature (K).

When designing products or structures that experience changes in temperature, thermal expansion is extremely important. If the product design uses different materials with different thermal expansion coefficients, the design must allow for a varying amount of component expansion and contraction. If not, the components experience a great amount of stress when they attempt to expand and cannot.

This makes the design and construction of bridges and aircraft extremely difficult. Bridges in regions that get relatively cold have metallic joints where the bridge starts and ends.

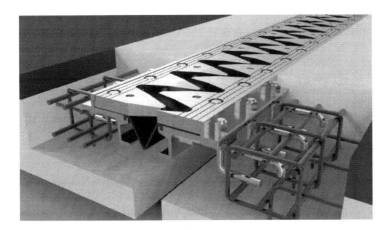

In the summer, these might be completely closed. However, in the winter, the thermal contraction of the bridge materials when subjected to cold air above and below cause the bridge to "shrink," and open a space up between these metal joints. This prevents the bridge from breaking because of material strain.

Notes

Phase Diagram: Pressure and Temperature

When an ice block is set out in the sun, it slowly absorbs the thermal energy through radiation and undergoes a series of phase changes. That is, it changes from a solid to a liquid, to a gas. Say the ice was in a freezer at a temperature of –20 °C.

Once it absorbs enough heat to melt (reaches 0 °C), its temperature remains constant until all of the molecules have reached a temperature of 0 °C. Only when this occurs does the ice melt (point C).

This is shown in the horizontal plateaus in the graph below. When the water changes to a gas (reaches 100 °C), it follows the same rule.

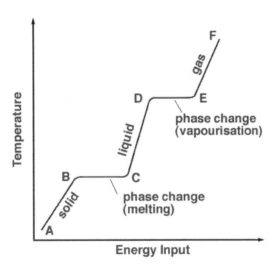

The *melting point* of a substance is the temperature at which it changes from a solid to a liquid, and it is the same temperature as the *freezing point*; the reverse reaction occurs at the same temperature.

The *boiling point* (vaporization) of a substance is the temperature at which it changes phase from a liquid to a gas, and it is the same temperature as the *condensation point*.

Although the energy input (heat) increases with temperature, it never stays constant as the temperature does during a phase change. As energy is constantly being added to the process, the substance uses the added heat to transition each molecule before increasing the temperature. Technically, it converts the potential energy stored within each atom to kinetic energy before it changes phase.

A common way to display the phases of a substance is through a *phase diagram*. This is a graph plotted on a pressure vs. temperature plane. The plane is split into three disproportionate parts, which represent the phases of the substance.

Every point on the plane represents a possible combination of pressure and temperature for the system.

Below is a figure of a typical phase diagram:

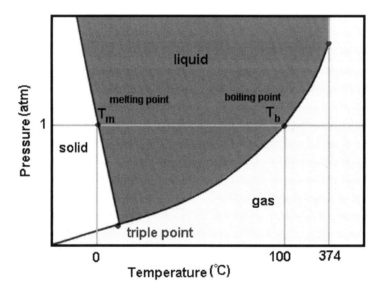

The melting point and boiling point of a substance are found by drawing a horizontal line at 1 atm of pressure, which is atmospheric pressure. Wherever the horizontal line intersects with a line on the phase diagram, the substance changes phases at that exact temperature.

The *triple point* is the point on the graph at which all three lines intersect and at which all three phases exist simultaneously.

The *critical point* on a phase diagram is the temperature, above which the substance is always a gas, regardless of pressure.

Latent Heat

The amount of heat required to perform a phase change is *latent heat*. The latent heat is known for most substances. In general, only computing the total heat is required for the reaction. The heat required to convert a substance from one phase to another is expressed as:

$$Q = m \cdot l$$

where *l* is the latent heat (J/kg), and *m* is the mass of the substance (kg).

If the particles get more excited (solid to liquid, liquid to gas) the change in entropy is always positive, because heat is being added to the system. For this process, the latent heat of fusion is used. The total heat required for this process is the *heat of fusion*.

If the particles get less excited (gas to liquid, liquid to solid) the change in entropy is always negative, because heat is being removed from the system. A negative change in entropy results in a more ordered molecular structure of the substance. The total heat required for this process is the *heat of vaporization*.

Occasionally, a solid skips the liquid phase right to the gas phase; this phenomenon is *sublimation*. The heat required for sublimation is the sum of the heat of fusion and the heat of vaporization. The reverse reaction of sublimation is a *deposition*.

$$Q_{sub} = Q_{fus} + Q_{vap}$$

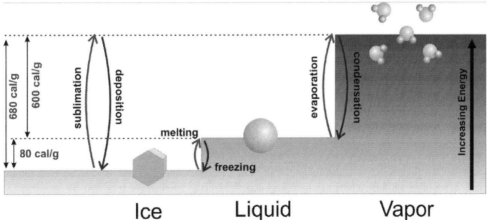

Latent heats are sometimes given in molar heat, or joules per mol (J/mol). Be sure to divide by the molecular weight of the substance if given a mass in grams. If any of these processes are reversed, the latent heat is given a negative sign.

For a process with multiple phase changes, the total heat of the reaction is the sum of the separate heats needed for each phase change and the addition of heat. For these types of problems, it is important to remember the First Law of Thermodynamics, which states that heat must be conserved (heat gained = heat loss), as well as the equation for heat ($Q = mc\Delta T$) where c is the specific heat capacity, and m is the mass. For example, to calculate the change in heat (change in entropy) when 2 kg of ice at 0 °C is warmed to 120 °C, a few equations must be set up, using a few known values.

- melting point = 0 °C

- boiling point = 100 °C

- latent heat of fusion = 3.33×10^5 J/kg

- latent heat of vaporization = 2.26×10^6 J/kg

- specific heat capacity = 4,186 J/kg·°C

Heat required to phase change the ice into liquid water:

$$Q = m \, l_{fusion} = (2kg) \cdot (3.33 \times 10^5 \text{ J/kg}) = 6.66 \times 10^5 \text{ J}$$

Heat required to heat the water to its boiling point:

$$Q = mc\Delta T = (2 \text{ kg}) \cdot (4186 \text{ J/kg °C}) \cdot (100 \text{ °C} - 0 \text{ °C}) = 837,200 \text{ J}$$

Heat required to phase change the liquid into gas:

$$Q = m \, l_{vap} = (2kg) \cdot (2.26 \times 10^6 \text{ J/kg}) = 4.52 \times 10^6 \text{ J}$$

Heat required to heat the water to 120 °C:

$$Q = mc\Delta T = (2 \text{ kg}) \cdot (4186 \text{ J/kg °C}) \cdot (120 \text{ °C} - 100 \text{ °C}) = 167,440 \text{ J}$$

Therefore, the total heat required for the process to occur is the sum of the separate heats:

$$Q_{total} = Q_{fusion} + Q_{heat\_1} + Q_{vap} + Q_{heat\_2}$$

$$= 6.66 \times 10^5 + 837,200 + 4.52 \times 10^6 + 167,440 = 6,190,640 \text{ J}$$

Chapter Summary

Heat and Temperature

- Heat is the total energy due to molecular motion, and the temperature is the average measure of the energy stored within a certain substance.

- The calorie is the amount of heat needed to raise the temperature of one gram of water by one degree Celsius (g/°C).

- Kelvin (K) is the measure of absolute temperature. Absolute zero = 0 K.

- Kelvin and Celsius use the same step in their degree measurements.

- Specific heat is the ratio of energy absorbed to the temperature rise per unit of mass.

- Heat required to perform a phase change is latent heat (*l*): $Q = m \times l$

- A calorimeter measures the heat of a reaction.

  - Temperature remains constant through a phase change.

- Phase diagram

  o Triple point: all three phases exist simultaneously.

  o Critical point: the substance is always a gas.

- Boltzmann's constant 1.381×10^{-23} J/K: $PV = NkT$

- Coefficient of expansion: the expansion per unit of length of a material for an increase in temperature under constant pressure:

$$\alpha = \frac{\Delta l}{l_i \cdot \Delta T}$$

Heat Transfer

- Conduction - direct contact. The rate of heat transfer (H) by conduction: $H = \frac{kA\Delta T}{L}$

- Convection (energized particles from one place to another).

- Radiation (electromagnetic waves).

Laws of Thermodynamics

- Zeroth Law: two systems in thermal equilibrium with a third system are in thermal equilibrium.

- First Law: energy is always conserved: $\Delta U = Q - W$

  o Work done by a system: $(-)$

  o Work done on a system: $(+)$

  o $Q < 0$: exothermic

  o $Q > 0$: endothermic

- Second Law: entropy increases or stays constant, never decrease;

  o Entropy (S) is a measure of disorder within a system.

  o Natural tendency of all things to move towards maximum disorder: $\Delta S \geq \frac{Q}{T}$

  o $\Delta S_{universe} > 0$: spontaneous

  o $\Delta S_{universe} > 0$: at equilibrium

  o $\Delta S_{universe} > 0$: reverse process spontaneous

- Third Law: as the temperature of a system approaches absolute zero; the entropy approaches a constant value (typically zero).

$$S = k \times ln\ (\Omega)$$

where S is the entropy (J/K), k is Boltzmann's constant (1.381×10^{-23} J/K), and Ω is the number of microstates.

- The entropy of a system at absolute zero is zero. However, some systems have more than one minimum energy state.

Enthalpy

- Amount of heat used at constant pressure: $\Delta U = \Delta H - P\Delta V$

- $\Delta H < 0$: exothermic

- $\Delta H > 0$: endothermic

- Hess' Law: $\Delta H_{rxn} = \sum H_{products} - H_{reactants}$

Gibb's Free Energy

- $\Delta G = \Delta H - T\Delta S$

- G < 0: spontaneous

- G = 0: at equilibrium

- G > 0: nonspontaneous.

PV Diagram

- Work is the area under the curve.

- Isothermal - constant temperature: hyperbola

- Adiabatic - no transfer of heat: steeper hyperbola

- Isobaric - constant pressure: horizontal line

- Isochoric - constant volume: vertical line

The Carnot Cycle

- Most efficient heat engine cycle

- Two isothermal processes and two adiabatic processes

- Carnot Efficiency: $\frac{T_H T_C}{T_H} \times 100\%$

The Kinetic Theory of Gases

1. Gases are made up of molecules. Molecules may be treated as perfect spheres of mass, and the space between each of these masses are many times greater than their diameters.

2. The motion of each molecule is random. There is no order or pattern to either their direction or magnitude of the velocity.

3. Molecules follow Newton's Laws of Motion. Each molecule moves in a straight line with a constant velocity. If they collide, the molecules exert an equal but opposite force on one another.

4. The collisions of molecules are perfectly elastic—they lose no kinetic energy.

Coefficient of Linear Expansion

- *The coefficient of expansion* is a measurement of the expansion or contraction per unit of length of a material that occurs when the temperature is increased or decreased by 1 °C. This term is referred to as expansivity.

$$\alpha_{linear} = \frac{\Delta l}{l_i \times \Delta T}$$

where α_{linear} is the coefficient of thermal expansion (K^{-1}), Δl is the change in length (m), l_i is the initial length (m), and ΔT is the change in temperature (K).

Phase diagram: Pressure and Temperature

- The *melting point* of a substance is the temperature at which it changes from a solid to a liquid, and it is the same temperature as the *freezing point*; the reverse reaction occurs at the same temperature.

- The *boiling point* (vaporization) of a substance is the temperature at which it changes phase from a liquid to a gas, and it is the same temperature as the *condensation point*.

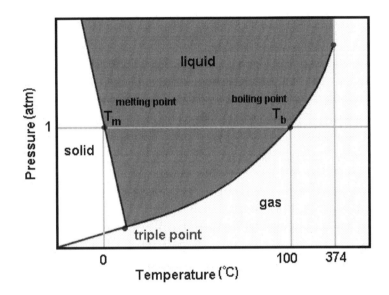

Latent Heat

- The amount of heat required to perform a phase change is *latent heat*. The latent heat is known for most substances.

The heat required to convert a substance from one phase to another is expressed as:

$$Q = m \times l$$

where *l* is the latent heat (J/kg), and *m* is the mass of the substance (kg).

Notes

$$t = -114.4 + 273 = 158.6 \text{ K}$$
$$Q = (0.2 \text{ kg})(1.04 \times 10^5) = 20,800$$

Chapter 1: Thermodynamics

Practice Questions

$\Delta S = \dfrac{Q}{t}$

$\dfrac{-20,800}{-158.6}$

$= -131.5$

1. A mass of 0.2 kg ethanol, in the liquid state at its melting point of −114.4 °C, is frozen at atmospheric pressure. What is the change in the entropy of the ethanol as it freezes? (Use the heat of fusion of ethanol $L_f = 1.04 \times 10^5$ J/kg)

    A. −360 J/K   **B.** 54 J/K   **C.** −131 J/K   **D.** −220 J/K

2. Isobaric work is: ⌃ pressure constant, volume changes

    A. $Q - W$ **B.** $P\Delta V$ **C.** $P\Delta T$ **D.** $V\Delta P$

3. An adiabatic process is performed on 9 moles of an ideal gas. The initial temperature is 315 K, and the initial volume is 0.70 m³. The final volume is 0.30 m³. What is the amount of heat absorbed by the gas? (Use the adiabatic constant for the gas = 1.44) $Q = 0$ bc adiabat

    A. −18 kJ   **B.** 32 kJ   **C.** 9 kJ   **D.** 0 kJ

4. An 80 g aluminum calorimeter contains 360 g of water at an equilibrium temperature of 20 °C. A 180 g piece of metal, initially at 305 °C, is added to the calorimeter. The final temperature at equilibrium is 35 °C. Assume there is no external heat exchange. What is the specific heat capacity of the metal? (Use the specific heat capacity of aluminum = 910 J/kg·K and the specific heat of water = 4,190 J/kg·K)

(0.08 kg) *293 k* $Q_{lost} = Q_{gained}$ $Q = mc\Delta T$

    A. 260 J/kg·K   **B.** 324 J/kg·K   **C.** 488 J/kg·K   **D.** 410 J/kg·K $= (0.08 \text{ kg})(910)(35-20)$

$23718 = (0.18)(x)(270)$ $Q = mc\Delta T = (4190)(3.6)(15) = 22626 + 1092 = 23718$ $Q_A = 1092$ aluminum

$x = 488$

5. A chemist uses 120 g of water that is heated using 65 W of power with 100% efficiency. How much time is required to raise the temperature of the water from 20 °C to 50 °C? (Use the specific heat of water = 4.186 J/g·°C)

    A. 136 s   **B.** 182 s   **C.** 93 s   **D.** 232 s

$Q = mc\Delta T = Pt$ $(0.12)(4.186)(30) = 65(x)$ 0.231

6. The Second Law of Thermodynamics leads to the following conclusion:

    A. the average temperature of the universe is increasing over time
    B. it is theoretically possible to convert heat into work with 100% efficiency
    C. disorder in the universe is increasing over time
    D. total energy of the universe remains constant

7. The statement that 'heat energy cannot be completely transformed into work' is a statement of which thermodynamic law?

    A. Third   **B.** Second   **C.** Zeroth   **D.** Fourth

Q = mHv = ΔST   (0.02)(22.6 × 10⁵) = (ΔS)(100+273)
= 121

8. What is the change in entropy when 20 g of water at 100 °C is turned into steam at 100 °C? (Use the latent heat of vaporization of water $L_v = 22.6 \times 10^5$ J/kg)

   A. −346 J/K   **B.** 346 J/K   **C.** −80.8 J/K   **D.** 121 J/K

9. A Carnot-efficiency engine is operated as a heat pump to heat a room in the winter. The heat pump delivers heat to the room at the rate of 32 kJ per second and maintains the room at a temperature of 293 K when the outside temperature is 237 K. The power requirement for the heat pump under these operating conditions is:

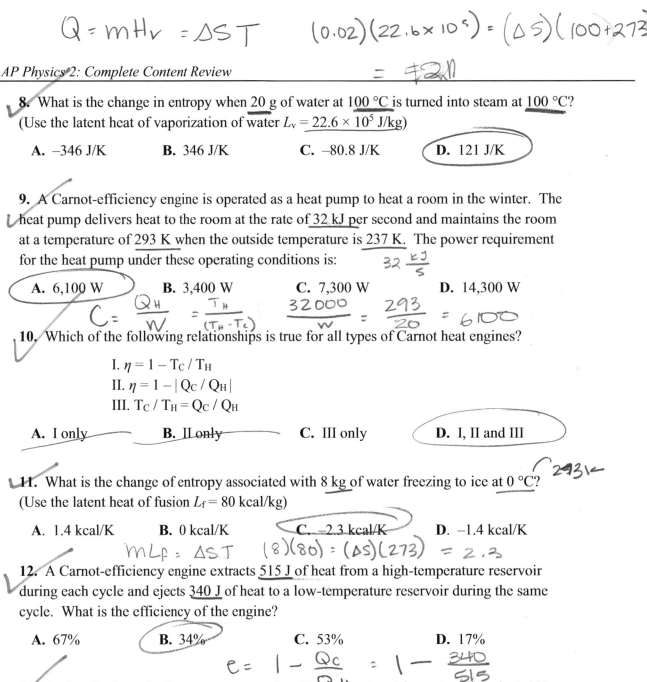

   A. 6,100 W   **B.** 3,400 W   **C.** 7,300 W   **D.** 14,300 W

$$C = \frac{Q_H}{W} = \frac{T_H}{(T_H - T_c)} \qquad \frac{32000}{W} = \frac{293}{20} = 6100$$

10. Which of the following relationships is true for all types of Carnot heat engines?

     I. $\eta = 1 - T_C / T_H$
     II. $\eta = 1 - |Q_C / Q_H|$
     III. $T_C / T_H = Q_C / Q_H$

   A. I only   **B.** II only   **C.** III only   **D.** I, II and III

293K

11. What is the change of entropy associated with 8 kg of water freezing to ice at 0 °C? (Use the latent heat of fusion $L_f = 80$ kcal/kg)

   A. 1.4 kcal/K   **B.** 0 kcal/K   **C.** −2.3 kcal/K   **D.** −1.4 kcal/K

$$mL_f = \Delta ST \qquad (8)(80) = (\Delta S)(273) = 2.3$$

12. A Carnot-efficiency engine extracts 515 J of heat from a high-temperature reservoir during each cycle and ejects 340 J of heat to a low-temperature reservoir during the same cycle. What is the efficiency of the engine?

   A. 67%   **B.** 34%   **C.** 53%   **D.** 17%

$$e = 1 - \frac{Q_c}{Q_h} = 1 - \frac{340}{515}$$

13. A glass beaker of unknown mass contains 65 ml of water. The system absorbs 1,800 cal of heat, and the temperature rises 20 °C. What is the mass of the beaker? (Use the specific heat of glass = 0.18 cal/g·°C and specific heat of water = 1 cal/g·°C)

   A. 342 g   **B.** 139 g   **C.** 546 g   **D.** 268 g

$$1800 \,cal = (X)(0.18)(293) + (65g)(1)(293)$$
$$X = 0.139$$

14. A 0.3 kg ice cube at 0 °C has sufficient heat added to result in total melting, and the resulting water is heated to 60 °C. How much total heat is added? (Use the latent heat of fusion for water $L_f = 334$ kJ/kg, the latent heat of vaporization for water $L_v = 2,257$ kJ/kg and the specific heat of water = 4.186 kJ/kg·K)

   A. 73 kJ   **B.** 48 kJ   **C.** 176 kJ   **D.** 144 kJ

$$Q = mL_f \qquad\qquad Q = mL_v \qquad\qquad Q = mc\Delta T$$
$$Q = (0.3 \,kg)(334) \qquad = (0.3)(2257) \qquad = (0.3)(4.186)(60-0)$$
$$= 100.2 \,kJ \qquad\qquad = 677.1 \qquad\qquad = 75.3$$

100.2 + 75.3 =
100.2 + 75.3 = 176

$$PE = mgh$$
$$mgh = mc\Delta T$$
$$(10)(60) = (4186)(\Delta T)$$
$$\Delta T = 0.14$$

Chapter 1: Thermodynamics

15. The water flowing over a large dam drops a distance of 60 m. If all the gravitational potential energy is converted to thermal energy, by what temperature does the water rise? (Use the acceleration due to gravity $g = 10$ m/s^2 and specific heat of water = 4,186 J/kg·K)

A. 0.34 °C   B. 0.44 °C   C. 0.09 °C   D. 0.14 °C

Solutions

1. C is correct.

Find heat from phase change:

$Q = mL_f$

$Q = (0.2$ kg$)\cdot(1.04 \times 10^5$ J/kg$)$

$Q = 20{,}800$ J

Because the ethanol is freezing, Q should be negative due to heat being released.

$Q = -20{,}800$ J

Find change in entropy:

$\Delta S = Q / T$

$\Delta S = -20{,}800$ J $/ (-114.4$ °C $+ 273$ K$)$

$\Delta S = -131$ J / K

2. B is correct.

$W = P\Delta V$

Isobaric means pressure is constant, and the volume is changing.

3. D is correct.

Adiabatic means that no heat enters or leaves the system.

$Q = 0$ kJ

4. C is correct.

$Q = mc\Delta T$

Find heat added to aluminum calorimeter:

$Q_A = (0.08$ kg$)\cdot(910$ J/kg·K$)\cdot(35$ °C $- 20$ °C$)$

$Q_A = 1{,}092$ J

Find the heat added to the water:

$Q_W = (0.36 \text{ kg}) \cdot (4{,}190 \text{ J/kg·K}) \cdot (35 \text{ °C} - 20 \text{ °C})$

$Q_W = 22{,}626 \text{ J}$

Find total heat added to the system:

$Q_{total} = Q_A + Q_W$

$Q_{total} = 1{,}092 \text{ J} + 22{,}626 \text{ J}$

$Q_{total} = 23{,}718 \text{ J}$

Find specific heat of the metal:

$Q = mc\Delta T$

$c = Q / m\Delta T$

$c = (23{,}718 \text{ J}) / [(0.18 \text{ kg}) \cdot (305 \text{ °C} - 35 \text{ °C})]$

$c = 488 \text{ J/kg·K}$

5. D is correct.

$\text{Watt} = 1 \text{ J/s}$

Thermal energy:

$Q = \text{Power} \times \text{time}$

$Q = mc\Delta T$

$P \times t = mc\Delta T$

$t = (mc\Delta T) / P$

$t = [(120 \text{ g}) \cdot (4.186 \text{ J/g·°C}) \cdot (50 \text{ °C} - 20 \text{ °C})] / (65 \text{ W})$

$t = 232 \text{ s}$

6. C is correct.

The Second Law of Thermodynamics states that entropy is either constant or increasing over time. A constant entropy process is an idealized process and doesn't exist. Thus, entropy is always increasing over time.

7. B is correct.

The Second Law of Thermodynamics states that through thermodynamic processes, there is an increase in the sum of entropies of the system and thus no engine process is 100% efficient.

8. D is correct.

Find heat from phase change:

$Q = mL_f$

$Q = (0.02 \text{ kg}) \cdot (22.6 \times 10^5 \text{ J/kg})$

$Q = 45,200 \text{ J}$

Because the water is vaporizing, Q should be positive due to heat being absorbed.

$Q = 45,200 \text{ J}$

Find the change in entropy:

$\Delta S = Q / T$

$\Delta S = 45,200 \text{ J} / (100 \text{ °C} + 273 \text{ K})$

$\Delta S = 121 \text{ J} / \text{K}$

A positive change in entropy indicates that the disorder of the isolated system has increased. When water evaporates into steam, the entropy is positive because the disorder of steam is higher than water.

9. A is correct.

Coefficient of performance assuming an ideal Carnot cycle:

$C_p = Q_H / W$

$C_p = T_H / (T_H - T_C)$

$Q_H / W = T_H / (T_H - T_C)$

$W = Q_H \cdot (T_H - T_C) / T_H$

$W = (32 \times 10^3 \text{ J/s}) \cdot (293 \text{ K} - 237 \text{ K}) / (293 \text{ K})$

$W = 6,116 \text{ J/s} \approx 6,100 \text{ W}$

10. D is correct.

Carnot efficiency engines are written as:

$\eta = 1 - T_C / T_H$

$\eta = 1 - | Q_C / Q_H |$

Thus:

$Q_C / Q_H = T_C / T_H$

11. C is correct.

Find the heat from the phase change:

$Q = mL_f$

$Q = (8 \text{ kg}) \cdot (80 \text{ kcal/kg})$

$Q = 640 \text{ kcal/kg}$

Because the water is freezing, Q should be negative due to heat being released.

$Q = -640 \text{ kcal/kg}$

Find the change in entropy:

$\Delta S = Q / \text{T}$

$\Delta S = -640 \text{ kcal/kg} / (0 \text{ °C} + 273 \text{ K})$

$\Delta S = -2.3 \text{ kcal/K}$

A negative change in entropy indicates that the disorder of the isolated system has decreased. When water freezes the entropy is negative because water is more disordered than ice. Thus, the disorder has decreased, and entropy is negative.

12. B is correct.

$Q_H = 515 \text{ J}$

$Q_C = 340 \text{ J}$

Carnot cycle efficiency:

$\eta = (Q_H - Q_C) / Q_H$

$\eta = (515 \text{ J} - 340 \text{ J}) / (515 \text{ J})$

$\eta = 0.34 = 34\%$

13. B is correct.

$Q = (mc\Delta \text{T})_{\text{water}} + (mc\Delta \text{T})_{\text{beaker}}$

Change in temperature is the same for both:

$Q = \Delta \text{T}[(mc)_{\text{water}} + (mc)_{\text{beaker}}]$

$1{,}800 \text{ cal} = (20 \text{ °C}) \cdot [(65 \text{ g}) \cdot (1 \text{ cal/g·°C}) + (m_{\text{beaker}}) \cdot (0.18 \text{ cal/g·°C})]$

$90 \text{ cal/°C} = 65 \text{ cal/°C} + (m_{\text{beaker}}) \cdot (0.18 \text{ cal/g·°C})$

$25 \text{ cal/°C} / (0.18 \text{ cal/g·°C}) = (m_{\text{beaker}})$

$m_{\text{beaker}} = 139 \text{ g}$

14. C is correct.

Heat to melt the ice cube:

$$Q_1 = mL_f$$

Heat to raise the temperature:

$$Q_2 = mc\Delta T$$

Total heat:

$$Q_{total} = Q_1 + Q_2$$

$$Q_{total} = mL_f + mc\Delta T$$

$$Q_{total} = (0.3 \text{ kg}) \cdot (334 \text{ kJ/kg}) + (0.3 \text{ kg}) \cdot (4.186 \text{ kJ/kg} \cdot \text{K}) \cdot (60 \text{ °C} - 0 \text{ °C})$$

$$Q_{total} = (100.2 \text{ kJ}) + (1.257 \text{ kJ/K}) \cdot (60 \text{ K})$$

$$Q_{total} = 175.55 \text{ kJ} \approx 176 \text{ kJ}$$

15. D is correct.

$$PE = Q$$

$$mgh = mc\Delta T$$

cancel m from both sides of the expression

$$gh = c\Delta T$$

$$gh / c = \Delta T$$

$$\Delta T = [(10 \text{ m/s}^2) \cdot (60 \text{ m})] / 4{,}186 \text{ J/kg} \cdot \text{K}$$

$$\Delta T = 0.14 \text{ °C}$$

Please, leave your Customer Review on Amazon

Notes

Chapter 2

Fluids Statics and Dynamics

- **Density, Specific Gravity**

- **Archimedes' Principle: Buoyancy**

- **Pressure**

- **Continuity Equation (Av = constant)**

- **Bernoulli's Equation**

- **Viscosity Poiseuille flow**

- **Surface Tension**

Density, Specific Gravity

The three common states of matter are solid, liquid and gas.

A *liquid* has a fixed volume, but can be any shape.

A *gas* can be any shape and compressed (variable volume). Since liquids and gases are both able to "flow," they are fluids.

The *density* (ρ) of an object is its mass per unit volume.

The equation for density is:

$$\rho = \frac{m}{V}$$

where ρ is density, m is mass, and V is volume.

Density is given in SI units of kg/m^3; depending on the situation it is sometimes given in g/cm^3.

To convert g/cm^3 to kg/m^3, dimensional analysis could be performed. However, it is easier to multiply by 1000 ($cm^3 kg\ /m^3 g$):

$$\left(\frac{g}{cm^3}\right)\left(\frac{100\ cm}{1\ m}\right)^3\left(\frac{1\ kg}{1000\ g}\right) = \left(\frac{g}{cm^3}\right)\left(\frac{1000\ cm^3 kg}{m^3 g}\right) = \frac{kg}{m^3}$$

The *specific gravity* of a substance is the ratio of its density to the density of the reference substance. Most of the time, specific gravity is referenced against water.

Thus the specific gravity of water is equal to 1.

The equation for specific gravity is written as:

$$\text{specific gravity} = \frac{\rho_{\text{object}}}{\rho_{\text{water}}}$$

Notes

Archimedes' Principle: Buoyancy

Archimedes' principle of buoyancy states that an object wholly or partially submerged in a fluid will be buoyed up by force equal to the weight of the fluid that it displaces. The equation for buoyancy is:

$$F_{\text{buoyant}} = \rho_{\text{fluid}} V_{\text{object}} g$$

where F_{buoyant} is the buoyant force (N), V is the volume of the fluid displaced (m^3), ρ is the density of the fluid it displaces (kg/m^3), and g is the value of gravity (9.8 m/s^2).

For a floating object, the fraction that is submerged is given by the ratio of the object's density to that of the fluid.

$$\frac{V_{\text{sub}}}{V_{\text{object}}} = \frac{\rho_{\text{object}}}{\rho_{\text{fluid}}}$$

The buoyancy force counteracts the weight of the object in the fluid making objects in water feel lighter than out of the water. This is the reason objects will float when their densities are less than that of the fluid in which they are submerged.

If an object's density is less than that of water, there will be an upward net force on it, and it will rise until it is partially out of the water.

The figure below depicts a log submerged in water ($\rho = 1000 \frac{kg}{m^3}$).

When fully submerged the net force on the log is greater than zero; thus the log floats until the buoyant force is equal to the weight of the log:

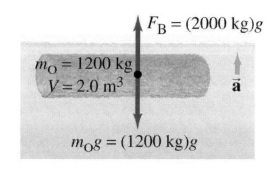

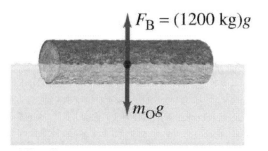

$$F_{net} = F_B - m_o g$$

$$F_{net} = \rho_F V_{displaced} g - m_o g$$

$$F_{net} = \left(1{,}000 \frac{kg}{m^3}\right) \times (2\ m^3)g - (1{,}200\ kg)g$$

$$F_{net} = (2{,}000\ kg)g - (1{,}200\ kg)g$$

$$F_{net} = (800\ kg)g$$

$$F_{net} > 0$$

This principle works in the air; this is why hot-air and helium balloons rise. Both hot air and helium have densities less than air at room temperature. The difference in densities causes the hot air or helium to exert a buoyant force and the balloon. The balloon rises because the buoyant force is greater than the weight of the object it is carrying. The graphic below shows that the net force on the object is the difference between the buoyant force and the gravitational force.

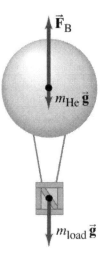

Remember, an object will float perfectly (where the top is level with the surface of the fluid) when the buoyant force is equal to the weight of the object. An object will rise upward out of the fluid when the buoyant force is greater than the weight of the object, and an object will sink when the buoyant force is less than the weight of the object.

Pressure

Pressure is the force exerted on the area over which the force acts. The equation for pressure is therefore written as:

$$P = \frac{F}{A}$$

where P is pressure (N/m^2), F is a force (N), and A is area (m^2).

The unit of pressure is N/m^2, which is the Pascal (Pa).

$$1 \text{Pa} = 1 \text{N/m}^2$$

Anything that can exert a force can exert a pressure; therefore, the concept of pressure can apply to solid objects, liquids, and gasses. When discussing fluids, the pressure exerted by the atmosphere, and measurements of pressure relative to it, are of particular concern.

At sea level, the atmospheric pressure is about 1.013×10^5 N/m^2; this is one atmosphere (atm). Another unit of pressure is the bar. 1 bar = 1.00×10^5 N/m^2. Standard atmospheric pressure is just over 1 bar. Atmospheric pressure does not crush organisms because their cells maintain an internal pressure that balances it.

When measuring pressure, two common types of are used: absolute pressure and gauge pressure. *Absolute pressure* is pressure zero-referenced against a perfect vacuum. *Gauge pressure* is pressure zero-referenced against atmospheric pressure. Most gauges measure pressure above the atmospheric pressure. Hence, most systems are measuring gauge pressure.

For example, if there are two pressure dials (with one displaying absolute pressure and the other displaying gauge pressure) at sea level, what would the reading be? The absolute pressure dial would read 1.013×10^5 Pa, and the gauge pressure dial would read 0 Pa. This is because the atmosphere exerts 1.013×10^5 Pa of pressure over a perfect vacuum; thus the absolute pressure gives this value. The gauge pressure reads 0 Pa because it is referenced at atmospheric pressure, and requires pressures above this to give a reading.

The equation for gauge pressure is the difference between absolute pressure and atmospheric pressure.

$$P_{gauge} = P_{abs} - P_{atm}$$

This can be solved for absolute pressure and gives the equation:

$$P_{abs} = P_{atm} + P_{gauge}$$

Pressure Versus Depth ($P = pgh$)

Below the surface of a liquid, pressure increases linearly with depth. Liquid pressure on an object is found only using the density of the liquid and the distance of the object below the surface, not the density of the object in the liquid nor the shape of the container. The equation for liquid pressure is expressed as:

$$P = \frac{F}{A} = \frac{\rho A h g}{A}$$

This simplifies to:

$$P_{liquid} = \rho g h$$

where P_{liquid} is the pressure exerted by the liquid (N/m^2 or Pa), g is the acceleration of gravity, ρ is the density of the liquid and h is the distance below the surface of the liquid (m):

Liquid pressure is useful in the operation of a number of types of pressure gauges. For example, the gauge pictured below is an open-tube manometer. The pressure in the open end is open to atmospheric pressure, and the pressure that is being measured causes the fluid to rise until the pressures on both sides are equal. Using the liquid pressure equation, the pressure being measured is calculated as:

$P_0 = P_{atm}$

$P = P_{atm} + P_{liquid}$

$P = P_{atm} + \rho g \Delta h$

(a) Open-tube manometer

Notice in this example that the pressure being measured is in absolute pressure because the equation includes atmospheric pressure. This is an important distinction, because if looking for the pressure on an object at depth, the gauge pressure gives only the liquid pressure on the object, whereas the absolute pressure gives the gauge pressure plus atmospheric pressure, so it will be more accurate.

For example, the figure below shows two different shaped containers holding water at equal levels. If points 1 and 2 are at equal height, what are the gauge and absolute pressure at point 1 and 2?

Notice that although the containers are different shapes, the two points are at equal depths within the water. Therefore, they will have equal gauge and absolute pressures. This is because the shape of the container has no influence on the liquid pressure, only the depth below the liquid contributes to liquid pressure. Thus, the gauge and absolute pressure are calculated as:

$$P_1 = P_2$$

$$P_{gauge} = \rho g \Delta h$$

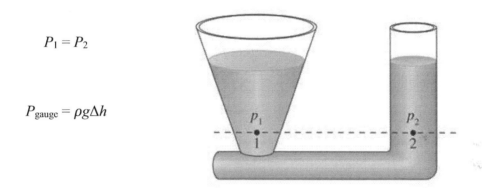

Pascal's Law

Pascal's Law states that a pressure exerted on an incompressible liquid transmits equally to all parts of the liquid. This has important implications because it explains why pressure differentials cannot be created within a closed volume of liquid.

For example, imagine as small cube within a beaker of water (consider the sides small enough that liquid pressure due to depth is equal on the top and bottom of the cube). The pressure on all sides is equal because the pressure is the same in every direction in a fluid at a given depth. If this were not the case, the fluid would flow because of the natural tendency of particle movement from high pressure to low pressure.

Although the pressures across an incompressible liquid are the same, the forces will vary depending on the area they are applied over (because of $P = F / A$). This is extremely useful because it allows the development of systems that impart mechanical advantage. If external pressure is applied to a confined fluid, the pressure at every point within the fluid increases by that amount.

This principle is used in hydraulic lifts and hydraulic brakes. The fluid is confined, so when a pressure is applied, the fluid is compressed, which raises the pressure throughout the system.

From the diagram below, if a small force is applied over a small area (F_1 over A_1), the output force (F_2) at the location with the larger area (A_2) is greater.

Energy must be conserved; thus, the work done on one end is the same as the work output at the other. Additionally, the volume of liquid displaced must be conserved, so that the volume displaced is equal from both the input and output.

Work Equivalence

$$W_1 = W_2$$

$$F_1 d_1 = F_2 d_2$$

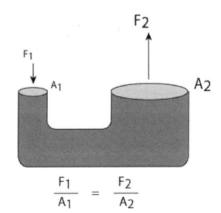

Volume Equivalence

$$V_1 = V_2$$

Continuity Equation

When liquids flow through pipes, the flow is considered incompressible, and the volume of the liquid remains constant regardless of pressure. As such, the volume of liquid flowing through a pipe in a given amount of time must always be equal.

This principle is the conservation of volume.

It is expressed by the *continuity equation*, which describes the volume flow rate of an incompressible liquid. Most often, the continuity equation is used to calculate the speed of the fluid flowing through pipes, and is given as:

$$A_1 v_1 = A_2 v_2$$

where A is an area of the pipe's cross-section (m^2), and v is the velocity of the fluid through that point (m/s).

For example, imagine an incompressible liquid flowing through a pipe which has a diameter reduction. The volume of fluid passing through the constriction over time cannot change.

Therefore the continuity equation is used to solve the resulting velocity of the liquid.

$$A_1 v_1 = A_2 v_2$$

$$v_2 = \frac{A_1 v_1}{A_2}$$

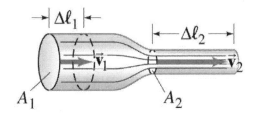

Notes

Bernoulli's Equation

The *Bernoulli equation* is a statement of conservation of energy within flowing fluids. More accurately, it states that the pressure energy, kinetic energy and potential energy of a flowing fluid must always be conserved. It is given by:

$$P_1 + \rho g h_1 + \frac{1}{2}\rho v_1^2 = P_2 + \rho g h_2 + \frac{1}{2}\rho v_2^2$$

where P is pressure (Pa), ρ is the density of the liquid, g is the acceleration due to gravity, h is the height of the fluid (m), and v is the velocity of the fluid through that point (m/s).

Bernoulli's equation is particularly helpful in analyzing fluid flow across pressure differentials, height differentials and the energy needed to transport volumes of fluid.

For example, in the diagram below, water is flowing into the left side at a pressure of P_1, a velocity of v_1, through an area of A_1, and at the height of y_1. The pipe rises in height and decreases in the area (circumference).

Bernoulli's Principle, given a few starting or ending conditions, is used to find any of the values needed.

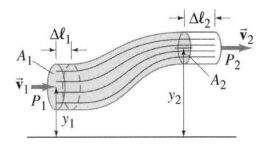

Bernoulli's principle can be used to correlate the speed of a fluid through an opening, to the height of the fluid above the opening. For example, suppose there is a spigot at the bottom of an open tank of water. The speed of this fluid is found by using Bernoulli's principle and making a few assumptions:

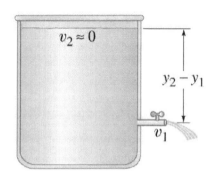

$$P_1 + \rho g y_1 + \frac{1}{2} \rho v_1^2 = P_2 + \rho g y_2 + \frac{1}{2} \rho v_2^2$$

Assume that the top of the container is much larger than the opening of the spigot:

$$A_{\text{top}} \gg A_{\text{spigot}}$$

By the continuity equation it is assumed that the velocity of fluid flow through the top is much smaller than the spigot, and is considered to be zero:

$$v_{\text{top}} \ll v_{\text{spigot}}$$

$$v_{\text{top}} \approx 0$$

Atmospheric pressure acts on both the top of the container and at the end of the spigot. This pressure is equal on both sides of the equation. It cancels out, leaving:

$$g y_1 + \frac{1}{2} v_1^2 = g y_2$$

Assume the height of the spigot as the reference height and, set it equal to zero.

Then solve for the velocity of fluid flow out of the spigot:

$$\frac{1}{2} v_1^2 = g y_2$$

$$v_1 = \sqrt{2 g y_2}$$

Notice that this is the same as the conservation of mechanical energy into kinetic energy. The Bernoulli equation can be used to explain the process of lift on airplane wings. When air strikes an airplane wing, it must separate to flow over both the top and bottom of the wing.

Due to its curvature, the air flowing over the top surface will have a slightly higher speed than the air flowing over the bottom surface.

The speed difference causes a pressure imbalance, and the top of the wing experiences less pressure than the bottom of the wing.

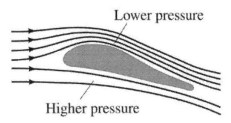

If the height of the wing is considered negligible, then the Bernoulli equation reduces to:

$$P_T + \frac{1}{2}\rho v_T^2 = P_B + \frac{1}{2}\rho v_B^2$$

The flow speed of air over the top of the wing is higher than the flow speed under the bottom, and thus by conservation of energy:

$$v_T > v_B$$

$$P_T < P_B$$

Venturi effect, pivot tube

The *Venturi effect* is the drop in fluid pressure that occurs when a fluid flows through a constriction in a pipe. As discussed earlier in the continuity principle, flow through a constriction in a tube will increase the velocity of the flow to conserve volume.

To adhere to the Bernoulli equation, the higher velocity gas must experience a drop in pressure.

This phenomenon is the Venturi effect and is used to measure fluid flow by measuring pressure differences.

For example, to measure the velocity of fluid flow through a pipe, a constriction is placed in the pipe, and two pressure meters are attached before the constriction and at the constriction.

If the areas of the pipe and the constriction are known, then the velocity of the fluid flow through the pipe is explained by solving for both the continuity and Bernoulli equation:

$$A_1 v_1 = A_2 v_2$$

$$P_1 + \frac{1}{2}\rho v_1^2 = P_2 + \frac{1}{2}\rho v_2^2$$

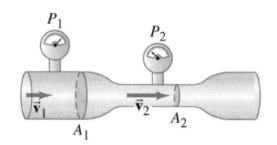

Viscosity Poiseuille Flow

When water poured out of a cup is compared to honey poured out of a jar, the pattern of flow is substantially different. Although water and honey are both liquids, they behave differently when flowing, due to their *viscosity*. The viscosity of a fluid is a measure of the internal frictional force within it. All fluids have some measure of viscosity, whether it be higher (such as that of honey), or lower (that of water). Viscosity of a fluid is a known value and is represented by the symbol η with units of (Pa·s).

When a viscous fluid is flowing through a pipe, the behavior is markedly different than when a fluid with lower viscosity flows through a pipe.

Specifically, the flow from viscous fluids forms a front that is shaped like a parabola bulging outward. This shape is due to the fact that the frictional forces on the fluid from the sides of the pipe are much higher than the frictional forces in the center.

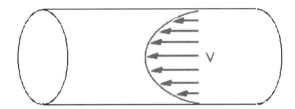

In addition to the flow shape, the flow rate of a liquid through a pipe must take into account the viscosity of the liquid. This is calculated by Poiseuille's Law, which is expressed as:

$$\dot{V} = \frac{\Delta P \pi r^4}{8 \eta L}$$

where $\dot{V}$ is the volumetric flow rate (m³/s), ΔP is the pressure differential across the pipe (Pa), r is the radius of the pipe (m), η is the viscosity of the pipe (Pa·s) and L is the length of the pipe (m).

Poiseuille's Law has important consequences for blood flow; if the radius of an artery is half what it should be, the pressure has to increase by a factor of 16 to keep the same flow. Usually, the heart cannot work hard enough to reach 16 times what it normally does, but blood pressure goes up as it tries.

Notes

Surface Tension

Sometimes small objects, such as paperclips, are placed lightly on the water surface, and they will float; however, if pushed down they will readily sink. These objects have higher densities than water, but how do they float on the surface? This phenomenon is due to the attraction between the molecules of the liquid, the *surface tension.*

Surface tension is due to cohesive forces within a liquid. This cohesion occurs because the molecules of the liquid are electrostatically attracted and try to stick. When a small object is placed on top of the water, it may not weigh enough to break the surface tension, and can, therefore, float despite its greater density.

Some insects, for example, can walk on water, not because they are less dense than the water, but because of surface tension.

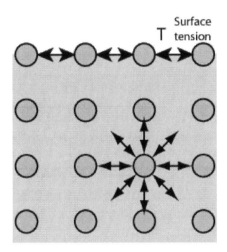

Often times, the surface of a liquid at rest in a container is not perfectly flat. This phenomenon is observed in a small container, such as a graduated cylinder, in which the liquid curves either up or down as it meets the walls of the container. This is the *meniscus* and is the result of surface tension and adhesion.

Adhesion is the property of a substance to be attracted to a dissimilar substance. Unlike cohesion, adhesion is caused by several mechanisms and may or may not be due to electrostatic forces. Regardless, the behavior of a liquid in a container is determined by the cohesive and adhesive forces the liquid experiences.

If the adhesive force between the liquid and the container is greater than the cohesive force between the liquid molecules, the liquid will curve up to meet the edges of the container, creating a concave meniscus.

If the cohesive force is greater than the adhesive force, the liquid will curve downward, creating a convex meniscus. For example, water molecules are more attracted to glass than they are to each other (adhesion > cohesion), so the surface of the water will curve upward toward the walls of its container.

The opposite is true for mercury (adhesion < cohesion), so its surface curves downward.

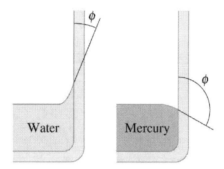

If a narrow tube is placed in a fluid, the fluid exhibits *capillarity*. This phenomenon is due to cohesive and adhesive forces. For example, if a narrow tube is placed in water (adhesion > cohesion), then the water will travel up the tube some distance. This is because the adhesive forces pull the water along the edge, and the cohesive forces pull water up the tube as well.

If the same tube is placed in mercury (adhesion < cohesion), then the cohesive forces of the mercury will attempt to keep the mercury together, rather than climb the wall of the tube. In this case, the mercury will lower itself in the capillary tube with regards to the height of the mercury level around it.

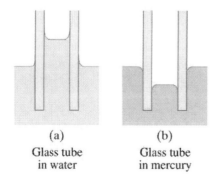

(a)	(b)
Glass tube in water	Glass tube in mercury

Chapter Summary

- States of matter: solid, liquid and gas phases. Liquids and gases are fluids.

- Density is mass per unit volume. Density is given by $\rho = \dfrac{m}{v}$

- Pressure is force per unit area. Pressure is given by $P = \dfrac{F}{A}$.

- External pressure applied to a confined fluid is transmitted throughout the fluid.

- Gauge pressure is the total pressure referenced at the atmospheric pressure, expressed as $P_{gauge} = \rho g \Delta h$.

- An object submerged partly or wholly in a fluid is buoyed up by force equal to the weight of the fluid it displaces.

  The buoyant force is an upward force experienced by an object submerged in a fluid, due to displacement.

  The buoyant force is given by $F_{buoy} = \rho V g$, where V is the volume of the fluid displaced.

- The Continuity Equation says that the flow rate through a pipe (area times velocity) is constant so that $A_1 v_1 = A_2 v_2$. This expresses the idea that a larger cross-sectional area of pipe will experience fluids traveling at a lower velocity.

- Bernoulli's Equation is a statement of conservation of energy. It states:

$$P + \rho g y + \frac{1}{2}\rho v^2 = \text{constant}$$

- Viscosity is an internal frictional force within fluids.

Notes

Practice Questions

1. The Bernoulli effect describes the lift force on an airplane wing. Wings must be designed to ensure that air molecules:

   A. move more rapidly past the lower surface of the wing than past the upper surface
   B. flow around wings that are smooth enough for an easy flow of the air
   C. are deflected upward when they hit the wing
   D. move more rapidly past the upper surface of the wing than past the lower surface

2. Two horizontal pipes (A and B) are the same length, but pipe B has twice the diameter of pipe A. Water undergoes viscous flow in both pipes, subject to the same pressure difference across the lengths of the pipes. If the flow rate in pipe A is Q, what is the flow rate in pipe B?

   A. 2Q   B. 4Q   C. 8Q   D. 16Q

   $$Q = \frac{\pi \, \Delta P \, r^{4}}{8 \eta L} \quad \text{equation}$$

   Questions **3-5** are based on the following:

A pressurized cylindrical tank is 5 m in diameter. Water exits from the pipe at point C with a velocity of 13 m/s. Point A is 10 m above point B, and point C is 3 m above point B. The cross-sectional area of the pipe at point B is 0.08 m², and the pipe narrows to a cross-sectional area of 0.04 m² at point C. Assume an ideal fluid in laminar flow. The density of water is 1,000 kg/m³. (Use the acceleration due to gravity $g = 9.8$ m/s²)

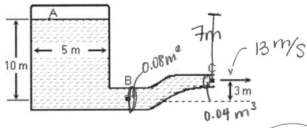

3. What is the mass flow rate in the pipe at point C?

   A. 520 kg/s   B. 440 kg/s   C. 570 kg/s   D. 610 kg/s

   $$A v = (0.04)(13) = 0.52 \text{ g/s}$$

4. What is the rate at which the water is falling into the tank?

   A. 12 mm/s   B. 26 mm/s   C. 86 mm/s   D. 44 mm/s

   $$A_1 V_1 = A_2 V_2$$
   $$2.5^2 \pi \, (v_1) = 0.52$$
   $$V_1 = 0.0265$$

5. What is the gauge pressure in the pipe at point B?

   A. 82 kPa   B. 167 kPa   C. 71 kPa   D. 98 kPa

$$\rho g h = (10 \text{ m})(9.8 \text{ m/s}^2)(1000 \text{ kg/m}^3)$$
$$= 98000$$

6. A closed cubical chamber resting on the floor contains oil and a piston. If the piston is pushed down hard enough to increase the pressure just below the piston by an amount ΔP, which of the following statements is correct?

A. The pressure at the top of the oil increases by less than ΔP

B. The pressure on the sides of the chamber remains the same.

C. The pressure in the oil increases by less than ΔP

D. The increase in the force on the top of the chamber equals the increase in the force on the bottom of the chamber

7. What is the gauge pressure in the water at the deepest point of the Pacific Ocean which is 11,030 m? (Use density of seawater $\rho = 1,025$ kg/m³ and acceleration due to gravity $g = 9.8$ m/s²)

A. 1.1×10^8 Pa **C.** 4.2×10^7 Pa

B. 3.1×10^8 Pa **D.** 7.6×10^7 Pa

$\rho g h$

$(1025)(9.8)(11030)$

$= 1.1 \times 10^8$

8. A cubical box with 25 cm sides is immersed in a fluid. The pressure at the top surface of the box is 108 kPa, and the pressure on the bottom surface is 114 kPa. What is the density of the fluid? (Use the acceleration due to gravity $g = 9.8$ m/s²)

$P_{TOP} = \rho g h$

$\dfrac{11020.4}{h} = \dfrac{11632.7}{h+25}$

A. 980 kg/m³ **C.** 2,452 kg/m³

B. 1,736 kg/m³ **D.** 2,794 kg/m³

$108,000 = (\rho)(9.8)(h)$

$114,000 = \rho(9.8)(h+25)$

$11020.4h + 275510 =$

$\rho h = 11020.4$

$\rho = 11020.4$

$\dfrac{11632.7}{25} = (\rho)(h+25)$

$\rho = \dfrac{11632.7}{h+25}$

$11632.7h$

9. A polar bear of mass 240 kg stands on a floating ice 100 cm thick. What is the minimum area of the ice that will just support the bear? (Use the specific gravity of ice = 0.98 and the specific gravity of saltwater = 1.03)

$612.3h = 275510$

$h = 44.929$

A. 2.6 m² **B.** 4.9 m² **C.** 4.8 m² **D.** 11.2 m²

$F_B = F_{Bear} + F_{ice}$

$\rho V g = mg + \rho V g$

$V_{ice} = \dfrac{m \cdot bear}{\rho_{salt} + \rho_{ice}}$

$\rho(44.929) = 11020.4$

$P = 245$

$SG = \dfrac{\rho_{substance}}{\rho_{water}}$ $0.98 = \dfrac{x}{1000}$ $\rho_{ice} = 980$ $\rho_{salt water} = 1030$

$= \dfrac{240}{1030-980}$

$= 4.8$

10. A 14,000 N car is raised using a hydraulic lift. The lift consists of a U-tube with arms of unequal areas, initially at the same level. The lift is filled with oil with a density of 750 kg/m³ with tight-fitting pistons at each end. The narrower arm has a radius of 6 cm, while the wider arm of the U-tube has a radius of 16 cm. The car rests on the piston on the wider arm of the U-tube. What is the force that must be applied to the smaller piston to lift the car after it has been raised 1.5 m? (Ignore the weight of the pistons and the acceleration due to gravity $g = 9.8$ m/s²)

$A = \dfrac{V}{h}$

$= 4.8$

$= \dfrac{4.8}{0.1}$

$= 4.8$

A. 4,568 N **B.** 3,832 N **C.** 2,094 N **D.** 1,379 N

$P = \dfrac{F}{A}$

$P_2 = P_1 + \rho g h$

$\dfrac{F_2}{A_2} = \dfrac{F_1}{A_1} + \rho g h$

$\dfrac{F_2}{0.06^2 \pi} = \dfrac{14,000}{0.16^2 \pi} + (750)(9.8)(1.5)$

$F_2 = 2094$

11. An object has a volume of 4.2 m³ and weighs 41,800 N. What is its apparent weight in water? (Use acceleration due to gravity $g = 9.8$ m/s² and density of water $\rho = 1,000$ kg/m³)

A. 1,140 N **B.** 230 N **C.** 800 N **D.** 640 N

$F_B = \rho g V$

$F_B = (1000)(9.8)(4.2)$

$F_B = 41160$

$41800 - 41160$

640

$F_B = F_g - F_T$

$\rho g V = mg - 42$

$(3650)(9.8)(V) = (9.2)(9.8) - 42$

$V = 0.001346$

$\rho = \dfrac{m}{V} = \dfrac{9.2}{0.001346}$

$\rho = 68833$

12. A solid sphere of mass 9.2 kg, made of metal whose density is 3,650 kg/m^3, hangs by a cord. When the sphere is immersed in a liquid of unknown density, the tension in the cord is 42 N. What is the density of the liquid? (Use acceleration due to gravity $g = 9.8$ m/s^2)

A. 1,612 kg/m^3

B. 1,468 kg/m^3

C. 1,950 kg/m^3

D. 1,742 kg/m^3

(100K @ AK)

13. A man is breathing through a snorkel while swimming in the ocean. When his chest is about 1 meter underwater, he has a difficult time breathing. What is the net pressure that his lungs must expand against for him to breathe? (Use the atmospheric pressure $P_{atm} = 1.01 \times 10^5$ Pa, the density of water $\rho = 10^3$ kg/m^3, the density of air $\rho = 1.2$ kg/m^3 and the acceleration due to gravity $g = 9.8$ m/s^2)

A. 3.2×10^5 Pa

B. 1.1×10^5 Pa

C. 4.1×10^5 Pa

D. 1×10^4 Pa

$P = \rho g h$

$= (1000)(9.8)(1m)$

$= 9800 = 1000$

14. A particular grade of motor oil, which has a viscosity of 0.3 N·s/m^2, is flowing through a 1 m long tube with a radius of 3.2 mm. What is the average speed of the oil, if the drop in pressure over the length of the tube is 225 kPa?

A. 0.82 m/s

B. 0.96 m/s

C. 1.2 m/s

D. 1.4 m/s

$Av = \dfrac{\Delta P A r^4}{8 n L}$

$(3.2^{-2})(\pi)(v) = \dfrac{225,000 \,(3.2)^4}{8\,(0.3)(1)}$

$v = 0.96$

15. Ice has a lower density than water because ice:

A. molecules vibrate at lower rates than water molecules

B. is made of open-structured, hexagonal crystals

C. is denser and therefore sinks when in liquid water

D. molecules are more compact in the solid state

check AK

Solutions

1. D is correct. According to the Bernoulli effect air moving with a higher velocity exerts less pressure against a surface then air with a lower velocity. Thus, to produce lift, the pressure on the underside of a wing should be higher, and thus the air should be slower on the bottom surface of the wing compared to air on the top surface.

2. D is correct.

Poiseuille's Law:

$Q = \pi \Delta P r^4 / 8\eta L$

$D_B = 2D_A$

$r_B = 2r_A$

$Q_A = \pi \Delta P r_A{}^4 / 8\eta L$

$Q_B = \pi \Delta P (2r_A)^4 / 8\eta L$

$Q_B = 16(\pi \Delta P r_A{}^4 / 8\eta L)$

$Q_B = 16 Q_A$

3. A is correct. Mass flow rate $\dot{m}$ is:

$\dot{m} = \rho v A_C$

where ρ = density of the fluid, v = velocity of flow, A_C = cross-sectional area

The dimensions of the tank are irrelevant to this answer, so $\dot{m}$ is calculated as:

$\dot{m} = (1{,}000 \text{ kg/m}^3) \cdot (13 \text{ m/s}) \cdot (0.04 \text{ m}^2)$

$\dot{m} = 520 \text{ kg/s}$

4. B is correct. Relationship between area and velocity of both exists:

$A_1 v_1 = A_2 v_2$

$v_1 = A_2 v_2 / A_1$

$v_1 = [(0.04 \text{ m}^2) \cdot (13 \text{ m/s})] / [(\pi / 4) \cdot (5 \text{ m/s})]$

$v_1 = 0.26 \text{ m/s} = 26 \text{ mm/s}$

5. D is correct. Gauge pressure is the pressure reference against the surrounding air pressure. Because of this, it is valid to ignore both the pressure in the tank and atmospheric pressure.

$P = \rho g h$

$P = (10^3 \text{ kg/m}) \cdot (9.8 \text{ m/s}^2) \cdot (10 \text{ m})$

$P = 98{,}000 \text{ Pa} = 98 \text{ kPa}$

6. D is correct. According to Pascal's Law, the pressure is transmitted undiminished in an enclosed static fluid. Thus the pressure increases by ΔP everywhere in the oil. If the chamber is cubic, the top and bottom sides have the same area and experience the same increase in force:

$A_{top} = A_{bottom}$

$\Delta P_{top} = \Delta P_{bottom}$

$P = F / A$

Thus, force is directly proportional to pressure, and if the area of the top is equal to the area of the bottom:

$\Delta F_{top} = \Delta F_{bottom}$

7. A is correct.

Gauge pressure is referenced relative to atmospheric pressure and is calculated by:

$P_{gauge} = \rho g h$

$P_{gauge} = (1{,}025 \text{ kg/m}^3)\cdot(9.8 \text{ m/s}^2)\cdot(11{,}030 \text{ m})$

$P_{gauge} = 1.1 \times 10^8 \text{ Pa}$

8. C is correct.

$P_{top} = \rho g h$

$P_{top} = 108 \times 10^3 \text{ Pa}$

$h = (1 / \rho)\cdot(108 \times 10^3 \text{ Pa} / 9.8 \text{ m/s}^2)$

$h = (1 / \rho)\cdot(11{,}020 \text{ kg/m}^2)$

$P_{bottom} = \rho g(h + 25 \text{ cm})$

$\rho g(h + 25 \text{ cm}) = 114 \times 10^3 \text{ Pa}$

$h = (1 / \rho)\cdot(114 \times 10^3 \text{ Pa} / 9.8 \text{ m/s}^2) - 0.25 \text{ m}$

$h = (1 / \rho)\cdot(11{,}633) - 0.25 \text{ m}$

Set equal and solve for ρ:

$(1 / \rho)\cdot(11{,}020 \text{ kg/m}^2) = (1 / \rho)\cdot(11{,}633 \text{ kg/m}^2) - 0.25 \text{ m}$

$(11{,}020 \text{ kg/m}^2) = (11{,}633 \text{ kg/m}^2) - 0.25 \text{ m}(\rho)$

$0.25 \text{ m}(\rho) = 613 \text{ kg/m}^2$

$\rho = (613 \text{ kg/m}^2) / (0.25 \text{ m})$

$\rho = 2{,}452 \text{ kg/m}^3$

9. C is correct.

Solve for density of ice and saltwater:

$SG = \rho_{substance} / \rho_{water}$

$SG_{ice} = 0.98 = \rho_{ice} / 10^3 \text{ kg/m}^3$

$\rho_{ice} = 980 \text{ kg/m}^3$

$SG_{saltwater} = 1.03 = \rho_{saltwater} / 10^3 \text{ kg/m}^3$

$\rho_{saltwater} = 1{,}030 \text{ kg/m}^3$

Solve for volume of ice:

$$F_B = F_{bear} + F_{ice}$$

$$\rho_{saltwater} V_{ice} \cancel{g} = m_{bear} \cancel{g} + \rho_{ice} V_{ice} \cancel{g}, \text{ cancel } g \text{ from all terms}$$

$$V_{ice} = m_{bear} / (\rho_{saltwater} + \rho_{ice})$$

$$V_{ice} = (240 \text{ kg}) / (1{,}030 \text{ kg/m}^3 - 980 \text{ kg/m}^3)$$

$$V_{ice} = 4.8 \text{ m}^3$$

Solve for area of ice:

$$A = V / h$$

$$A = (4.8 \text{ m}^3) / (1 \text{ m})$$

$$A = 4.8 \text{ m}^2$$

10. C is correct. $P_1 = P_2 + \rho g h$

$$F_1 / A_1 = F_2 / A_2 + \rho g h$$

$$F_1 = A_1(F_2 / A_2 + \rho g h)$$

$$F_1 = \pi(0.06 \text{ m})^2 \cdot [(14{,}000 \text{ N}) / \pi(0.16 \text{ m})^2 + (750 \text{ kg/m}^3) \cdot (9.8 \text{ m/s}^2) \cdot (1.5 \text{ m})]$$

$$F_1 = \pi(0.0036 \text{ m}^2) \cdot [(14{,}000 \text{ N}) / \pi(0.0256 \text{ m}^2) + (750 \text{ kg/m}^3) \cdot (9.8 \text{ m/s}^2) \cdot (1.5 \text{ m})]$$

$$F_1 = (0.0036 \text{ m}^2) \cdot [(14{,}000 \text{ N}) / (0.0256 \text{ m}^2) + (11{,}025 \text{ N})\pi]$$

$$F_1 = 1{,}969 \text{ N} + 125 \text{ N}$$

$$F_1 = 2{,}094 \text{ N}$$

11. D is correct. $F_B = \rho V g$

$$F_{net} = F_{object} - F_B$$

$$F_{net} = (41{,}800 \text{ N}) - (1{,}000 \text{ kg/m}^3)(4.2 \text{ m}^3)(9.8 \text{ m/s}^2)$$

$$F_{net} = (41{,}800 \text{ N}) - (41{,}160 \text{ N})$$

$$F_{net} = 640 \text{ N}$$

12. C is correct. $F_{net} = F_{object} - F_B$

$$F_{net} = mg - \rho_{fluid} V g$$

$$\rho_{fluid} = -(F_{net} - mg) / V_{sphere} g$$

$$\rho_{fluid} = -[42 \text{ N} - (9.2 \text{ kg}) \cdot (9.8 \text{ m/s}^2)] / [(9.2 \text{ kg} / 3{,}650 \text{ kg/m3}) \cdot (9.8 \text{ m/s}^2)]$$

$$\rho_{fluid} = 1{,}950 \text{ kg/m}^3$$

13. D is correct.

$P = \rho g h$

$P = (10^3 \text{ kg/m}^3) \cdot (9.8 \text{ m/s}^2) \cdot (1 \text{ m})$

$P = 9{,}800 \text{ Pa} \approx 1 \times 10^4 \text{ Pa}$

14. B is correct.

By Poiseuille's Law, the volumetric flow rate of a fluid is given by:

$V = \Delta P A r^2 / 8\eta L$

The volumetric flow rate is the volume of fluid that passes a point per unit time:

$V = Av$

where v is the speed of the fluid.

Therefore:

$Av = \Delta P A r^2 / 8\eta L$

$v = \Delta P r^2 / 8\eta L$

$v = (225 \times 10^3 \text{ Pa}) \cdot (0.0032 \text{ m})^2 / [8 \, (0.3 \text{ Ns/m}^2) \cdot (1 \text{ m})]$

$v = 0.96 \text{ m/s}$

15. B is correct.

For most substances, the solid form is denser than the liquid phase. Therefore, a block of most solids sinks in the liquid. With regards to pure water though, a block of ice (solid phase) floats in liquid water because ice is less dense.

Like other substances, when liquid water is cooled from room temperature, it becomes increasingly dense. However, at approximately 4 °C (39 °F), water reaches its maximum density, and as it's cooled further, it expands and becomes less dense. This phenomenon is negative thermal expansion and is attributed to strong intermolecular interactions that are orientation-dependent.

The density of water is about 1 g/cm^3 and depends on the temperature. When frozen, the density of water is decreased by about 9%. This is due to the decrease in intermolecular vibrations, which allows water molecules to form stable hydrogen bonds with other water molecules around.

As these hydrogen bonds form, molecules are locking into positions similar to form hexagonal structures. Even though hydrogen bonds are shorter in the crystal than in the liquid, this position locking decreases the average coordination number of water molecules as the liquid reaches the solid phase.

Notes

Chapter 3

Electrostatics

- **Charges, Electrons, Protons, Conservation of Charge**

- **Conductors, Insulators**

- **Coulomb's Law**

- **Electric field *E***

- **Potential Difference, Electric Potential at Point in Space**

- **Equipotential Lines**

- **Electric Dipole**

- **Electrostatic Induction**

- **Gauss's Law**

Charges, Electrons and Protons, Conservation of Charge

What is charge?

Like mass, the *charge* is an innate property of all matter. Every particle in the universe has a mass and a charge, measured in coulombs (C). Unlike mass, however, three distinct types of charges exist: positive charge, negative charge, and neutral charge. (Note: neutral charge does NOT mean that the particle has no charge; the net charge is neutral.)

Where does charge come from?

Today, it is known that the basic unit of matter is the atom, which is made up of electrons orbiting a nucleus of protons and neutrons. These subatomic particles, specifically the electron and proton, are the basis of all macroscopically observed charge phenomenon.

The electron is negatively charged and has a charge of -1.60×10^{-19} coulombs.

Conversely, the proton is positively charged and has an equal but opposite charge of $+1.60 \times 10^{-19}$ coulombs. When dealing with macroscopic objects that contain a charge, it is important to note that only the electrons contribute to the charge, because they are mobile. Protons are part of the nuclei of the atom and are not mobile.

Therefore any charge on an object is either due to an excess of electrons (if the observed charge is negative) or shortage of electrons (if the observed charge is positive).

Negative charge: # electrons > # protons

Positive charge: # electrons < # protons

Neutral charge: #electrons = # protons

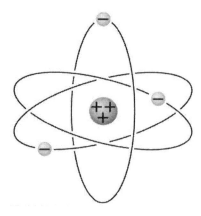

What are the properties of charge?

Charges have several unique properties that govern the laws of nature. Most importantly, charges exhibit force upon each other according to the charge. Same charges exhibit repulsive forces, and opposite charges exhibit attractive forces.

For example, the figure below shows a ruler that is negatively charged (excess of electrons) and a glass rod that is positively charged (shortage of electrons).

In diagram (a) two negatively charged rulers are brought close and repel due to their like charges. Diagram (b) demonstrates the same effect with two positively charged glass rods.

However, in diagram (c), the charged ruler and glass rod attract due to their opposite charges.

(a) Two charged plastic rulers repel

(b) Two charged glass rods repel

(c) Charged glass rod attracts
charged plastic ruler

Additionally, the charge is always conserved. Like mass and energy, the charge cannot be created or destroyed, only transferred from one source to another.

Thus, if a charged object, such as the ruler in the above example, is placed on a table for some time, and later found to be neutrally charged, it is concluded that the charge was not destroyed, but rather transferred to the surroundings (air and table).

Another unique property of charge is that all charge is quantized. The magnitude of the electron's charge (or proton), is the *fundamental charge* and is the smallest unit of charge that exists.

This means that all macroscopically charged objects have a net charge equal to an integer multiple of the fundamental charge. This is expressed as:

$$q = ne$$

where q is the net charge (C), n is the integer multiple (i.e., excess electrons or protons), and e is the magnitude of the fundamental charge (1.60×10^{-19} C).

The quantization of charge enables one to calculate the excess or shortage of electrons in an object that contributes to its net charge.

For example, if the negatively charged ruler from the earlier example is measured to have one coulomb of charge, then the number of excess electrons in the ruler is:

$$n = \frac{q}{e}$$

$$n = \frac{1.00 \text{ Coulomb}}{1.60 \times 10^{-19} \text{Coulomb}} = 6.25 \times 10^{18} \text{ electrons}$$

Notes

Conductors, Insulators

Conductivity is a measure of a material's ability to transmit charge through itself. Materials which have a high conductivity are *conductors*. These types of materials allow electrical charge (electrons) to "flow" through the material.

An example of a good conductor is copper. Notice that in most wires for electrical equipment, the electricity is provided via copper wires, which allow the electrical charges to flow through it easily.

If a material does not transmit charge well, then it is considered a poor conductor and is an *insulator*. Common insulators are wood, glass, and paper.

In the example below, there are two spheres. One has been charged positively (deficit of electrons), and the other has been left neutral (a).

In diagram (b), a metal nail is placed on top of both spheres. As a conductor, the metal nail allows electrons to flow through itself (from the neutral to the positive sphere) until the charges in each sphere are equal.

In diagram (c), a piece of wood is placed across the spheres instead of the nail. The piece of wood is an insulator and does not allow the free flow of electrons into the right sphere.

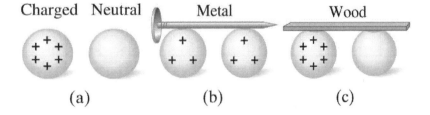

Notes

Coulomb's Law

As mentioned earlier, charges will either repel or attract one another, depending if the charges are similar or opposite.

This force is the electrostatic force (Coulomb force) and is found using *Coulomb's Law*, which describes the interaction between two charged particles:

$$F = \frac{1}{4\pi \in_0} \frac{q_1 q_2}{r^2}$$

Which simplifies to:

$$F = k \frac{q_1 q_2}{r^2}$$

where F is the electrostatic force between the two charges (N), q is the magnitudes of the charges (C), r is the distance between them (m), $\in_0$ is the permittivity of free space ($8.854 \times 10^{-12} \frac{C^2}{N \cdot m^2}$) and k is Coulomb's constant, with a value of 9×10^9 N·m²/C².

Coulomb's Law strictly applies only to point charges. If two object has a net charge, then they must be approximated as point charges to calculate the force they exert on each other.

Moreover, the electrostatic force will always be along the line connecting the charges.

Remember, if the charges have the same sign, the force is repulsive, and if the charges have opposite signs, the force is attractive.

To find the electrostatic force on more than two point charges, use the superposition principle and sum the force from each charge in all axial directions.

For example, what is the net force on Q_3 in the example below?

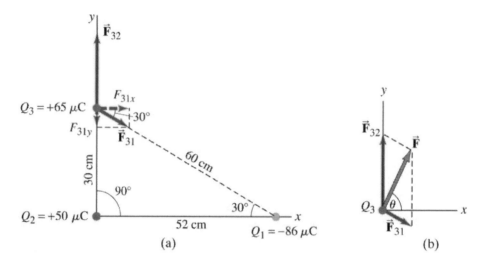

$$F_{32} = k \frac{q_1 q_2}{r^2} = \frac{(9 \times 10^9 \text{Nm}^2) \cdot (65 \times 10^{-6}\text{C}) \cdot (50 \times 10^{-6}\text{C})}{(0.3 \text{ m})^2} = 325 \text{ N}$$

$$F_{31y} = \sin \theta \, k \frac{q_1 q_2}{r^2} = \left| \frac{\sin 30 \, (9 \times 10^9 \text{Nm}^2) \cdot (65 \times 10^{-6}\text{C})(-86 \times 10^{-6}\text{C})}{(0.6 \text{ m})^2} \right| = 70 \text{ N}$$

$$F_{31x} = \cos \theta \, k \frac{q_1 q_2}{r^2} = \left| \frac{\cos 30 \, (9 \times 10^9 \text{Nm}^2)(65 \times 10^{-6}\text{C})(-86 \times 10^{-6}\text{C})}{(.6 \text{ m})^2} \right| = 121 \text{ N}$$

$$F_{net} = \sqrt{(121 \text{ N})^2 + (325 \, N - 70 \, N)^2} = 282 \text{ N}$$

Electric Field *E*

Every charge is surrounded by *electric fields* (*E*), which emanate in all directions around the charge. These fields are directional, vector fields. The orientation of any field is always in the direction that a positive charge would be pushed if placed in the field.

Consequently, for positive charges, the electric field points outward in every direction, and for negative charges, the electric field points inward in every direction.

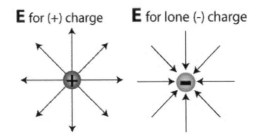

The electric field (*E*) is expressed as the force (*F*) on a charge, divided by the magnitude of the charge (*q*):

$$\vec{E} = \frac{\vec{F}}{q}$$

where (E) is the electric field in Newtons/Coulombs (N/C).

Substituting in the electrostatic equation for force, the electric field from a single point charge (*Q*):

$$\vec{E} = \frac{\vec{F}}{q} = \frac{kqQ/r^2}{q} = k\frac{Q}{r^2}$$

These equations are rearranged to solve for the force on a point charge in an electric field (*E*):

$$\vec{F} = q\vec{E}$$

For example, in figure (a) below, an electric field points in an arbitrary direction.

If a positive charge is placed in the electric field, as in diagram (b), then the force on charge will be in the direction of the electric field. If a negative charge is placed in the same electric field, then the force will be in the opposite direction, as in diagram (c).

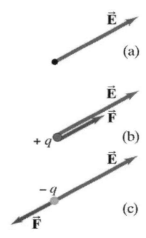

When solving problems in electrostatics, with electric forces and electric fields, make sure to draw a diagram of the entire situation.

Show all charges with signs, electric fields, and force. Be sure to include the directions. Then calculate forces using Coulomb's Law, and add forces as vectors.

Remember, like all vectors, the net strength of multiple electric fields on a point charge is calculated by the superposition principle:

$$\vec{E} = \vec{E_1} + \vec{E_2} + \dots$$

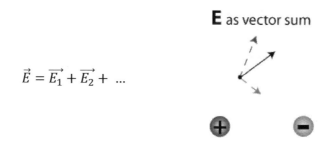

Field lines

Like all field lines, the density of electric field lines denotes the strength of the field. Simply put, if there are certain places where the field lines are closer, the electric field is stronger.

If the lines are spread out, the field is weaker.

The density of field lines can be used to determine the magnitude of the charge emitting the field. If the density of field lines is high, then the charge must have a higher magnitude.

If the density is low, the charge must have a lower magnitude.

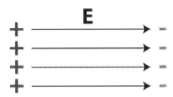

Field due to the charge distribution

When two charges are brought close, their electric fields will interact depending on the types of charge. For example, if two positive charges are brought close, the field lines will repel, not intersect.

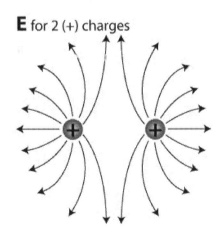

If the two charges were negative, the field lines would be the same as those for two positive charges, except that the direction of the field lines would be reversed.

When two opposite charges are brought near, an *electric dipole* will be created. In an electric dipole, the field lines will come out of the positive charge and go into the negative charge, as pictured below:

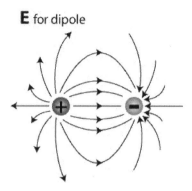

The net charge on a conductor is always on its surface, which radiates electric field lines.

For a charged cylinder, the electric field runs radially perpendicular to the cylinder and is zero (nonexistent) inside the cylinder. This is true for all conducting objects; the net electric field is always from the surface and nonexistent within the object.

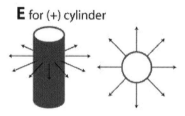

Summary of field lines:

1. Field lines indicate the direction of the field; the field is tangent to the line.

2. The magnitude of the field is proportional to the density of the lines.

3. Field lines start on positive charges and end on negative charges; the number is proportional to the magnitude of the charge.

4. Net electric field within a conductor is zero

Potential Difference, Electric Potential at Point in Space

Because charges exert a force on each other in relation to the distance between the charges, charges must have potential energy. The *electric potential energy* has units of joules (J) and is written as:

$$U = \frac{kQq}{r}$$

where U is the electric potential energy (J), Q and q are the point charges (C), r is the distance between the point charges (m) and k is Coulomb's constant, with a value of 9×10^9 N·m²/C².

The electric potential energy of a single point charge is related but different from its electric potential. The *electric potential* is the amount of energy per charge that something possesses. The unit for electric potential is joules per coulomb (J/C) or volts (V) and is a scalar field associated with potential energy.

An electric potential is found using either of two equations.

$$V = \frac{U}{q} \quad or \quad V = \frac{kQ}{r}$$

where V is the electric potential (V), Q is the charge that is causing the potential (C), q is the charge experiencing the potential (the magnitude of q is small), U is the electrical potential energy possessed by q (J), k is Coulomb's constant and r is the distance between the two charges (always positive).

If there are multiple charges contributing to the electric potential, then the total electric potential is the sum of the potentials caused by the individual components.

Remember that positive charges cause positive potentials, and negative charges cause negative potentials.

These plots show the potential due to (a) positive and (b) negative charge.

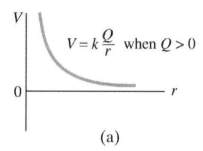

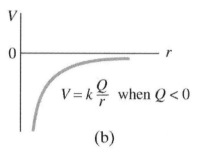

The potential difference is important in producing forces and moving charges. The process is analogous to moving masses in gravitational fields. The potential difference is given by ΔV and is the difference between the two potentials.

$$\Delta V = V_B - V_A$$

The potential difference is used in scenarios such as the difference in potential between the two plates of a capacitor, or the positive and negative terminals of a battery. Using potentials instead of fields can make solving problems much easier— the potential is a scalar quantity, whereas a field is a vector. For example, the Coulomb force is conservative.

Therefore the work in an electric field is conservative. As such, the work required to move a point charge in an electric field is only dependent upon the displacement of the charge, not the path taken by it. An easy way to calculate this work is to use electric potential difference, which is written to relate it to work involved in positioning charges.

$$\Delta V = \frac{W}{q}$$

where ΔV is the electric potential difference (V), W is the work needed to move the charge (J), and q is the magnitude of the moving charge (C).

Equipotential Lines

Equipotential lines are placed around a charge and mark where the electric potential is the same. Equipotential lines are always perpendicular to electric field lines.

In 3D, equipotential lines will form a "surface" called an equipotential surface. Any movement along an equipotential surface requires no work because the movement is perpendicular to the electric field.

The figure below depicts equipotential lines under different circumstances.

On the left is a single charge, along with its electric field and corresponding equipotential lines.

On the right, there is a dipole with its bent electric field lines and mirrored equipotential lines.

Notice that in both instances, the equipotential lines are perpendicular to the electric field lines at every point.

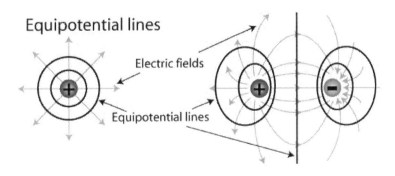

Notes

Electric Dipole

Definition of dipole

A dipole is an interaction between a positive charge and a negative charge that are separated by some distance.

Behavior in an electric field

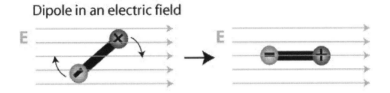

A dipole in an electric field will want to align itself with the electric field, such that the positive end of the dipole is in the direction of the electric field (furthest from the source of the electric field). It will spin or rotate until it reaches such a position.

Many molecules exhibit electric dipoles and are *polar molecules*.

The water molecule is an example of a polar molecule that exhibits a dipole.

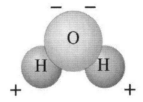

Oxygen is partially negative (∂^-) due to its high electronegative value and draws electrons in the polar covalent bond from the hydrogens; hydrogens are partial positive (∂^+).

In this water molecule, the dipole moment arises from the partial (delta) negative charge near the location of the oxygen atom, and two (delta) positive charges near the hydrogen atoms. The asymmetric distribution of charge creates an electric dipole, which plays an important role in the physical and chemical properties of water.

For example, a microwave heats food by heating the water in the food. This occurs because the oscillating electric field of a microwave rotates the water molecule such that the electric dipole is in line with the electric field.

The movement of the water molecule creates heat, which increases the temperature of the food.

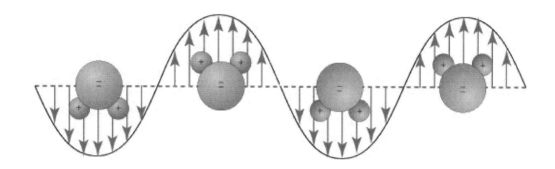

Electrostatic Induction

Electrostatic energy is a charge more or less fixed in a single place. However, this charge can be transferred to other objects in two ways.

Energy can be transferred through *conduction*, which means there is a point of direct contact between two objects (as discussed earlier), or through *induction*, which is a transfer of energy across an open space between two objects.

Electrostatic induction is where a charged object induces the movement or redistribution of charges in another object. This occurs whenever an object is placed in or near an electric field.

Metal objects can be charged by conduction. In the diagram (a) below, the metal rod B is initially neutral. When the neutral rod B touches a charged rod A, negatively charged electrons flow from B to A.

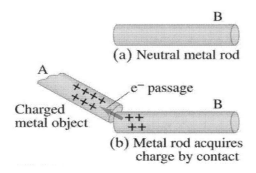

(a) Neutral metal rod

(b) Metal rod acquires charge by contact

The rods can be charged by induction. In the figure below, the two rods never touch, and the neutral rod is grounded. This means that electrons from the neutral rod can be transferred to the ground and leave the surface of their object.

In diagram (b), when the negatively charged rod is brought near the neutral rod, the electric field will attract positive charge and cause the negatively charged electrons to be repelled and go into the ground.

If the connection to ground is cut (such that electrons cannot flow back into the system) and the negatively charged rod is removed, the neutral rod will now have a positive charge evenly distributed across its surface (c).

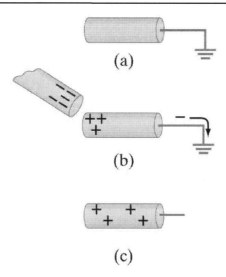

Insulators will not become charged by conduction or induction but will experience a charge separation as *polarization.*

Unlike conductors, insulators do not have electrons that can move freely about the material. Instead, when a strong charge is brought near the insulator, the molecules become polarized and orient themselves such that charges on the molecule align themselves with the electric field (like electric dipoles in an electric field).

This is seen in the figure below.

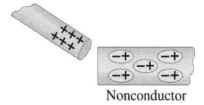

Nonconductor

A device called an electroscope can be used for detecting charge in an object. Below is a picture of a gold leaf electroscope. The gold arms in the middle will hang together if there is no charge, and spread apart when there is a charge present.

An object is held near to (a) or touching (b) the metal knob on top.

If electrons flow one way or the other due to induction or conduction (diagrams (a) and (b) respectively), the gold leaves become similarly charged, and repel.

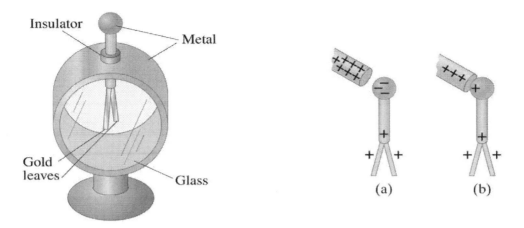

The charged electroscope can be used to determine the sign of an unknown charge.

If a negatively charged object is held near the knob and the leaves expand wider still, it means that even more electrons are trying to get away from the like-charged object, causing an even stronger negative charge in both of the two leaves.

If a positively charged object is held near the knob and the leaves swing in toward each other, it means electrons are cramming into the knob to be close to the presence of the opposite charge; the leaves will not be as negatively charged as before, and there will be less of a force driving them apart.

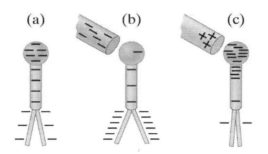

Notes

Gauss's Law

Gauss's Law relates the flow of a vector field through a surface to the behavior of the vector field inside the surface.

In this case, the vector field in question will be an electric field:

$$\Phi_E = EA \cos (\theta)$$

where Φ_E is the electric flux (V·m), E is the electric field (N/C), A is the area that the field covers and θ is the angle between the field and plane that runs perpendicular to the direction of field flow.

For an enclosed surface, the electric flux is equal to the charge inside the enclosure (q), over the permittivity of free space (ε_0).

$$\Phi_E = \frac{q}{\varepsilon_0}$$

The net electric flux through any enclosed surface is totally dependent on the charge inside. If there is no charge inside, then the net electric flux through the enclosure is zero.

Electric flux through an area is proportional to the total number of field lines crossing the area. In diagram (a) below, an electric field passes through an area A that is at an angle with respect to the electric field.

The electric flux is either proportional to the electric field that is perpendicular to that area, as in diagram (b), or to the electric field passing through the projection of the area perpendicular to the electric field, as in diagram (c).

Regardless of the method, the two values will be equal.

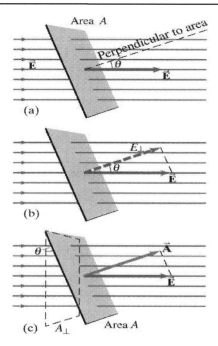

The flux through a closed surface of multiple electrical fields is found by the sum:

$$\Phi_E = E_1 \Delta A_1 \cos(\theta_1) + E_2 \Delta A_2 \cos(\theta_2) + \ldots = \sum E\Delta\ A\cos(\theta) = \sum E_\perp \Delta A$$

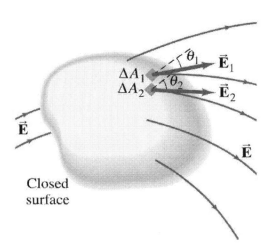

The net number of field lines through the surface is proportional both to the charge enclosed and the flux, giving Gauss's Law:

$$\sum_{\substack{closed \\ surface}} E_\perp \Delta A = \frac{Q_{encl}}{\epsilon_0}$$

This is used to find the electric field in situations with a high degree of symmetry.

Chapter Summary

Charge

- There are two kinds of electric charge — positive and negative.

- Charge is always conserved.

- The charge on an electron is: $e = 1.602 \times 10^{-19}$ C

- Charge is quantized in units of e (how many times greater than the charge on an electron).

- Conductors are materials in which electrons are free to move.

- Insulators are nonconductors and do not allow electrons to move freely.

- Objects can be charged by conduction or induction.

Electric Fields

- Coulomb's Law gives the magnitude of the electrostatic force: $F = k \times \frac{Q_1 Q_2}{r^2}$

- Electric field is force per unit charge: $\vec{E} = \frac{\vec{F}}{q}$

- Electric field is given by a single point charge: $E = \frac{F}{q} = \frac{kqQ/r^2}{q} = k \times \frac{Q}{r^2}$

- Electric fields are represented by electric field lines.

- Static electric field inside a conductor is zero; the surface field is perpendicular to the surface.

- Electric flux (flow of a field through a closed surface):

$$\Phi_E = E_\perp A = E A_\perp = E A \cos(\theta)$$

- Gauss's Law (electric flux through a closed surface):

$$\sum_{\substack{closed \\ surface}} E_\perp \Delta A = \frac{Q_{encl}}{\epsilon_0}$$

Notes

Practice Questions

1. In the figure, $Q = 5.1$ nC. What is the magnitude of the electrical force on the charge Q? (Use Coulomb's constant $k = 9 \times 10^9$ N·m²/C²)

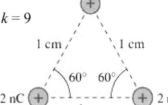

 A. 4.2×10^{-3} N   **C.** 1.6×10^{-3} N

 B. 0.4×10^{-3} N   **D.** 3.2×10^{-3} N

2. Two uncharged metal spheres, A and B, are mounted on insulating support rods. A third metal sphere, C, carrying a positive charge, is then placed near B. A copper wire is momentarily connected between A and B, and then removed. Finally, sphere C is removed. In this final state:

 A. spheres A and B both carry equal positive charges
 B. sphere A carries a negative charge and B carries a positive charge
 C. sphere A carries a positive charge and B carries a negative charge
 D. spheres A and B both carry positive charges, but B's charge is greater

3. Two charges separated by 1 m exert a 1 N force on each other. What is the force on each charge when they are pulled to a separation distance of 3 m?

 A. 3 N   **B.** 0 N   **C.** 9 N   **D.** 0.11 N

4. A balloon after being rubbed on a wool rug can stick to a wall. This illustrates that the balloon has:

  I. magnetism
  II. net charge
  III. capacitance

A. I only   **B.** II only   **C.** III only   **D.** I, II and III

5. The diagram shows two unequal charges $+q$ and $-Q$, of opposite sign. Charge Q has a greater magnitude than charge q. Point X is midway between the charges.

In what section of the line is the point where the resultant electric field could equal zero?

 A. VW   **B.** WX   **C.** XY   **D.** YZ

6. One coulomb of charge passes through a 6 V battery. Which of the following is the correct value for the increase of some property of the battery?

   A. 6 watts   **B.** 6 ohms   **C.** 6 amps   **D.** 6 J

7. What travels through a conductor at near the speed of light when a current is established?

   A. Protons   **B.** Photons   **C.** An electric field   **D.** Electrons

8. Which statement is accurate for a proton that moves in a direction perpendicular to the electric field lines?

   A. it is moving from high potential to low potential and gaining electric potential energy
   B. it is moving from high potential to low potential and losing electric potential energy
   C. it is moving from low potential to high potential and gaining electric potential energy
   D. both its electric potential and electric potential energy remain constant

9. An object with a 6 μC charge is accelerating at 0.006 m/s^2 due to an electric field. If the object has a mass of 2 μg, what is the magnitude of the electric field?

   A. 0.002 N/C   **B.** –0.005 N/C   **C.** 2 N/C   **D.** –2 N/C

10. Two Gaussian surfaces, A and B, enclose the same positive charge $+Q$. The Gaussian surface A has an area two times greater than surface B. Compared to the flux of the electric field through Gaussian surface B, the flux of the electric field through surface A is:

   A. two times smaller   **B.** equal   **C.** two times larger   **D.** four times larger

---

Solutions

1. C is correct.

$$F_e = kQ_1Q_2 / r^2$$

$$F_e = [(9 \times 10^9 \text{ N·m}^2/\text{C}^2)\cdot(5.1 \times 10^{-9} \text{ C})(2 \times 10^{-9} \text{ C})] / (0.1 \text{ m})^2$$

$$F_e = 9.18 \times 10^{-4} \text{ N}$$

$F_e \sin (60°)$ represents the force from one of the positive 2 nC charges.

Double to find the total force:

$$F_{total} = 2F_e \sin (60°)$$

$$F_{total} = 2(9.18 \times 10^{-4} \text{ N}) \sin (60°)$$

$$F_{total} = 1.6 \times 10^{-3} \text{ N}$$

The sine of the angle is used since only the vertical forces are added because the horizontal forces are equal and opposite and therefore they cancel.

---

2. C is correct.

When the positively charged sphere C is near sphere B, it polarizes the sphere causing its negative charge to migrate towards C and a positive charge to build on the other side of sphere B.

The wire between sphere A and sphere B allows negative charge to flow to B and create a net positive charge on sphere A. Once the wire is removed and sphere C is removed, sphere A will have a net positive charge and B has a net negative charge.

3. D is correct.

Coulomb's Law:

$$F_e = kQ_1Q_2 / r^2$$

If r is increased by a factor of 3:

$$F_{new} = kQ_1Q_2 / (3r)^2$$

$$F_{new} = kQ_1Q_2 / (9r^2)$$

$$F_{new} = (1/9)kQ_1Q_2 / r^2$$

$$F_{new} = F_{original}(1/9)$$

$$F_{new} = (1 \text{ N}) \cdot (1/9)$$

$$F_{new} = 0.11 \text{ N}$$

4. B is correct.

The balloon sticks to the wall because the rubbing on the wool has transferred charges to the balloon, leading to an electrostatic force.

5. A is correct.

If the charge Q is of a greater magnitude than charge q then the electric field points toward Q (because its negative) in section W to Z.

In section VW the electric field is the difference in magnitude between q and Q. If Q has a large enough charge, then the difference could equal zero, and there is no electric field.

6. D is correct.

A volt is defined as the potential difference that causes 1 C of charge to increase potential energy by 1 J. Therefore, moving 1 C through 6 V causes the potential energy of the battery to increase by 6 J.

7. C is correct.

A current is caused by a voltage (potential difference) across a conductor.

Whenever a voltage exists an electric field exists, and this travels at near the speed of light. Electrons do not travel quickly when a current is established and only travel at their drift speed which is proportional to voltage.

8. D is correct.

A proton moving perpendicular to electric field lines does not get close to the charges creating the electric field. Thus its electric potential and potential energy remain constant because these values are related to distance from other charges.

Electric Potential Energy:

$$U = kQq \,/\, r$$

Electric Potential:

$$V = kQ \,/\, r$$

9. A is correct.

Convert all units to their correct form:

$$F = ma$$
$$F = (2 \times 10^{-6} \text{ kg}) \cdot (0.006 \text{ m/s}^2)$$
$$F = 1.2 \times 10^{-8} \text{ N}$$

Substituting into the equation for electric field:

$$E = F \,/\, q$$
$$E = (1.2 \times 10^{-8} \text{ N}) \,/\, (6 \times 10^{-6} \text{ C})$$
$$E = 0.002 \text{ N/C}$$

Note: $1 \text{ N} = 1 \text{ kg} \cdot \text{m/s}^2$, not $1 \text{ g} \cdot \text{m/s}^2$

10. B is correct.

$$\Phi = Q \,/\, E_0$$

For an enclosed charge, the area of the surface does not affect the flux.

Please, leave your Customer Review on Amazon

Chapter 4

DC and RC Circuits

- **Electric Circuits**

- **Batteries, Electromotive Force, Voltage**

- **Current**

- **Resistance**

- **Power**

- **Kirchhoff's Laws**

- **Capacitance**

- **Inductors**

- **DC Circuits**

- **Alternating Currents and Reactive Circuits**

- **LCR circuits**

- **Transformers and Transmission of Power Transformers**

- **Measuring Devices**

Electric Circuits

An *electric circuit* is a series of connections between a voltage source, circuit elements and conducting wires, which result in a flow of current.

The voltage source is the energy input and is necessary for continuing the flow of energy.

The circuit elements can use some of the energy from the voltage source as heat or light. The current in a circuit will always flow from high potential to low potential through the external circuit.

A complete circuit is one where current can flow in a complete loop. Below, the left image shows a complete circuit. The battery provides a potential difference, which causes current to flow from its positive terminal, through the light bulb, then to its negative terminal, completing the loop.

The figure on the right is a schematic circuit drawing of the circuit on the left.

Note that the schematic drawing does not look much like the physical circuit.

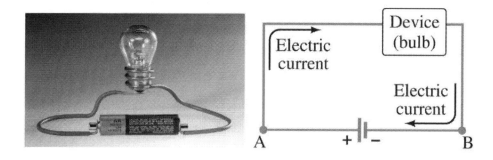

Notes

Batteries, Electromotive Force, Voltage

The electric potential difference is particularly important in solving circuit problems. The *electromotive force* (EMF) is used to describe the measure of energy that causes the flow of current in a circuit. It is defined as the potential difference between two points in a circuit and is the energy per unit of charge given by an energy source.

This is the same as the amount of work done on one unit of electric charge, given in volts (V).

Batteries are physical devices that produce an electric potential difference and are used to provide the EMF in electric circuits. These devices operate by transforming chemical energy into electrical energy.

Chemical reactions within the battery cell create a potential difference between two terminals. This potential difference can be maintained, even if a current is kept flowing until eventually the chemical reaction has exhausted itself and the battery can no longer maintain a potential difference.

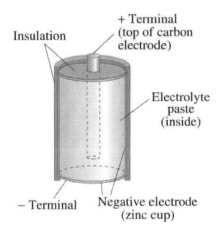

Internal resistance of a battery

Although batteries are depicted as having no resistance, all non-ideal batteries will have some internal resistance. The internal resistance of a battery is like a resistor right next to the battery, connected in series.

If the battery in a circuit has no internal resistance (ideal case), the potential difference across the battery equals the EMF.

If the battery does have an internal resistance, the potential difference across the battery equals the EMF, minus the voltage drop due to internal resistance.

This is *terminal voltage* and is given by:

$$V_{ab} = V_0 - IR_{battery}$$

where V_{ab} is the terminal voltage of the battery (V), V_0 is the voltage before internal resistance (V), I is the current through the battery (A) and $R_{battery}$ is the internal resistance of the battery (Ω).

The figure below depicts a non-ideal battery with internal resistance and resulting terminal voltage.

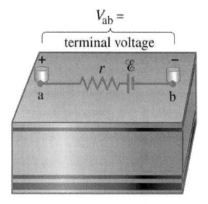

Batteries in series and parallel

When two or more batteries are in series, the total potential difference provided is the sum of the EMF provided by each battery. It is important to note that this is only the case if the terminals are aligned such that the batteries' terminals go from positive to negative, or vice versa. For example, the figure below shows two batteries in series (note that these batteries have internal resistance and the voltage shown is the terminal voltage). The total voltage provided by the two batteries is:

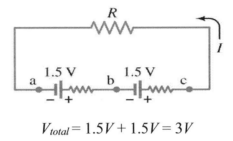

$$V_{total} = 1.5V + 1.5V = 3V$$

When the batteries are in series but aligned such that the positive terminal goes to positive or negative to negative, then the total voltage provided is the difference between the two batteries. In this case, however, the battery with less voltage is being charged:

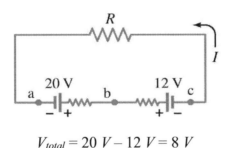

$$V_{total} = 20\ V - 12\ V = 8\ V$$

Batteries in parallel will produce the same voltage but can support larger current draws depending upon the resistance of the circuit.

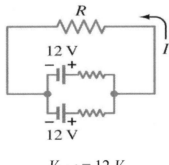

$$V_{total} = 12\ V$$

Notes

Current

Current is the result of electron flow through a conductor. Electrons in a conductor are loosely bound to the nuclei and have large, random speeds dependent upon the temperature of the conductor. For example, metals are well-known conductors because one electron from each atom is loosely bound and free to move through the metal lattice. When an electric potential difference is applied across a metal or any conducting material, it creates an electrical field that passes through the conductor at near the speed of light.

Accordingly, the free electrons in the conductor are attracted against the line direction of the electric field due to Coulomb attraction forces. As they pass through the conduction material, these electrons acquire an average drift velocity, which although considerably smaller than the thermal velocity of the electrons, creates the electric current through the conductor.

Observe the diagram below of a conductor with an applied potential difference and subsequent electric field.

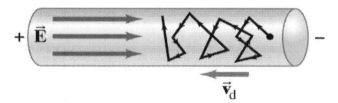

The current through the conductor is calculated as the number of electrons drifting through a unit's volume at the drift velocity:

$$I = nq_eAv_d$$

where I is the current (A), n is the number of electrons per unit volume (electrons/m^3), A is the area of the conductor (m^2), v_d is the drift velocity (m/s) and q_e is the charge of an electron (1.6×10^{-19} C).

More generally, the electric current is defined as the rate at which charge flows through a conductor, and can be expressed as:

$$I = \frac{\Delta q}{\Delta t}$$

There are two types of current: direct current (DC), and alternating current (AC).

A *direct current* is when a constant potential difference is applied to the circuit, and the current moves only in one direction. This is characteristic of electronic devices, batteries, and solar cells.

However, nearly all generated electricity is an *alternating current*, in which the potential difference is quickly cycled between high and low, creating an oscillatory current flow. It is transmitted over high voltage lines and "stepped down" for use in homes and industry.

Resistance

Resistivity ($\rho = RA/l$)

Electrical resistance is the loss of current energy (electron flow) through a material. There are two sources of electrical resistance: collisions with other electrons in current, or collisions with other charges in the material. These factors are taken into account as the resistance, which is determined by the resistivity of a material (a measure of conductance) and several other factors, including geometry and temperature. For instance, in most electronic circuit applications, wires are used to transmit current from one point to another.

The resistance of a wire depends upon the length, the cross-sectional area, the temperature, and the material:

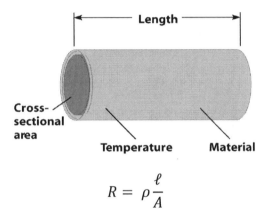

$$R = \rho \frac{\ell}{A}$$

where R is the resistance (Ohms or Ω), ρ is the resistivity ($\Omega \cdot$m), ℓ is the length of the wire (m) and A is the cross-sectional area of the wire (m^2).

Notice the resistivity is directly proportional to the resistance; therefore, the greater the resistivity, the greater the resistance of the material. Additionally, resistance is inversely proportional to the area (inverse square to the radius and diameter).

Therefore, the greater the diameter, the less resistance there will be. This is logical, as there is a larger area for electrons to flow. As shown mathematically in the equation above, a wire of low resistance will be short, of large diameter and made from a material that has low resistivity. For this reason, extension cords are made thicker to keep the resistance low.

The resistance of a wire is dependent upon the temperature of the material. This is because, for any given material, the resistivity increases with temperature:

$$\rho_T = \rho_0[1 + \alpha(T - T_0)]$$

where ρ_T is the resistivity at a temperature T ($\Omega \cdot m$), ρ_0 is the standard resistivity at a standard temperature of T_0 ($\Omega \cdot m$), α temperature coefficient of resistivity (K^{-1}) and T is temperature (K)

Ohm's Law (I = V/R)

Ohm's Law gives the relationship between the potential difference across a resistance and the current through the resistance.

In electrical circuits, Ohm's Law states that the current through a conductor between two points is directly proportional to the potential difference, or voltage across, the two points, and inversely proportional to the resistance between them:

$$I = \frac{V}{R} \quad \text{or} \quad V = IR$$

where V is the potential difference (V), I is the current (A), and R is the resistance (Ω).

Resistors in series

In a circuit, *resistors* may be arranged in series or parallel.

In a series arrangement, the resistors have a current pass through the first resistor, then into the second, into the third and so on:

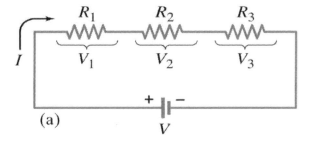

When in series, the total resistance of the circuit is the sum of all the resistances of the components, which means that as more elements are added to the circuit, the total resistance increases, and the total current drops. The equivalent resistance of resistors in series is found by:

Resistance in a Series Circuit $= R_{equivalent} = R_1 + R_2 + R_3 + ...$

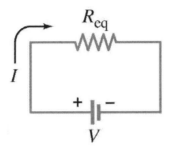

In a series circuit, the current through each resistor is the same ($I_{series} = I_1 = I_2 = I_3$); however, the voltage drops across each resistor. The voltage drop among resistors in series is split according to the resistance—a greater resistance equals a greater voltage drop ($V = IR$).

This can be expanded for more than one resistor, by splitting it into components:

$$V = V_1 + V_2 + V_3 = IR_1 + IR_2 + IR_3$$

Resistors in parallel

Parallel resistors are arranged such that all resistors (in parallel) experience the same voltage drop across them, but have different currents through them according to their resistances.

In a parallel circuit, there is more than one available path for the current to take.

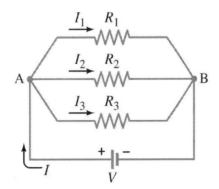

The equivalent resistance of resistors in parallel is found by:

$$\frac{1}{R_{equivalent}} = \frac{1}{R_1} + \frac{1}{R_2} + \frac{1}{R_3} + \cdots$$

As stated earlier, in an arrangement of parallel resistors, the voltage across each resistor is the same ($V_{parallel} = V_1 = V_2 = V_3$) however the current across each resistor is not.

The total current is found as the sum of the currents across each resistor:

$$\frac{V}{R_{eq}} = \frac{V}{R_1} + \frac{V}{R_2} + \frac{V}{R_3}$$

$$I = \frac{V}{R_{eq}}$$

Most common circuits are combinations of series and parallel circuits.

For example, household circuits are a combination of series and parallel circuits.

Generally, outlets in the same room are in series, but the separate rooms are in parallel. This is the reason why a blown fuse may cut the power to an entire room, but not the entire house.

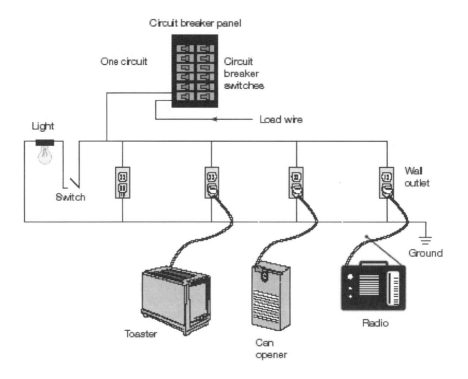

Power

The *power* (P) in a circuit is the rate at which energy is converted from electrical energy into some other form, such as heat or mechanical energy. The SI unit is the watt, which is equal to joules per second. For a component in a DC circuit, power is given by:

$$P = IV$$

where P is the power (W), I is the current (A), and V is the voltage (V).

Using Ohm's Law, power in an electrical circuit can be expressed as:

$$P = I^2 \times R$$

Notes

Kirchhoff's Laws

Kirchhoff's Laws are useful to solve for unknown components within a circuit.

Kirchhoff's Current Law

Kirchhoff's Current Law is an expression of the conservation of charge. By the Law of Conservation of Charge, a charge cannot be created or destroyed.

Therefore, in a circuit, the sum of all currents entering a junction must be equal to the sum of all currents exiting the junction.

$$I_{entering,total} = I_{exiting,total}$$

Kirchhoff's Voltage Law

Kirchhoff's Voltage Law is an expression of the conservation of energy.

The voltage law states that the sum of all voltage drops, across any resistive elements within a closed circuit loop, must equal the EMF in the same loop.

$$\sum V_{drop} = EMF_{total}$$

When solving problems that require the use of Kirchhoff's rules, follow these steps:

1. Label each current.

2. Identify unknowns.

3. Apply junction and loop rules; as many independent equations will be needed as there are unknowns.

4. Solve the equations, being careful with signs.

For example, apply Kirchhoff's circuit laws to the circuit below:

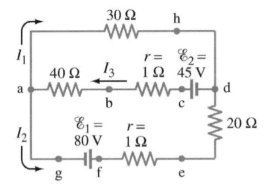

Apply Kirchhoff's Current Law:

$$I_1 + I_2 = I_3$$

Apply Kirchhoff's Voltage Law:

Loop CBAHD: $45V = I_3(1\Omega) + I_3(40\Omega) + I_1(30\Omega)$

Loop FEDCBAG: $80V = I_2(1\Omega) + I_2(20\Omega) + 45V + I_3(1\Omega) + I_3(40\Omega)$

Loop FEDHAG: $80V = I_2(1\Omega) + I_2(20\Omega) - I_1(30\Omega)$

Capacitance

A *capacitor* is a device used to store electrical charge. A basic capacitor usually consists of two conductors that are close but not touching. The two conducting plates can be separated by an insulator of a dielectric, or by air.

In diagram (a), a parallel plate capacitor has no insulator, and only air is between the plates.

Diagram (b) depicts a variation of the parallel plate capacitor in which there is an insulating material.

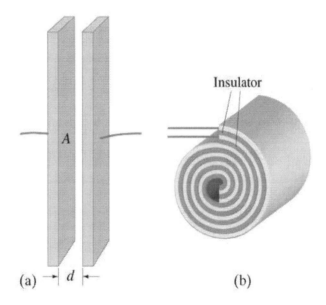

A capacitor's ability to store charge is *capacitance*, measured in Farads (F).

The capacitance does not depend on the voltage; it is a function of the geometry and materials of the capacitor.

Capacitance is expressed by:

$$C = \frac{Q}{V}$$

where C is the capacitance (F), Q is the charge (J), and V is the voltage (V).

Parallel-plate capacitor

The simplest form of a capacitor is that of the parallel-plate capacitor. It consists, as its name implies, of two conductors in the form of plates, which are parallel and separated by air or a dielectric material.

In the diagrams below, a parallel-plate capacitor is connected to a battery, and the equivalent circuit diagram is on the right.

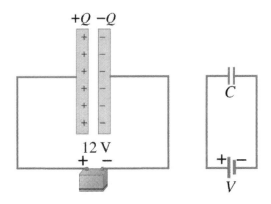

The capacitance of a parallel plate capacitor is expressed as:

$$C = \frac{Q}{V} = \frac{\epsilon_0 \, A}{d}$$

where ϵ_0 is the permittivity of space (8.854×10^{-12} F/m), k is the relative permeability of the dielectric material; A is the area of the plates, not the sum of the areas (m^2) and d is the plate separation (m).

The voltage (V) across the capacitor is found as the product of the electric field between the plates and the plate separation:

$$V = E \times d$$

where E is the electric field between the capacitor (V·m^{-1}).

Dielectrics

A *dielectric* is a non-conductive material that does not readily allow a current to pass through the material. Inserting a dielectric between the plates of a capacitor increases the capacitance by allowing more charge to be stored on the plates of the capacitor. For example, the diagrams below shows an air-filled parallel plate capacitor and a dielectric-filled parallel plate capacitor.

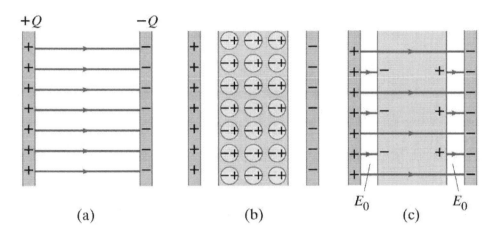

(a)   (b)   (c)

In an air-filled parallel plate capacitor (a), the amount of charge stored is limited by the strength of the electric field between the plates.

If too much charge is stored between the plates (b), a strong electric field will develop which will ionize the air and cause an arc of charge to jump across the plates.

When a dielectric is placed between the plates, the dielectric material becomes polarized (insulator in an electric field) and inhibit the formation of a strong electric field between the plates (c).

Accordingly, more charge (and thus a higher capacitance) can be stored on the plates before the dielectric material breaks down and allows current to pass through it.

The capacitance of a parallel plate capacitor with a dielectric is expressed as:

$$C = \frac{Q}{V} = \frac{k \, \epsilon_0 \, A}{d}$$

where k is the relative permeability of the dielectric material (unitless).

Energy of charged capacitor

A charged capacitor stores electric energy; the energy stored is equal to the work done to charge the capacitor.

$$U = \frac{1}{2}QV = \frac{1}{2}CV^2 = \frac{1}{2}\frac{Q^2}{C}$$

where U is the potential energy of the charged capacitor (J), Q is the charge stored (magnitude of either $+Q$ or $-Q$ on one of the plates) (C), and C is capacitance (F).

The energy density of the capacitor is defined as the energy of the electric field per unit volume, and is expressed as:

$$energy\ density = \frac{PE}{volume} = \frac{1}{2}k\,\epsilon_0\,E^2$$

Capacitors in series

Like resistors, capacitors can be connected in series or parallel in a circuit. For capacitors in series, the equivalent capacitance is found as the sum of the reciprocals of the individual capacitance:

$$\frac{1}{C_{eq}} = \frac{1}{C_1} + \frac{1}{C_2} + \frac{1}{C_3}$$

Additionally, all capacitors in series have the same charge, but the voltage across each capacitor is different:

$$V_1 \neq V_2 \neq V_3$$

$$Q_1 = Q_2 = Q_3$$

Capacitors in parallel

Capacitors may be connected in parallel, as depicted below:

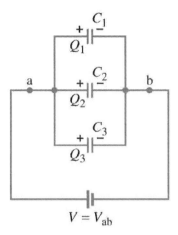

In this case, all the capacitors will have the same voltage, and the equivalent capacitance will be the sum of the individual capacitances.

$$V_1 = V_2 = V_3$$

$$C_{equivalent} = C_1 + C_2 + C_3$$

However, capacitors in parallel will hold different charges:

$$Q_1 \neq Q_2 \neq Q_3$$

Notes

Inductors

Inductors are circuit devices that resist changes in current, through the application of Faraday's Law.

Typical inductors consist of coils of wire wrapped around different types of the core material. They operate by producing a back EMF against a change in a current (according to Lenz's Law and Faraday's Law).

Unit for the inductor is the *H*enry (H), and the back EMF produced is expressed as:

$$EMF = -L\frac{\Delta I}{\Delta t}$$

where *EMF* is the opposing voltage produced (V), *L* is the inductance of the inductor (H) and $\frac{\Delta I}{\Delta t}$ is the change in current over the change in time (A/s).

The magnetic field produced by an inductor stores energy similar to the electric field of a capacitor. The energy stored in this magnetic field is expressed as:

$$U = \frac{1}{2} \times \frac{B^2}{\mu_0}$$

where *U* is the stored energy (J), *B* is the magnetic field (T), and μ_0 is the permeability of free space (1.2566×10^{-6} m kg/s^2 A^2)

Notes

DC Circuits

RC Circuits

A simple RC circuit consists of a resistor and capacitor in series, connected to a potential difference; the capacitor begins to charge when the switch is closed, and the circuit forms a complete loop.

Below is a diagram of an RC circuit with the switch open.

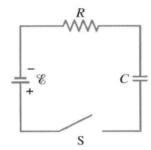

When the switch is closed, the capacitor will begin to charge over time. The voltage across the capacitor increases with time and is expressed as:

$$V_C = V(1 - e^{-t/RC})$$

where V_C is the voltage across the capacitor (V), V is the potential difference across the circuit (V), t is time (s), R is resistance (Ω), and C is the capacitance (F).

The charge follows a similar curve:

$$Q_C = CV_b(1 - e^{-t/RC})$$

where $V_b = V_R + V_C$. V_R is the voltage across the resistor (V), and Q_C is the charge across the capacitor (C).

The current through the circuit is the same everywhere (series circuit) and is expressed as:

$$I = \frac{V_b}{R}(e)^{-t/RC}$$

where I is the current through the circuit (A).

This curve has a characteristic time constant:

$$\tau = RC$$

where τ is the time constant (s).

The graphs below display the voltage across the charging capacitor and current across the circuit.

Diagram (b) illustrates the growth curve of voltage over time. Notice that the capacitor reaches 63% voltage in one time constant and is ~100% voltage after three-time constants.

Diagram (c) displays the decay in current over time. Notice that after one time constant, the current is 37% of its original value (t = 0 seconds), and after three-time constants, the current is nearly zero amps.

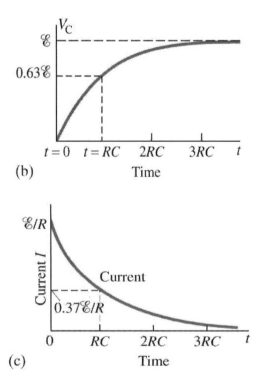

During the discharge of a capacitor, the capacitor acts as a battery and drives current flow, which decreases with time as the capacitor discharges.

In this case, the capacitor voltage decays and is expressed as:

$$V_C = V_0(e)^{-t/RC}$$

where V_0 is the charged voltage across the capacitor (V).

The charge through the discharging capacitor follows a similar decay and is expressed as:

$$Q = CV_0(e)^{-t/RC}$$

The current in the circuit when the capacitor is discharging is expressed as:

$$I = \frac{V_0}{R}(e)^{-t/RC}$$

When the capacitor is discharging, the voltage, charge and current all follow a similar decay curve.

The figure below shows the voltage decay curve of a discharging capacitor. Although this curve represents the voltage, both the charge and current would have exponential decay curves that follow this pattern.

Also notice that by one time constant the voltage, charge, and current would be at 37% of the max value (t = 0 seconds), and by three-time constants, all three will have decayed to nearly zero.

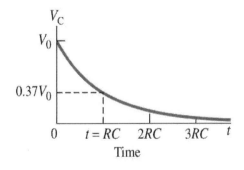

LR Circuits

A simple *LR circuit* consists of an inductor in series with a resistor, connected to a potential difference. In this configuration the inductor will resist change in current through the circuit, therefore causing a gradual, rather than abrupt, rise in current when the loop is closed.

After a period, the current remains steady and be equal to that if the circuit were a resistor alone (assuming ideal inductor with no resistance).

Below is a figure of an LR circuit with a switch that can either connect or disconnect the circuit to a potential difference.

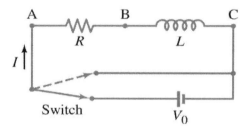

When the switch is initially open such that there is no potential difference, there will be no current through the circuit.

When the switch is closed, the voltage across the capacitor is:

$$V_\text{L} = V_b e^{-tR/L}$$

where V_L is the voltage across the inductor (V), R is the resistance of the resistor (Ω), and L is the inductance of the inductor (H).

$V_b = V_L + V_R$ and V_R is the voltage across the resistor (V)

The current across the circuit is expressed as:

$$I = \left(\frac{V_b}{R}\right)(1 - e^{-tR/L})$$

where I is the current across the circuit (A).

The time constant of an LR circuit is:

$$\tau = \frac{L}{R}$$

where τ is the time constant (s).

The growth curve of the current through the circuit is below. Although it is not displayed, the maximum current is reached in approximately three-time constants (like the RC circuit), and after one time constant, the circuit has reached 63% of its maximum current.

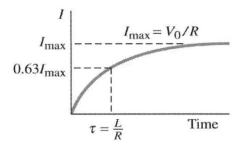

If the switch is opened, such that the potential difference is no longer across the circuit, but the circuit remains closed, the current will decay according to:

$$I = I_{max}e^{-t/\tau}$$

In this case, the current decays from its maximum value, and after one time constant will be at 37% of its maximum; after three-time constants, the circuit will have approximately zero current through it.

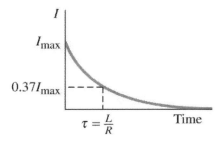

Notes

Alternating Currents and Reactive Circuits

As mentioned in the introduction to this chapter, the current provided by a battery flows steadily in one direction. This is where *direct current*, or DC, gets its name. However, the power supplied by an electrical generation plant is always delivered in alternating current. The two figures below demonstrate current vs time for DC and. AC systems.

Diagram (a) shows a DC system in which the current is held steadily over time. Conversely, in diagram (b) the current varies sinusoidally, and the result is *alternating current*. An alternating current may vary as a function of a square wave or triangular wave. However, in the vast majority of applications, the current is supplied as a sinusoidal function.

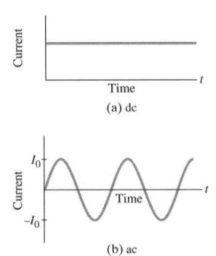

The sinusoidal variation in current is expressed as a function of the frequency:

$$I = I_0 \sin \omega t = I_0 \sin 2\pi f t$$

where I_0 is the max current (amplitude) given in (A), ω is the frequency (rad/s) and f is the frequency (Hz).

Like the current, the voltage varies in a sinusoidal motion when graphed against time. This is expressed as:

$$V = V_0 \sin 2\pi f t = V_0 \sin \omega t$$

where V_0 is the max voltage (amplitude) given in (V).

The power delivered is found through the multiplication of the current squared and the voltage:

$$P = IV = I(IR) = I^2R = I^2_0R \sin^2 \omega t$$

Usually, the average power is of most interest, which is found by using:

$$\bar{P} = \frac{1}{2}I_0^2R = \frac{1}{2}\frac{V_0^2}{R}$$

where $\bar{P}$ is the average power (W) and R is the resistance (Ω).

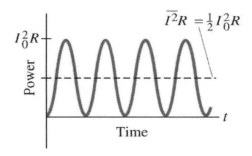

The current and voltage both have average values of zero. Thus they are expressed as root-mean-square values, which is calculated by:

$$I_{rms} = \sqrt{\bar{I^2}} = \frac{I_0}{\sqrt{2}} = 0.707\,I_0$$

$$V_{rms} = \sqrt{\bar{V^2}} = \frac{V_0}{\sqrt{2}} = 0.707\,V_0$$

where I_{rms} is the root-mean-square current (A), and V_{rms} is the root-mean-square voltage (V).

Ohm's Law can then be rewritten using the root-mean-square values:

$$V_{rms} = I_{rms}R$$

The average power can be found using the root-mean-square values:

$$P_{avg} = I_{rms}V_{rms} = I^2_{rms}R$$

LRC Circuits

Resistors, capacitors, and inductors have different phase relationships between current and voltage when placed in an AC circuit instead of a DC circuit. Below is a diagram of a simple AC circuit with an inductor, resistor, and capacitor (LRC circuit):

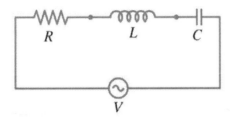

Unlike DC circuits, the current vs. voltage through the different elements of an LRC circuit is time-dependent. As such, the unique characteristics of each element must be known before the entire circuit is analyzed.

For example, the current through a resistor in an AC circuit is in phase with the voltage, meaning both change sign at the same time.

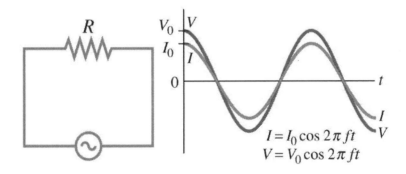

$$I = I_0 \cos 2\pi ft$$
$$V = V_0 \cos 2\pi ft$$

However, the phase relationship between current and voltage in inductors is different. Inductors resist changes in current, therefore the current lags behind the voltage by 90°.

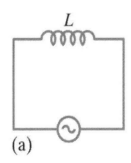

(a)

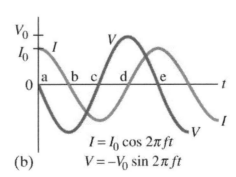

(b)

$$I = I_0 \cos 2\pi ft$$
$$V = -V_0 \sin 2\pi ft$$

Conversely, the capacitor's current leads the voltage by 90°.

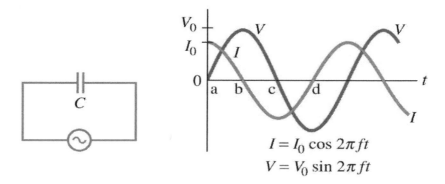

$$I = I_0 \cos 2\pi f t$$
$$V = V_0 \sin 2\pi f t$$

Because both the inductor and capacitor have phase differences with respect to the voltage of their effective resistance (ratio of voltage to current), the root-mean-square current is calculated differently.

The *reactance* is the effective resistance of an inductor or capacitor and is given by:

$$X_L = \omega L = 2\pi f L$$

where X_L is the reactance of the inductor (Ω).

The reactance of the capacitor (X_C) is given by:

$$X_c = \frac{1}{\omega C} = \frac{1}{2\pi f C}$$

where X_c is the reactance of the capacitor (Ω).

Note that both of these equations depend on frequency. From the ratio of voltage to current, the effective resistance (i.e., *impedance*) of the circuit is given by:

$$Z = \sqrt{R^2 + (X_L - X_C)^2}$$

where Z is the impedance (Ω).

The root-mean-square current in an AC circuit is:

$$I_{rms} = \frac{V_{rms}}{Z} = \frac{V_{rms}}{\sqrt{R^2 + (2\pi f L - \frac{1}{2\pi f C})^2}}$$

Clearly, I_{rms} depends on the frequency. I_{rms} is at a maximum when $X_c = X_L$; the frequency at which this occurs is:

$$f_0 = \frac{1}{2\pi}\sqrt{\frac{1}{LC}}$$

where f_0 is the resonant frequency of the circuit (Hz).

This is the *resonant frequency*.

The figure below illustrates the current peak at the resonant frequency for large resistances and small resistances:

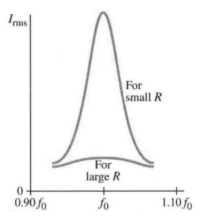

Notes

Transformers and Transmission of Power

Power is transmitted in alternating current for various reasons, but a significant factor is the reduced power losses through power lines when transporting the electricity. If electricity was transported at high current, the result would be large Ohmic power losses through the power lines themselves. These losses are reduced by transporting electricity at high voltages rather than higher currents. This is because according to the power loss equation:

$$P = I^2 R$$

However, how can the voltage be manipulated such that the electricity is transported at high voltage, and then reduced to lower voltages for the consumer? This is possible through electrical devices known as *transformers*. Transformers work only if the current is changing; this is an important reason why electricity is transmitted as AC.

A transformer operates according to Faraday's Law of Electromagnetic Induction and can step-up or step-down the voltage through a line, allowing power companies to reduce power loss during electricity delivery. The device consists of an iron core around which an input wire and output wire are wrapped around. In a step-up transformer (increase voltage) the input wire will have a few primary coils around the iron core, whereas the output wire will have many secondary coils.

When an AC current runs through the input coil, the changing current (sinusoidal variation in current) will induce a magnetic field in the iron core. The magnetic field will loop through the iron core and induce a voltage in the output wire wrapped around the core.

The output voltage is proportional to the number of coils wrapped around the core.

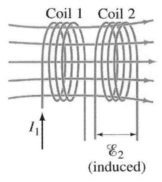

The figure below shows a basic power delivery system. The power station generates electricity, which it sends through a step-up transformer to reduce power loss in transit. The electricity runs the high voltage transmission line to a step-down transformer near the consumer. The electricity is then sent to homes on low voltage lines, where a final step-down transformer lowers the voltage to 240 volts.

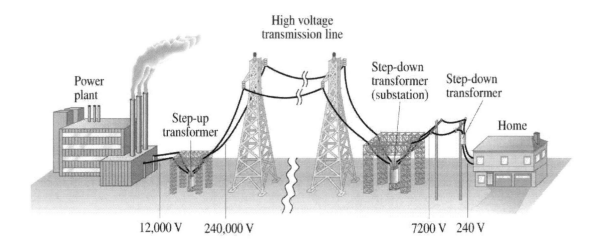

The ratio of the voltages in the primary and secondary coils of a transformer is equal to the ratio of the number of turns in each coil:

$$\frac{V_S}{V_P} = \frac{N_S}{N_P}$$

where V_s is the voltage through the secondary (V), V_P is the voltage through the primary (V), N_S is the number of turns in the secondary and N_P is the number of turns in the primary.

Given that power is found by calculating the product of voltage (V) and current (I), the input power in the primary coil must equal the output power in the secondary coil; this is found through the following relationship:

$$V_p I_p = V_s I_s$$

where I_p is the current through the primary coils (A) and I_s is the current through the secondary coils (A).

Energy must be conserved; therefore, in an ideal system, the ratio of the currents must be the inverse of the ratio of turns:

$$\frac{I_P}{I_S} = \frac{N_S}{N_P}$$

For example, the diagram below is of a step-up transformer. These types of transformer are used at power-generating stations to increase the voltage of the power lines, to reduce Ohmic losses in the lines.

Notice that the primary coil has far fewer turns than the secondary coil.

Accordingly, the voltage through the secondary coil will be much higher, and the electricity can be sent down power lines at a higher voltage with less power loss.

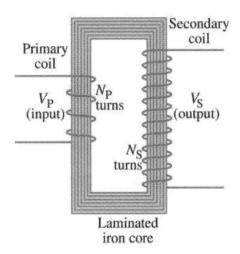

Notes

Measuring Devices

Electric meters are instruments used to measure various aspects of an electric circuit. There are many types; the ammeter and the voltmeter are two of the most commonly used.

Ammeters

An *ammeter* is a device used to measure the current through a circuit. Ammeters usually have two connecting electrodes that are placed alongside the point in the circuit where current is to be measured. A current passes through the ammeter and is recorded and displayed. It is important that an ammeter should have almost no resistance within it. This is because the current in the circuit passes through the ammeter, so the ammeter needs to have low resistance as not to affect the current.

An older but accurate type of ammeter is the galvanometer. The figure below displays a typical galvanometer. The two electrodes are placed at a point in the circuit, and current flows through them.

As the current passes through the coil, it creates a magnetic field whose direction depends upon the direction of the flow of current. The permanent magnets on the side of the coil produce a torque about the coil, which then rotates to display the measured current against a calibrated dial.

The symbol for an ammeter in a circuit diagram is shown below:

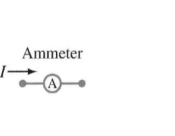

Ammeter

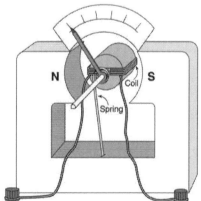

Voltmeters

Voltmeters measure the voltage through two points within a circuit. Like ammeters, they have two connecting electrodes, which are placed on either side of the element to be measured.

However, voltmeters are designed such that they have infinitely high resistance, theoretically pushing all the current through the circuit element and not letting any flow through the voltmeter.

The figure below depicts a voltmeter connected across opposite sides of a resistor to measure the voltage through it.

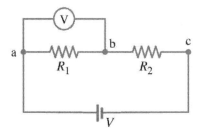

Ohmmeter

An *ohmmeter* is a device used to measure electrical resistance.

Unlike ammeters and voltmeters, it has a battery that allows it to pass current through resistive elements to measure their resistance.

The figure below depicts an ohmmeter symbol:

Chapter Summary

Electric Potential

- Electric potential is potential energy per unit charge: $V_a = \frac{PE_a}{q}$

- A source of EMF transforms energy from another form to electrical energy.

- A battery is a source of constant potential difference.

- Electric potential of a point charge: $V = k\frac{Q}{r}$

  [single point charge V=0 at r=∞] $= \frac{1}{4\pi\epsilon_0}\frac{Q}{r}$

- Kirchhoff's rules:

  − sum of currents entering a junction equals the sum of currents leaving.

  − total potential difference around a closed loop is zero.

Magnetic Fields and Flux

- Magnetic flux: $\Phi_B = B_\perp A = BA\cos(\theta)$

- Changing magnetic flux induces EMF: $\mathcal{E} = -N\frac{\Delta\Phi_B}{\Delta t}$

- An induced EMF produces current that opposes original flux change.

- A changing magnetic field produces an electric field.

- Energy density stored in a magnetic field: $u = energy\ density = \frac{1}{2}\times\frac{B^2}{\mu_0}$

Transformers

- Transformers use induction to change voltage: $\frac{V_S}{V_P} = \frac{N_S}{N_P}$

- Mutual inductance: $\mathcal{E}_2 = -M\frac{\Delta I_1}{\Delta t}$, $\mathcal{E}_1 = -M\frac{\Delta I_2}{\Delta t}$

Circuits

- Electric current is the rate of flow of electric charge.

- Conventional current is in the direction that positive charge would flow.

- A direct current is constant.

- An alternating current varies sinusoidally:

$$I = \frac{V}{R} = \frac{V_0}{R} \sin \omega t = I_0 \sin \omega t$$

- Power in an electric circuit: $P = IV$

- An RC circuit has a characteristic time constant: $\tau = RC$

Resistance

- Resistance is the ratio of voltage to current: $V = IR$

- Ohmic materials have constant resistance, independent of voltage.

- Resistance is determined by shape and material:

$$R = \rho \frac{\ell}{A} \quad (\rho \text{ is the resistivity})$$

- A battery is a source of EMF in parallel with internal resistance.

- Resistors in series: $R_{eq} = R_1 + R_2 + R_3$

- Resistors in parallel: $\frac{1}{R_{eq}} = \frac{1}{R_1} + \frac{1}{R_2} + \frac{1}{R_3}$

Capacitance

- Capacitors are non-touching conductors carrying an equal and opposite charge.

- Capacitance is given by the equation: $Q = CV$

- The capacitance of a parallel-plate capacitor is: $C = \epsilon_0 \frac{A}{d}$

- A dielectric is an insulator (usually used between the plates of a parallel-plate capacitor)

- Dielectric constant gives a ratio of total field to an external field.

- Energy density in an electric field: energy density $= \frac{PE}{volume} = \frac{1}{2} \epsilon_0 E^2$

- Capacitors in parallel:

  o $V = C_{eq} V = C_1 V + C_2 V + C_3 V = (C_1 + C_2 + C_3)V$

  o $C_{eq} = C_1 + C_2 + C_3$

- Capacitors in series:

  o $\frac{Q}{C_{eq}} = \frac{Q}{C_1} + \frac{Q}{C_2} + \frac{Q}{C_3} = Q\left(\frac{1}{C_1} + \frac{1}{C_2} + \frac{1}{C_3}\right)$

  o $\frac{1}{C_{eq}} = \frac{1}{C_1} + \frac{1}{C_2} + \frac{1}{C_3}$

Average RMS

- Current: $I_{rms} = \sqrt{\overline{I^2}} = \frac{I_0}{\sqrt{2}} = 0.707\, I_0$

- Voltage: $V_{rms} = \sqrt{\overline{V^2}} = \frac{V_0}{\sqrt{2}} = 0.707\, V_0$

- $I = \frac{\Delta Q}{\Delta t} = neAv_d$

- LRC series circuit: $z = \sqrt{R^2 + (X_L - X_c)^2}$

Notes

Practice Questions

1. Two parallel circular plates with radii 7 mm carrying equal-magnitude surface charge densities of ± 3 μC/m² are separated by a distance of 1 mm. How much stored energy do the plates have? (Use dielectric constant $k = 1$ and electric permittivity $\mathcal{E}_0 = 8.854 \times 10^{-12}$ F/m)

A. 226 nJ   **B.** 17 nJ   **C.** 127 nJ   **D.** 78 nJ

2. The potential difference between the plates of a parallel plate capacitor is 75 V. The magnitude of the charge on each plate is 3.5 μC. What is the capacitance of the capacitor?

A. 116×10^{-6} F   **B.** 37×10^{-6} F   **C.** 0.7×10^{-6} F   **D.** 4.7×10^{-8} F

3. An electron is released from rest at a distance of 5 cm from a proton. How fast will the electron be moving when it is 2 cm from the proton? (Use Coulomb's constant $k = 9 \times 10^9$ N·m²/C², the mass of an electron $= 9.1 \times 10^{-31}$ kg, the charge of an electron $= -1.6 \times 10^{-19}$ C and the charge of a proton $= 1.6 \times 10^{-19}$ C)

A. 92 m/s   **B.** 123 m/s   **C.** 147 m/s   **D.** 1.3×10^3 m/s

4. A current of 5 A flows through an electrical device for 12 seconds. How many electrons flow through this device during this time? (Use the charge of an electron $= -1.6 \times 10^{-19}$ C)

A. 5.2×10^{18} electrons   **C.** 6.3×10^{19} electrons
B. 3.8×10^{20} electrons   **D.** 1.2×10^8 electrons

5. Two parallel plates are separated by 1 mm. If the potential difference between them is 3 V, what is the magnitude of their surface charge densities? (Use electric permittivity $\mathcal{E}_0 = 8.854 \times 10^{-12}$ F/m)

A. 64×10^{-9} C/m²   **B.** 33×10^{-9} C/m   **C.** 27×10^{-9} C/m²   **D.** 16×10^{-9} C/m²

6. A 3 Ω resistor is connected in parallel with a 6 Ω resistor; both resistors are connected in series with a 4 Ω resistor, and all three resistors are connected to an 18 V battery as shown. If 3 Ω resistor burnt out and exhibits infinite resistance, which of the following is true?

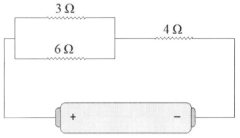

A. The power dissipated in the circuit increases
B. The current provided by the battery remains the same
C. The current in the 6 Ω resistor decreases
D. The current in the 6 Ω resistor increases

7. Each plate of a parallel-plate air capacitor has an area of 0.005 m², and the separation of the plates is 0.08 mm. What is the potential difference across the capacitor when an electric field of 5.6×10^6 V/m is present between the plates?

   A. 367 V   **B.** 578 V   **C.** 448 V   **D.** 227 V

8. What is the current in a wire if a total of 2.3×10^{13} electrons pass a given point in a wire in 15 s? (Use charge of an electron = -1.6×10^{-19} C)

   A. 0.25 µA   **B.** 3.2 µA   **C.** 7.1 µA   **D.** 1.3 µA

9. The resistivity of gold is 2.44×10^{-8} Ω·m at a temperature of 20 °C. A gold wire, 0.6 mm in diameter and 48 cm long, carries a current of 340 mA. What is the number of electrons per second passing a given cross-section of the wire? (Use charge of an electron = -1.6×10^{-19} C)

   A. 2.1×10^{18} electrons   **C.** 1.2×10^{22} electrons
   B. 2.8×10^{14} electrons   **D.** 2.4×10^{17} electrons

10. When the frequency of the AC voltage across a capacitor is doubled, the capacitive reactance of that capacitor will:

   A. become zero   **C.** increase to 4 times its original value
   B. decrease to ½ its original value   **D.** decrease to ¼ its original value

11. A charged particle of mass 0.006 kg is subjected to a 6 T magnetic field, which acts at a right angle to its motion. If the particle moves in a circle of radius 0.1 m at a speed of 3 m/s, what is the magnitude of the charge on the particle?

   A. 3 C   **B.** 30 C   **C.** 3.6 C   **D.** 0.03 C

12. When a current flows through a metal wire, the moving charges are:

   I. protons   II. neutrons   III. electrons

   A. I only   **B.** II only   **C.** III only   **D.** I and II only

13. A kilowatt-hour is equivalent to:

   A. 3.6×10^6 J/s   **B.** 3.6×10^6 J   **C.** 3.6×10^3 W   **D.** 3.6×10^3 J

14. For the graph shown, what physical quantity does the slope of the graph represent?

   A. 1 / Voltage
   B. Resistance
   C. Power
   D. Charge

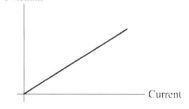

15. What is the voltage across a 15 Ω resistor that has 5 A current passing through it?

A. 3 V   **B.** 5 V   **C.** 15 V   **D.** 75 V

Solutions

1. D is correct.

Find area:

$$A = \pi r^2$$

$$A = \pi (7 \times 10^{-3} \text{ m})^2$$

$$A = 1.54 \times 10^{-4} \text{ m}^2$$

Find capacitance:

$$C = A\mathcal{E}_o k \,/\, d$$

$$C = [(1.54 \times 10^{-4} \text{ m}^2) \cdot (8.854 \times 10^{-12} \text{ F/m}) \cdot (1)] \,/\, (1 \times 10^{-3} \text{ m})$$

$$C = 1.36 \times 10^{-12} \text{ F}$$

Find charge:

$$\sigma = 3 \times 10^{-6} \text{ C/m}^2$$

$$\sigma = Q \,/\, A$$

$$Q = \sigma A$$

$$Q = (3 \times 10^{-6} \text{ C/m}^2) \cdot (1.54 \times 10^{-4} \text{ m}^2)$$

$$Q = 4.6 \times 10^{-10} \text{ C}$$

Find potential energy:

$$U = \tfrac{1}{2} Q^2 \,/\, C$$

$$U = \tfrac{1}{2} (4.6 \times 10^{-10} \text{ C})^2 \,/\, (1.36 \times 10^{-12} \text{ F})$$

$$U = 78 \times 10^{-9} \text{ J}$$

2. D is correct.

Use the relationship:

$$Q = CV$$

$$C = Q \,/\, V$$

$$C = (3.5 \times 10^{-6} \text{ C}) \,/\, (75 \text{ V})$$

$$C = 4.7 \times 10^{-8} \text{ F}$$

3. B is correct.

Use energy relationship: $PE_{before} = PE_{after} + KE$

Electrostatic Potential Energy: $PE = kQq / r$

Solve:

$$kQq / r_1 = kQq / r_2 + \tfrac{1}{2}mv^2$$

$$\tfrac{1}{2}mv^2 = kQq(1 / r_1 - 1 / r_2)$$

$$v^2 = (2kQq / m)\cdot(1 / r_1 - 1 / r_2)$$

$$v = \sqrt{[(2kQq / m)\cdot(1 / r_1 - 1 / r_2)]}$$

$$v = \sqrt{[(2)\cdot(9 \times 10^9 \text{ N·m}^2/\text{C}^2)\cdot(1.6 \times 10^{-19} \text{ C})\cdot(1.6 \times 10^{-19} \text{ C})} /$$

$$(9.1 \times 10^{-31} \text{ kg})]\cdot[(1 / 0.02 \text{ m}) - (1 / 0.05 \text{ m})]$$

$$v = 123 \text{ m/s}$$

Note: only the magnitude of the charge is used.

5. B is correct.

$$1 \text{ amp} = 1 \text{ C/s}$$

# of electrons $= (5 \text{ C/s})\cdot(12 \text{ s} / 1)\cdot(1 \text{ electron} / 1.6 \times 10^{-19} \text{ C})$

# of electrons $= 3.8 \times 10^{20}$ electrons

5. C is correct.

$$Q = A\mathcal{E}_o V / d$$

$$Q / A = \mathcal{E}_o V / d$$

$$Q / A = (8.854 \times 10^{-12} \text{ F/m})\cdot(3 \text{ V}) / (1 \times 10^3 \text{ m})$$

$$Q / A = 27 \times 10^{-9} \text{ C/m}^2$$

6. D is correct. The equivalent resistance of the 3 Ω and 6 Ω resistors is:

$$1 / R_{eq} = 1 / (3 \text{ Ω}) + 1 / (6 \text{ Ω})$$

$$R_{eq} = 2 \text{ Ω}$$

The voltage across the equivalent resistor (i.e., the 6 Ω resistor) is given by the voltage divider relationship:

$$V_6 = 18 \text{ V} (2 \text{ Ω}) / (2 \text{ Ω} + 4 \text{ Ω}) = 6 \text{ V}$$

The current through the 6 Ω resistor is:

$I_6 = V_6 / 6\ \Omega = 1$ A

After the 3 Ω resistor burns out, the voltage across the 6 Ω resistor is found using the voltage divider relationship:

$V_6' = 18$ V $(6\ \Omega) / (6\ \Omega\ +\ 4\ \Omega) = 10.8$ V

Now the current through the 6 Ω resistor is:

$I_6' = V_6' / 6\ \Omega = 1.8$ A

The current has increased.

7. C is correct. Parallel-plate capacitor voltage:

$V = Ed$

$V = (5.6 \times 10^6$ V/m$) \cdot (0.08 \times 10^{-3}$ m$)$

$V = 448$ V

8. A is correct.

1 amp = 1 C/s

$I = (2.3 \times 10^{13}$ electrons $/ 1) \cdot (1.6 \times 10^{-19}$ C $/ 1$ electron$) \cdot (1 / 15$ s$)$

$I = 0.25 \times 10^{-6}$ amps

$I = 0.25$ μA

9. A is correct.

Use definition of one ampere: 1 amp = 1 C/s

Let the current expressed in electrons per second be denoted by I_e.

Solve: $I_e = (340 \times 10^{-3}$ C $/ 1$ s$) \cdot (1$ electron $/ 1.6 \times 10^{-19}$ C$)$

$I_e = 2.1 \times 10^{18}$ electrons/s

10. B is correct. Capacitive Reactance formula: $X_c = 1 / (2\pi Cf)$

If f is doubled: $X_{c2} = 1 / [2\pi C(2f)]$

$X_{c2} = \frac{1}{2}[1 / (2\pi Cf)]$

$X_{c2} = \frac{1}{2}X_c$

Capacitive reactance is halved.

11. D is correct.

Find forces acting on particle:

$$F_{\text{centripetal}} = F_{\text{magnetic}}$$

$$ma_{\text{centripetal}} = qvB$$

$$mv^2 / r = qvB$$

$$q = mv / Br$$

$$q = (0.006 \text{ kg})\cdot(3 \text{ m/s}) / (6 \text{ T})\cdot(0.1 \text{ m})$$

$$q = 0.03 \text{ C}$$

12. C is correct.

In a solid, the locations of the nuclei are fixed; only the electrons move.

13. B is correct.

$$1 \text{ kW} = 1,000 \text{ W}$$

$$1,000 \text{ W} = 1,000 \text{ J/s}$$

$$1 \text{ hr} = (60 \text{ min})\cdot(60 \text{ sec/min})$$

$$1 \text{ hr} = 3,600 \text{ s}$$

$$\text{kW}\cdot\text{hr} = (1,000 \text{ J/s})\cdot(3,600 \text{ s})$$

$$\text{kW}\cdot\text{hr} = 3.6 \times 10^3 \text{ J}$$

14. B is correct.

$$V = IR$$

$$R = V / I$$

15. D is correct.

Voltage = current × resistance

$$V = IR$$

$$V = (5 \text{ A})\cdot(15 \text{ Ω})$$

$$V = 75 \text{ V}$$

Chapter 5

Electromagnetism

- **Magnetic Fields and Poles**

- **Magnetic Field Force**

- **Faraday's Law**

- **Torque on Current-Carrying Wire**

- **Properties of Electromagnetic Radiation**

- **Classification of Electromagnetic Spectrum, Photon Energy**

Magnetic Fields and Poles

Magnetism is a natural phenomenon that has important applications in the modern world. For example, navigation with a compass, memory storage on a computer and high-speed trains all require magnetism and the understanding of the properties of magnets.

The earliest assumption about magnetism was that it was associated with naturally occurring magnetic materials such as iron, cobalt or nickel. Now, it is known that there are a few different ways in which magnetism can be produced. On the atomic level, the electrons of material can produce magnetism due to their motion (the electron spin and revolution). Magnets can be created by electric currents. This is the basis behind electromagnetism.

All magnetic objects emit magnetic fields, which can be visualized using magnetic field lines. These lines are similar to electric field lines in their behavior and always start from the north pole (think positive charge), and go towards the south pole (think negative charge). Unlike the electric field, magnetic fields always form closed loops because all magnets have a north pole and south pole. The figure below shows a bar magnet with a closed loop so that the magnetic field is created from north to south pole.

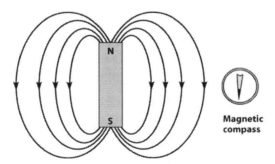

Another example is Earth's magnetic field. Earth's magnetic field originates deep beneath the surface layer and is caused by currents of conductive elements in the molten core. The magnetic field lines originate at the geographic south pole (magnetic north pole) and terminate at the geographic north pole (magnetic south pole). A compass operates by aligning itself with the magnetic field of Earth (because magnetic fields will always form complete loops), allowing the user to navigate with respect to a known axis.

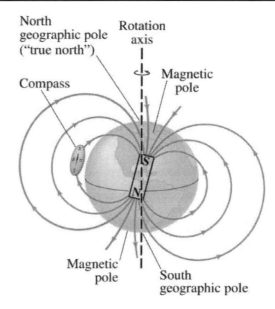

Another important aspect of magnets is that they can never have only one pole, all magnets must have a north and south pole. If a large magnet is broken into two equal halves, it will not produce two   single polarity magnets. Instead, the two fragments will each have their north and south poles. If these pieces are broken again, the process will repeat itself.

Magnets have some other similar behaviors to electrically-charged particles. Most importantly, the poles of two magnets exert a force on each other according to their polarity. Opposite poles will attract, while like poles will repel.

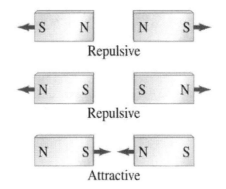

Magnetic fields around a current-carrying wire

As discussed previously, the charge can be made to travel across a conductor if an electric potential difference exists. When this occurs, the traveling charge is the *electric current*, and is the rate of flow of charge through a conductor over time:

$$I = \frac{\Delta q}{\Delta t}$$

where I is the electric current given in amperes (A), and Δt is time (s).

Current is conventionally considered to be the movement of positive charge through a conductor. Although this is technically wrong (protons are immobile, only electrons can "flow"), all diagrams and calculations of current follow this convention.

Remember that the movement of electrons is opposite to that shown. When a current flows through a wire, a magnetic field is formed that circulates the wire.

Direction of the magnetic field is found by the *right-hand rule* (diagram below).

According to the right-hand rule, the thumb goes in the direction of positive charge (i.e., the direction of current by convention), and the direction the fingers curl around in the direction of the magnetic field.

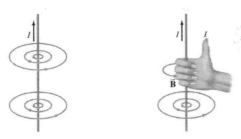

To understand the flow of electrons through the conductor, In the figure below, notice the direction of the magnetic field.

The magnetic field is clockwise because current flows down the wire from top to bottom.

However, the electron flow is opposite to the conventional current flow. Thus electrons flow from bottom to top.

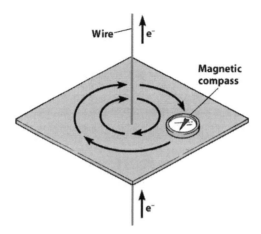

When a magnetic field is induced by a current in a straight wire, the magnetic field strength is calculated by *Ampère's Law*:

$$B = \frac{\mu_0 I}{2\pi r}$$

where μ_0 is the constant of permeability of free space ($4\pi \times 10^{-7}$ T·m/A), I is the current (A), and r is the distance away from the wire (m).

Magnetic fields in solenoids

When a current-carrying wire is wrapped around, such that it forms a loop, it is a *solenoid*. Solenoids have many applications and are the basis for common electromagnets.

The primary importance of a solenoid is that the magnetic field is manipulated, as in the diagrams:

In this configuration, the net magnetic field created by the loop is imagined as:

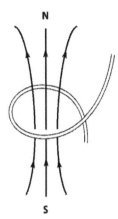

If the number of loops is increased in the solenoid, the magnetic field will increase proportionally with the number of loops. Additionally, if a piece of iron is inserted in the solenoid, the magnetic field greatly increases.

Using the equation for the magnetic field strength of a wire, the magnetic field strength through a solenoid (not outside of) is expressed as:

$$B = \frac{\mu_0 \mu_r n I}{l}$$

where n is the number of loops, μ_r is the relative permeability of core material ($\mu_r = 1$ in air) and l is the length of the solenoid (m).

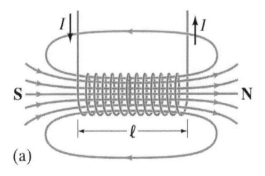

(a)

Notes

Magnetic Field Force

Particles

When a charged particle passes through a magnetic field with a specific velocity, which must be perpendicular to the magnetic field) it will experience a force from the magnetic field. This only occurs if the charge has a velocity perpendicular to the magnetic field.

If its speed is zero or its direction is parallel to the field, then no force is exerted:

$$F = qvB \sin (\theta)$$

where q is the electric charge (C), v is the velocity of the charge (m/s), B is the strength of the magnetic field given in the Tesla (T), and θ is the angle between the charge velocity and the magnetic field (degrees). Sometimes the $\sin(\theta)$ is omitted, as θ is assumed to be 90°.

The magnetic force is always perpendicular to both the magnetic field and the velocity of the charge:

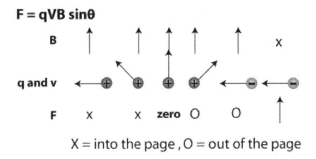

Again, an easy way to remember this is the right-hand rule. The thumb of the right-hand goes in the direction of a positive charge, the middle finger is the direction of the magnetic field, and the palm faces the direction of the force.

If the charge is negative, then the direction of the force is opposite.

Right –hand rules (RHR)

Physical Situation	Example	How to Orient Right Hand	Result
1. Magnetic field produced by current (RHR-1)		Wrap fingers around wire with thumb pointing in direction of current *I*	Fingers curl in direction of $\vec{B}$
2. Force on electric current *I* due to magnetic field (RHR-2)		Fingers first point straight along current *I*, then bend along magnetic field $\vec{B}$	Thumb points in direction of the force $\vec{F}$
3. Force on electric charge +*q* due to magnetic field (RHR-3)		Fingers point along particle's velocity $\vec{v}$, then along $\vec{B}$	Thumb points in direction of the force $\vec{F}$

Motion of charged particles in magnetic fields

When a charged particle travels through a magnetic field, it will be deflected according to the magnitude and direction of the field. The deflection of the particle has important applications, such as mass spectrometers, because it is related to the centripetal force to solve for the mass of the particle.

For example, the equations for centripetal force and magnetic field force on a charged particle are:

$$F_C = \frac{mv^2}{r} \qquad F_M = qvB \sin(\theta)$$

If the particle is assumed to be traveling perpendicular to the magnetic field, then the magnetic field force becomes:

$$F_M = qvB$$

Thus, if a particle with some velocity perpendicular to a magnetic field travels in a circular orbit, the mass is solved for by:

$$\frac{mv^2}{r} = qvB$$

$$m = \frac{qBr}{v}$$

When $qvB < mv^2 / r$, there is not enough centripetal force, and the charged particle will fly out of orbit.

When $qvB > mv^2 / r$, there is too much centripetal force, and the charged particle spirals inward.

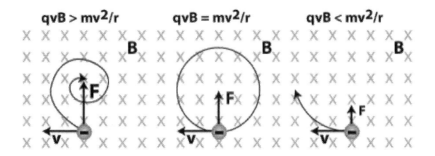

Current-carrying wires

Wires carrying current have charged particles in motion through them.

Consequently, a magnetic field exerts a calculable force on a current-carrying wire.

This is expressed as:

$$F = I\ell B \sin (\theta)$$

where I is the current through the wire (A) and l is the length of wire exposed to the magnetic field (m).

Again, the direction of the force is given by the right-hand rule.

For example, in the diagrams below a length of current-carrying wire is exposed to a magnetic field.

In diagram (a), the current flows in such a manner that the magnetic field exerts a downward force.

If the current is reversed, then the magnetic force will be opposite its original direction and point upwards.

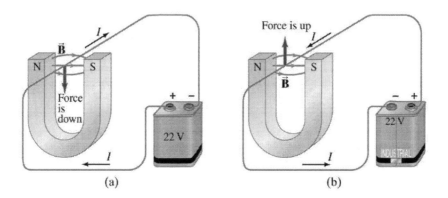

Parallel current-carrying wires

When two current-carrying wires are parallel and close enough such that their magnetic field can interact, they will exert a force on each other according to the magnitude and direction of their respective currents.

The magnitude of the force per unit length of the parallel wire section is given by:

$$\frac{F}{l} = \frac{\mu_0}{2\pi} \frac{I_1 I_2}{d}$$

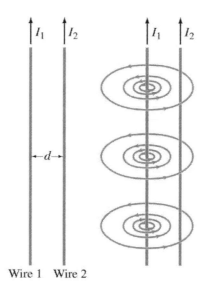

Wire 1   Wire 2

The direction of the force between the wires depends upon the direction of the currents in the wires with respect to each other.

Parallel currents (currents moving in the same direction) create an attractive force; anti-parallel currents (currents moving in opposite directions) create repulsive forces.

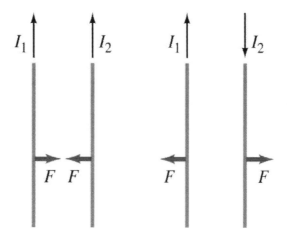

Notes

Faraday's Law

Michael Faraday identified the relationship that linked the induced electromotive force (EMF) in a wire loop proportionally to the rate of change of magnetic flux through the loop. He called this the *Law of Induction*. To understand the full meaning of this law, magnetic flux must first be investigated.

The magnetic flux (Φ_B) is similar to the electric flux and is defined as the amount of magnetic field passing through an area of a surface. The Weber (Wb) is the SI unit of magnetic flux, which is equal to volt-seconds. It may be given in tesla-meters-squared (T·m²).

The equation for computing magnetic flux is:

$$\Phi_B = B_\perp A = BA \cos (\theta)$$

where $B_\perp$ is the magnitude of the magnetic field that is perpendicular to the area (A).

If the field lines are not perpendicular to the area, then the right-hand equation must be used where θ is the angle between the field lines and the vector normal to the surface.

The diagrams below demonstrate the varying amounts of magnetic flux through the coiled wire as it is rotated with respect to the magnetic field.

In diagram (a), the magnetic flux is equal to zero because the coil area is perpendicular to the applied field. Diagram (b) has some magnetic flux because the area of the coil is at an angle to the field, while diagram (c) has the maximum flux because its area is fully parallel to the magnetic field.

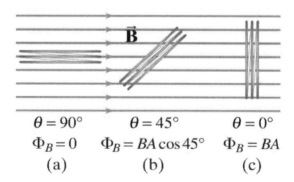

Using an equation for magnetic flux, one can investigate how *Faraday's Law* pertains to the voltage induced in a coiled wire under certain situations. This law states that the induced voltage in a coil is proportional to the number of loops it contains, multiplied by the rate at which the magnetic field changes within those loops.

The magnitude of the current is related to the resistance of the coil, its circuit and the voltage induced. The more coils a wire has, the greater the induced voltage.

However, the higher the voltage, the greater the current that pushes back against the magnet. The rapid motion of the magnet also induces a greater voltage. This relationship is explained in the equation of Faraday's Law of Induction (sometimes referred to as Lenz's Law, named after the scientist who, after more experimentation, added the negative sign):

$$EMF = -N\frac{\Delta\Phi_B}{\Delta t}$$

For example, the diagrams below show a loop of wire exposed to a magnetic field. In diagram (b), the loop is stretched such that the area exposed to the flux changes. According to Faraday's Law, an EMF is induced and current results through the loop.

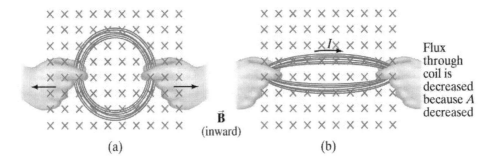

(a)   (b)

An EMF can be formed by a moving conductor.

In diagram (a) below, the rectangle represents a conductor with a movable slide. If the slide is moved outward, then the magnetic flux will change.

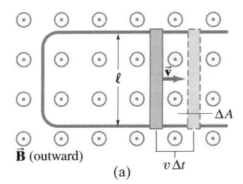

(a)

The induced current from the movement of the sliding bar causes a current to form, as in the diagram below.

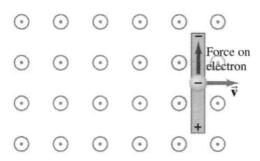

The induced EMF in such a situation has a magnitude of the following form:

$$EMF = \frac{\Delta\Phi_B}{\Delta t} = \frac{B\Delta A}{\Delta t} = \frac{B\ell v\Delta t}{\Delta t} = B\ell v$$

Solving problems with Faraday's Law:

1. Determine whether the magnetic flux is increasing, decreasing or unchanged.

2. The magnetic field due to the induced current points is in the opposite direction to the original field if the flux is increasing, in the same direction if it is decreasing and is zero if the flux is not changing.

3. Use the right-hand rule to determine the direction of the resulting current. To do so, point the thumb in the direction of a vector normal to the area on the side the flux is exiting. The direction curled by the fingers as they close toward the palm is the direction of the current.

4. Remember that the external field and the field due to the induced current are different.

Notes

Torque on Current-Carrying Wire

When a wire carrying a current forms a loop, the current will reverse directions (with respect to the *x* and *y*-axes) as it travels in the loop and out of the loop.

If the loop is exposed to a magnetic field, a torque will be generated about the axis of the loop, due to the opposing forces on each side of the loop. This concept has many applications and is used in equipment such as galvanometers, motors, and loudspeakers.

For example, a galvanometer takes advantage of the torque on a current loop to measure current. Observe the figure below of a galvanometer:

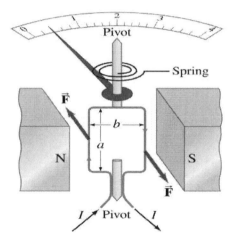

If the current increases in the loop, the force from the magnetic field increases in proportion, and the dial twists more because of increased torque.

The magnitude of the produced torque is calculated by:

$$\tau = nIAB \sin(\theta)$$

where the quantity *nIA* is the magnetic dipole moment, *n* is the number of loops (this equation works for a solenoid), *I* is the current (A), *A* is the area of the enclosed space (m^2) and θ is the angle of the loop area with respect to the magnetic field (degrees).

Notes

Properties of Electromagnetic Radiation

What is electromagnetic radiation?

Electromagnetic radiation is a form of energy that propagates through space as an oscillating electric and magnetic field. Classically, electromagnetic radiation is considered to be a wave; however, in quantum mechanics, electromagnetic radiation is considered as packets of energy as *photons*. Below is a figure of the wave nature of electromagnetic radiation.

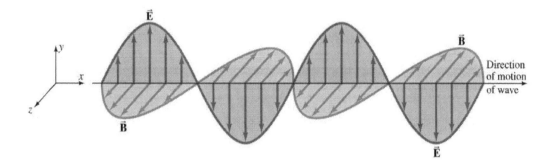

Radiation velocity equals constant *c* in a vacuum

Unlike sound and mechanical waves, electromagnetic radiation does not need a medium in which to propagate. In a vacuum, it has a constant speed of:

$$c = 2.99792458 \times 10^8 \text{ m/s} \approx 3 \times 10^8 \text{ m/s}$$

This is the standard value is the *speed of light*. Nothing in the universe can travel faster than light in a vacuum. Electromagnetic radiation travels slower than this speed in other mediums, according to the value of the mediums' refractive index.

The speed in these mediums is calculated by:

$$v = \frac{c}{n}$$

where *v* is the speed of light in the medium and *n* is the refractive index of that medium.

Production, energy, and momentum of electromagnetic waves

Electromagnetic waves are produced by accelerating charges. The acceleration produces oscillations of electric and magnetic fields (electromagnetic radiation), which propagate through space indefinitely until absorbed.

Like all waves, electromagnetic waves are related by their speed, frequency, and wavelength by:

$$c = \lambda f$$

where c is the speed of light, λ is the wavelength (m), and f is the frequency of the electromagnetic radiation (Hz).

Additionally, when considering electromagnetic radiation from the quantum mechanical viewpoint, the photons have discrete, quantifiable energies related to their frequency. This is found via:

$$E = hf = \frac{hc}{\lambda}$$

where E is the energy per photon (J or eV), and h is Planck's constant (6.626×10^{-34} J·s or 4.135×10^{-15} eV).

Electromagnetic radiation carries momentum. Although the wave has no mass, it still can exert a force as *radiation pressure*. When the radiation is fully absorbed, the radiation pressure is at a minimum, and is expressed as:

$$P_{minimum} = \frac{\bar{I}}{c}$$

When the radiation is fully reflected, the radiation pressure is at a maximum, expressed as:

$$P_{maximum} = \frac{2\bar{I}}{c}$$

where P is the radiation pressure (N/m^2) and I is the intensity of the electromagnetic radiation (W/m^2).

Classification of Electromagnetic Spectrum, Photon Energy

Electromagnetic radiation varies significantly in properties and energies depending on the frequency of the radiation. Observe the figure below showing the spectrum of electromagnetic radiation according to wavelength and frequency. Notice that as frequency increases, the wavelength decreases due to the inverse proportionality of the wavelength vs. frequency. The higher frequency forms of electromagnetic radiation (ultraviolet, X-rays, gamma rays) are all known carcinogens and are harmful to one's health. This is because the high frequency of these forms of radiation gives them high energies, which can cause damage to cells and DNA.

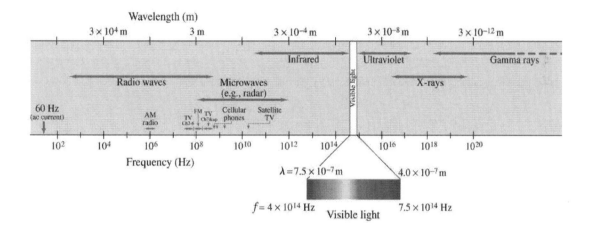

Lower frequency = longer wavelength = less energy	
Radio	Causes electronic oscillations in the antenna
Microwave	Causes molecular rotation
Infrared	Causes molecular vibration
Visible	Can excite electrons to orbits of higher energy. Visible light ranges from 400-700 nm. 400 being violet, 700 is red.
Ultraviolet	Can break bonds and excite electrons so much as to eject them, which is why UV is considered ionizing radiation.
X-rays	Ionizing radiation, the photoelectric effect
Gamma rays	Even more energetic than X-rays
Higher frequency = shorter wavelength = more energy	

Notes

Chapter Summary

Magnets

- Magnets have north and south poles.

- Like poles repel, unlike attract.

- Electric currents produce magnetic fields.

Magnetic Fields

- Given in units of Tesla (T).

- Parallel currents attract, anti-parallel currents repel.

- A magnetic field exerts a force on an electric current in the form:

$$F = I\ell B\sin(\theta)$$

- A magnetic field exerts a force on a moving charge in the form:

$$F = qvB\sin(\theta)$$

- Magnitude of the field of a long, straight current-carrying wire:

$$B = \frac{\mu_0}{2\pi} \times \frac{I}{r}$$

- Ampère's Law (magnitude of a field):

$$\sum B_{\parallel}\Delta\ell = \mu_0 I_{encl}$$

- Magnetic field inside a solenoid: $B = \frac{\mu_0 NI}{\ell}$

Torque

- Torque on a current loop: $\tau = NIAB\sin(\theta)$

Notes

Practice Questions

1. Which one of the following statements is correct?

   A. The north pole of a magnet points towards Earth's geographic North Pole
   B. The north pole of a magnet points towards Earth's geographic South Pole
   C. Earth's geographic North Pole is the north pole of Earth's magnetic field
   D. None of the above

2. With all other factors remaining constant, how does doubling the number of loops of wire in a coil affect the induced emf?

   A. The induced emf increases by a factor of $\sqrt{2}$
   B. The induced emf doubles
   C. There is no change in the induced emf
   D. The induced emf quadruples

3. A proton is traveling to the right and encounters a region S which contains an electric field or a magnetic field or both. The proton is observed to bend up the page. Which of the statements is true regarding region S?

   I. There is a magnetic field pointing into the page
   II. There is a magnetic field pointing out of the page
   III. There is an electric field pointing up the page
   IV. There is an electric field pointing down the page.

   A. I only   **B.** II only   **C.** I and III   **D.** II and IV

4. A light bulb is connected to a circuit and has a wire leading to it in a loop. What happens when a strong magnet is quickly passed through the loop?

   A. The brightness of the light bulb dims or gets brighter due to an induced emf produced by the magnet
   B. The light bulb's brightness remains the same although current decreases
   C. The light bulb gets brighter because more energy is being added to the system by the magnet inside the coil
   D. The light bulb gets brighter because there is an induced emf that drives more current through the light bulb

5. A loop of wire is rotated about a diameter (which is perpendicular to a given magnetic field). In one revolution, the induced current in the loop reverses direction how many times?

   A. 2   **B.** 1   **C.** 0   **D.** 4

6. A charged particle is observed traveling in a circular path in a uniform magnetic field. If the particle had been traveling twice as fast, the radius of the circular path would be:

A. three times the original radius

B. twice the original radius

C. one-half of the original radius

D. four times the original radius

7. A proton, moving in a uniform magnetic field, moves in a circle perpendicular to the field lines and takes time T for each circle. If the proton's speed tripled, what would now be its time to go around each circle?

A. T/3 **B.** T **C.** 6T **D.** 3T

8. A charged particle moves and experiences no magnetic force. What can be concluded?

A. Either no magnetic field exists, or the particle is moving parallel to the field

B. No magnetic field exists in that region of space

C. The particle is moving at right angles to a magnetic field

D. The particle is moving parallel to a magnetic field

9. Which of these electromagnetic waves has the shortest wavelength?

A. γ rays **B.** Visible light **C.** Radio waves **D.** Infrared

10. Which type of electromagnetic (EM) wave travels through space the slowest?

A. Visible light

B. Ultraviolet light

C. Gamma rays

D. All EM waves travel at the same speed

11. A circular loop of wire is rotated about an axis whose direction at constant angular speed can be varied. In a region where a uniform magnetic field points straight down, what orientation of the axis of the rotation guarantees that the emf will be zero (regardless of how the axis is aligned to the loop)?

A. It must be vertical

B. It must make an angle of 45° to the direction South

C. It could have any horizontal orientation

D. It must make an angle of 45° to the vertical

12. Which form of electromagnetic radiation has the highest frequency?

A. Gamma radiation

B. Ultraviolet radiation

C. Visible light

D. Radio waves

Solutions

1. D is correct.

2. B is correct.

Faraday's Law states that the electromotive force (emf) in a coil is:

emf = $N\Delta BA \cos \theta / \Delta t$

where N = number of loops of wire.

If N doubles, the emf doubles.

3. C is correct.

There is a force on the proton up to the page. The electric field points in the direction of the force on positive particles, therefore it is pointed upwards.

The direction of the magnetic field is determined by the right-hand rule.

$F = qvB$, where q is a charge, v is velocity and B is a magnetic field

When F is oriented upwards, curling your fingers from the direction of velocity gives B into the page.

4. A is correct.

According to Lenz's Law, inserting a magnet into the coil causes the magnetic flux through the coil to change. This produces an emf in the coil which drives a current through the coil:

Lenz's Law:

emf = $-N\Delta BA / \Delta t$

The brightness of the bulb changes with a change in the current, but it cannot be known if the bulb gets brighter or dimmer without knowing the orientation of the coil with respect to the incoming magnetic pole of the magnet.

5. A is correct.

Initially, the current will flow clockwise, but after 180° of rotation, the current will reverse itself. After 360° of rotation, the current will reverse itself again. Thus there are 2 current reverses in 1 revolution.

6. B is correct.

$$F = qvB$$

$$F = mv^2 / r$$

$mv^2 / r = qvB$, cancel v from both sides of the expression

$$mv / r = qB$$

$$r = (mv) / (qB)$$

If the velocity doubles, the radius doubles.

7. B is correct.

The time taken for one revolution around the circular path is $T = 2\pi R/v$, where R is the radius of the circle and v is the speed of the proton. If the speed is increased, the radius increases. The relationship between speed and radius follows from the fact that the centripetal force here is provided by the magnetic interaction:

$$mv^2 / R = qvB$$

Thus:

$$R = mv / qB$$

If the speed is tripled, the radius triples, other things being equal. The final period for a revolution is:

$$T_f = 2\pi R_f / v_f$$

$$= 2\pi(3R) / 3v = 2\pi R / v = T$$

8. A is correct.

A charged particle only experiences a magnetic force if it moves with a perpendicular velocity component to the field. Thus, there must not be a magnetic field, or the particle moves parallel to the field.

9. A is correct.

10. D is correct.

All the electromagnetic waves travel through space (vacuum) at the same speed:

$$c = 3 \times 10^8 \text{ m/s}$$

11. A is correct.

Faraday's Law states that electromotive force (emf) is equal to the rate of change of magnetic flux. Magnetic flux is the product of the magnetic field and projected area:

$$\Phi = BA_\perp,$$

where $A_\perp$ is the area of the loop projected on a plane perpendicular to the magnetic field.

In this problem, B is vertical (and constant), so the projection plane is horizontal. Therefore, find the orientation of the axis of rotation that guarantees that as the loop rotates, the projection of its area on a horizontal plane does not change with time.

Notice that if the orientation of the axis is at an arbitrary angle to the field, the emf can be made to be zero by aligning the axis of rotation with the axis of the loop (i.e., perpendicular to the loop). With this orientation, the projection of the area never changes, which is not true of other alignments to the loop. Although the emf can be made to be zero, it is not *guaranteed* to be zero.

The only orientation of the axis that *guarantees* that the projected area is constant is the vertical orientation. One way to see this is to notice that because of the high symmetry of the vertical-axis orientation, rotating the loop about a vertical axis is equivalent to changing the perspective of the viewer from one angle to another.

The answer cannot depend on the perspective of the viewer.

Therefore, the projected area cannot change as the loop is rotated about the vertical axis; the emf is guaranteed to be zero.

12. A is correct.

Gamma rays have the highest frequency on the electromagnetic spectrum, with frequencies greater than 3×10^{19} Hz.

Please, leave your Customer Review on Amazon

Notes

Chapter 6

Geometric and Physical Optics

- **Visual Spectrum**

- **Double Slit Diffraction**

- **Diffraction Grating**

- **Single Slit Diffraction**

- **Thin Films**

- **Other Diffraction Phenomena, X-Ray Diffraction**

- **Polarization of Light**

- **Doppler Effect**

- **Reflection from Plane Surface**

- **Refraction, Refractive Index N, Snell's Law**

- **Dispersion**

- **Conditions for Total Internal Reflection**

- **Mirrors**

- **Thin Lenses**

- **Combination of Lenses**

- **Lens Aberration**

- **Optical Instruments**

Visual Spectrum

The visible light spectrum is an important topic within physics because it contributes extensively to the way humans perceive and interact with the world. For example, red stop signs, masterpiece paintings, and glasses are a couple of objects that characterize the diverse range that visible light occupies in life. As stated an in earlier chapters, electromagnetic radiation is a form of energy that consists of oscillating electric and magnetic fields, without any need of a medium to propagate.

Visible light is a thin spectrum of electromagnetic radiation that humans are able to perceive as colors. For perspective, the electromagnetic radiation spectrum spans from long radio waves to high energy gamma rays with wavelengths ranging from 10^4 m to 10^{-14} m, respectively. Out of this spectrum, the human eye can only perceive a narrow range of wavelengths between 400 nm to 750 nm. This range is the *visible light spectrum* and consists of all the colors that humans can see.

Light of different frequencies is perceived as different colors. The figure below depicts the visible light range with respect to frequency, wavelength, and color. Lower frequency light consists of red, orange and yellow hues, while higher frequency light consists of greens, blues, and violets. Not only do different frequencies give different color, but the different frequencies of light give more or less energy (i.e., $E = hf$).

An easy way to remember the spectrum of visible light, with respect to increasing frequency (and thus energy), is by the mnemonic ROYGBIV. This stands for the lowest frequency light (red), through orange, yellow, green, blue, indigo and up to the highest frequency (highest energy) light – violet.

The sun, candles, and light bulbs are a few examples of objects that emit light. However, most objects absorb and reflect light, but do not emit light. When an object is perceived to be a certain color, it is usually not emitting light, but rather reflecting that specific frequency of light.

Likewise, if an object absorbs specific frequencies of light, those colors would not be visible at all. This is an important distinction because it determines the perceived colors of most objects.

For example, sunlight is considered white light, because it contains all the frequencies within the visible light spectrum. Therefore, it is perceived as white. Similarly, a white tablecloth reflects all frequencies of the visible range and is perceived as white. If the tablecloth were red, however, then that cloth reflects predominately red light.

Conversely, a black tablecloth absorbs every color of light, and therefore, it is perceived as black.

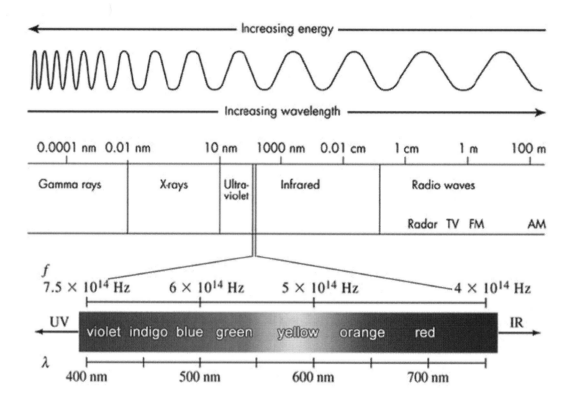

The sky is blue because of *Rayleigh scattering* (when the blue light gets scattered in the atmosphere). Sunlight hits the nitrogen and oxygen molecules and gets bounced all around; it is reemitted at a high frequency. Violet scatters the most, and then on down the spectrum to red. Because human eyes are not violet-sensitive, the next color down on the spectrum (blue) is perceived.

This scattering process is affected by the composition of the atmosphere. In the Mediterranean areas where the air is dry, a deep blue is seen. When dust, water vapor or other large particles are present, the light of lower frequency is scattered, and the sky appears paler or hazier.

In large cities, smog makes particles so large that they absorb light instead of scattering it, giving off a brownish haze.

Sunsets appear red because red, orange and yellow are transmitted better than colors at the other end of the visible light spectrum. When the sun is lower on the horizon, its light has to travel through the largest distance of the Earth's atmosphere.

The more atmosphere it travels through, the more that violet and blue are scattered, causing red to be perceived more intensely.

Primary Colors

Yellow, blue and green are considered the "primary" colors because they are detected by the eye independent of intensity but based instead on frequencies and the ocular receptors.

If any two of these colors are added together, all of the other colors can be made.

Red + blue = magenta

Red + green = yellow

Blue + green = cyan

If two secondary colors are added together, and they create white, they are complementary.

Magenta + green = white (magenta = red + blue)

Notes

Double Slit Diffraction

Like all waves, visible light can constructively and destructively interfere. This was famously observed in an iconic experiment known as Young's *double slit diffraction experiment*. This experiment proved that light was indeed a wave, as it displayed the wave property of interference. In addition, this helped establish the wave nature of light in the particle-wave duality disagreement of the time.

Observe the figure below of the double slit diffraction experiment. Two slits, S1 and S2, are positioned on an opaque wall, such that the distance between them is known. A viewing screen is placed a known distance away from the wall with the slits.

When a light source is shone at the wall with the slits, the expected behavior of light, according to particle theory, seen in diagram (b).

In reality, the light that passes through the slits will constructively and destructively interfere, producing the pattern in diagram (c).

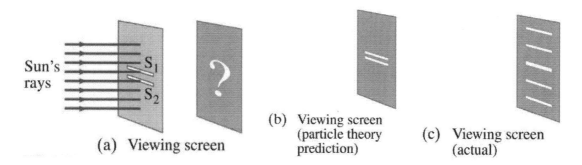

This result proves that light is indeed a wave because the resulting pattern is consistent with interference patterns seen in waves. The interference occurs because each point on the screen is not the same distance from both slits. Depending on the path length difference, the wave can interfere constructively (leaving a bright spot on the wall) or destructively (leaving a dark spot on the wall).

This is seen in the figure below. Diagrams (a, b) illustrate constructive interference spots on the viewing screen. At these points, the light waves coming through the screen are in phase and constructively interfere.

Notice in the diagram (b) that the wave from the lower slit traveled an extra wavelength compared to the upper wave. This is the path length difference and is important in identifying if a spot will be bright or dark (constructive or destructive).

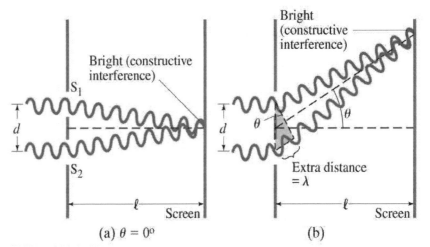

(a) $\theta = 0^\circ$ (b)

Geometry is used to find the conditions for constructive and destructive interference:

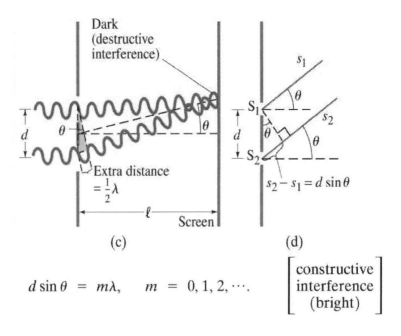

(c)   (d)

$$d \sin \theta = m\lambda, \quad m = 0, 1, 2, \cdots. \qquad \begin{bmatrix} \text{constructive} \\ \text{interference} \\ \text{(bright)} \end{bmatrix}$$

The occurrence of bright and dark spots is predicted by:

$$D \sin \theta = m\lambda$$

where d is the slit separation distance (m), θ is the angle of the bright or dark spot with respect to the center between the two slits (degrees), λ is the wavelength of the light passing through the slits (m), and m is the order value and determines whether or not the spot will be bright or dark (constructive or destructive interference).

If $m = 0,1,2,3\ldots$ then the interference will be constructive, and the spot will be bright.

If $m = \frac{1}{2}, \frac{3}{2}, \frac{5}{2} \ldots$ then the interference will be destructive, and the spot will be dark.

The figure below depicts the relation of the order number to constructive interference spots and destructive interference spots.

The maxima represent constructive interference, and the minima represent destructive interference.

Although only the order values for constructive interference are shown, it is seen that the values for destructive interference occur between these.

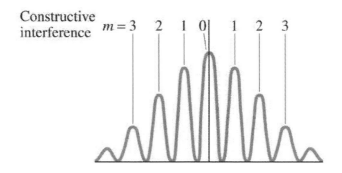

Notes

Diffraction Grating

A *diffraction grating* is similar to the double slit experiment except that instead of two slits, the grating has many slits close together. Diffraction gratings operate via the same principle as the double slit experiment, and the equation for a diffraction grating interference spots is the same as the double-slit experiment, including order values for destructive and constructive interference.

However, diffraction gratings are better able to separate wavelengths of incoming light than a double slit. Additionally, the peaks of the maxima from a diffraction grate will be much sharper and more pronounced than those of a double slit.

Observe the two figures below of a double slit maxima pattern and a diffraction grating maxima pattern. The figure on the left is the maxima pattern produced by double slits and the figure on the right is the maxima pattern for the diffraction grating.

Notice the sharper peaks of the maxima produced by the diffraction grating, and that the order values are the same as for the double slit.

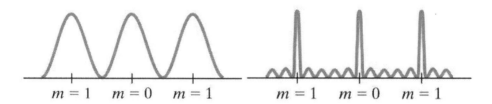

Notes

Single Slit Diffraction

Single slit diffraction is another method of diffraction where light is passed through a single slit, and the resulting diffraction pattern is observed. Like other diffraction techniques, single slit diffraction is the result of interference of the incoming wave as it bends around the slit through which it passes.

Unlike the double slit and diffraction grates, the maxima pattern produced by single slit diffraction does not follow the same order values or equation. This is because the light waves in single slit diffraction are in-phase (constructive) and out-of-phase (destructive) at different points than diffraction grates and double slit diffraction.

The maxima of the diffraction pattern are defined by:

$$a \sin (\theta) = m\lambda$$

where a is the width of the slit (m).

If $m = 0, \frac{3}{2}, \frac{5}{2} \dots$ then the interference will be constructive and the spot will be bright.

If $m = 1, 2, 3 \dots$ then the interference will be destructive, and the spot will be dark.

The diffraction pattern of single slit diffraction will be slightly different. The figure below compares the diffraction patterns produced by all three diffraction methods.

The single slit diffraction pattern produces the widest maxima; all subsequent maxima after the m = 0 value are substantially reduced.

The pattern produced by the diffraction grating and double slit are sharper and do not fade nearly as much after the m = 0 value.

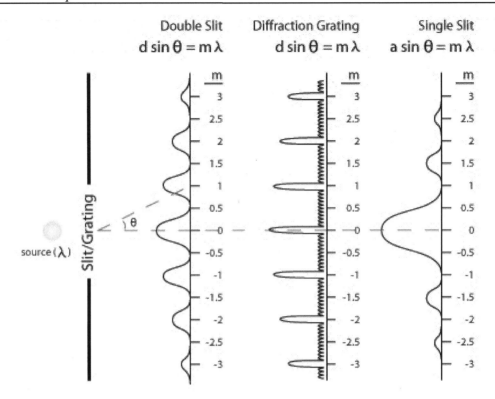

Thin Films

When observing an oil slick on water or on the ground, one sees various swirling colors on top of the slick. This phenomenon is *thin film interference* because the observed colors are not the color of the oil, but rather an effect of light interference when reflecting off the slick.

The figure below illustrating thin film interference. The interference of the light (both destructive and constructive) occurs because the incoming light partially reflects off the oil surface and partially transmits through the oil.

The transmitted light is then reflected off the substance below the oil (water, in this case) and the observer sees both the oil-reflected light and the water-reflected light.

However, because the two reflected light rays traveled slightly different distances, according to the material they reflected off, they will have a path difference and therefore interfere.

The most visible swirling colors are seen on top of the oil slick are a result of constructive interference, and the dim colors (or those not seen altogether) are a result of destructive interference.

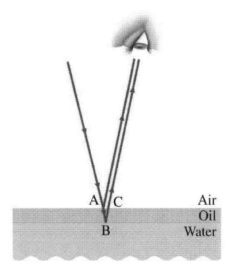

The wavelengths of light that will be displayed are found by the equation:

$$(2) \cdot (n) \cdot (d) = m\lambda$$

where n is the index of refraction for the thin film, d is the thickness of the thin film (m), λ is the wavelength of the light source (m) and m is the order value dependent upon the material underneath the thin film.

Let $n_{thin\,film}$ be the index of refraction of the thin film material, and n_{under} be the index of refraction of the material underneath the thin film.

If $n_{thin\,film} > n_{under}$ then:

Destructive interference: $m = 1, 2, 3 \ldots$

Constructive interference: $m = \dfrac{1}{2}, \dfrac{3}{2}, \dfrac{5}{2} \ldots$

If $n_{thin\,film} < n_{under}$ then:

Destructive interference: $m = \dfrac{1}{2}, \dfrac{3}{2}, \dfrac{5}{2} \ldots$

Constructive interference: $m = 1, 2, 3 \ldots$

Other Diffraction Phenomena, X-Ray Diffraction

Another interesting form of diffraction is X-ray diffraction. Although X-rays are not visible light, they are waves which can have interference patterns caused by phase differences. This is particularly useful when investigating the structure of crystal lattices and molecular arrangements. X-rays have incredibly small wavelengths. Thus they are able to diffract off these objects at the molecular level, revealing the pattern of their structure.

For example, the experiment below illustrates X-ray crystal diffraction. When X-rays are shone upon a crystal structure, the wavelengths are small enough such that the waves reflect off individual atoms within the crystal structure.

If two or more waves reflect off the crystal surface, they will interfere due to their path length difference. The resulting diffraction pattern gives information into the crystal structure of the specimen being examined.

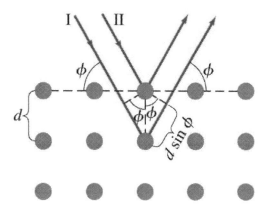

The pattern of maxima produced by X-ray diffraction is calculated *via* Bragg's Law, which is expressed as:

$$n\lambda = 2d \sin \phi$$

where n is the order number (1, 2, 3…), λ is the wavelength of the X-ray (m), d is the lattice spacing of the crystal (m) and ϕ is the reflection angle (degrees).

Notes

Polarization of Light

Light from the sun and from common sources is un-polarized. *Polarization* refers to the planes in which the electric field and magnetic field oscillate. When light is unpolarized, as it is from the sun, all the light waves oscillate randomly in different directions. If the light were to become polarized, then the oscillation of the electric and magnetic field would be uniform amongst all the light waves. For example, in the diagram below, when light is emitted from the sun, it is unpolarized, and its electric field will oscillate in many directions, as indicated by the arrows of the unpolarized light. When the light strikes the surface of the water, it reflects and becomes horizontally polarized. The horizontally-polarized light only has its electric field oscillating in one direction, rather than all directions.

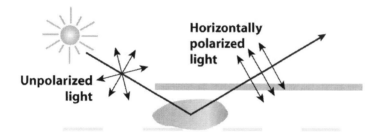

Polarized light and materials which polarize light have many applications. For example, diagram (a) below shows rope that represents a vertically polarized wave, which is transmitted through a vertically polarized filter.

In diagram (b) the wave is horizontally polarized and cannot pass through the vertical polarizer. This is exactly how polarized glasses work to remove glare from the water. Light reflected off the water (glare) is usually horizontally-polarized and is eliminated by a vertical polarizer.

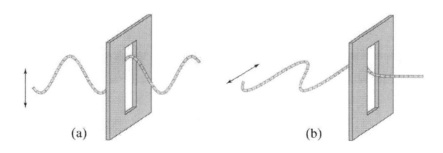

Polarized sunglasses allow the wearer to see through water because they have a vertical polarizer, and therefore reduce/eliminate the horizontally-polarized light reflecting off the water.

The intensity of light after passing through a polarizer filter is calculated by:

$$I = I_0 \cos^2(\theta)$$

where I_0 is the original intensity of the light (W/m²), I is the intensity of the light after passing through the polarizer, and θ is the angle of the original light wave electric field with respect to the axis of the polarizer, the transmission axis (degrees).

When unpolarized light is incident upon any polarizing filter, the intensity is reduced by half:

$$I = \frac{1}{2}I_0$$

If the light is incident upon crossed polarizers (90° angle between transmission axis) no light will pass through.

For example, in the diagram below, the unpolarized light is initially polarized such that its electric field oscillates only vertically after it passes through a filter with a vertical transmission axis.

Next, it is passed through a polarizer with a horizontal transmission axis. As a result, no light is transmitted because none of the light's electric field oscillates in the horizontal axis.

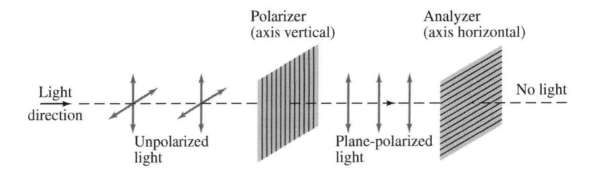

Doppler Effect

All electromagnetic radiation (light, in this case), can undergo the *Doppler effect*. The Doppler effect for light is commonly used in astronomy. When observing stars, galaxies, and other interstellar bodies, astronomers noted that sometimes the observed colors of these bodies shifted in regards to different periods of the year. This was found to be because of the Doppler effect.

When the Earth moves towards, and away from these stellar bodies during the year, the color would shift as a result of the Earth's speed in relation to that of the observed body.

Specifically, two types of shifts were noted: the redshift and the blue shift.

A redshift occurs when the source of light and the observer are moving away. In this case, like the Doppler effect for sound, the frequency of the observed wave decreases.

Since lower frequencies of visible light are red, these sources appear to be redder than they are because the Doppler effect shifts the source frequency to a lower frequency for the observer.

The blue shift is the opposite of the redshift. When the source of light and the observer are moving towards each other, the observer sees a higher frequency than the source light itself.

Blues and violets are the higher frequency colors in the visible color spectrum. Thus the sources of light appear bluer than they are.

Notes

Reflection from Plane Surface

When light strikes various surfaces, it is absorbed, transmitted or reflected. Mirrors are the most identifiable examples of surfaces that reflect all incoming light (ideal mirror).

When someone looks in a mirror, he or she see his or her image because the light incident upon the mirror is completely reflected back. Many other surfaces provide reflection, such as shiny metal or calm water.

However, these images are usually not nearly as clear as the mirror and tend to be somewhat blurry. All these effects, from the clear image presented in the mirror to the blurry image provided by other surfaces, are due to the Law of Reflection.

The Law of Reflection states that the angle of incidence of a light ray, with respect to the normal of the surface, will be equal to the angle of reflection. When this occurs, it is a *specular reflection* and is what is observed in flat mirrors.

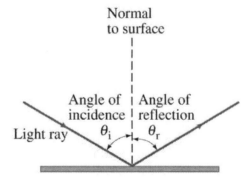

Blurry images are formed according to the Law of Reflection. When the reflecting surface is irregular rather than smooth, the light rays will reflect off the irregularities.

However, in this case, the reflected rays will not be parallel, but rather in every direction.

This is a *diffuse reflection* and results in a blurry image being formed.

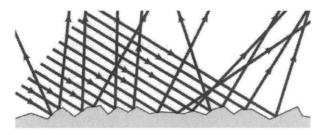

With diffuse reflection, a person's eye sees reflected light at all angles. With specular reflection (from a mirror), the eye must be in the correct position. Think about a person positioning themselves in the mirror to see something behind them—where they place themselves determines what they can see.

This is seen in the two diagrams below. Diagram (a) demonstrates diffuse reflection, in which the observer can see the reflected light from the source in multiple locations; diagram (b) demonstrates specular reflection, in which the reflected light can only be seen in a specific location.

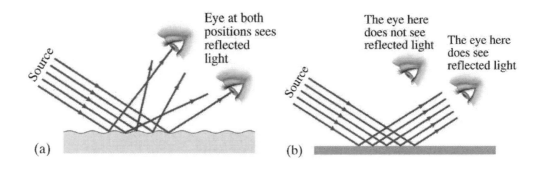

Refraction, Refractive Index N, Snell's Law

When light transmits from one medium to another, it changes direction slightly based upon the properties of the two mediums. This phenomenon is *refraction* and is observed in many everyday experiences. The angle that the light ray bends, with respect to the normal, depends upon the indices of refraction for each medium.

The angle of refraction is given by *Snell's Law*, where each *n* is the index of refraction for its respective medium:

$$n_1 \sin(\theta_1) = n_2 \sin(\theta_2)$$

where *n* is the index of refraction and θ is the angle of the wave with respect to the normal of the medium interface.

The index of refraction is a relation of the light propagation speed in a medium to that of the speed of light in a vacuum (*n* is always greater than 1 because light cannot go faster than in a vacuum)

$$n = \frac{c}{v}$$

Observe the figures below, which depict the refraction of light from water to air and vice versa. When a wave moves to a denser medium (with a greater refractive index), it bends toward the normal. When it moves to a less dense medium (with a smaller refractive index), it bends away from the normal.

Accordingly, when the light is refracted from water into the air, in diagram (b), it will be refracted away from the normal. If the light is refracted from air to water, in diagram (a), it bends toward the normal.

Given the angle of incidence, the angle of refraction is computed by Snell's Law.

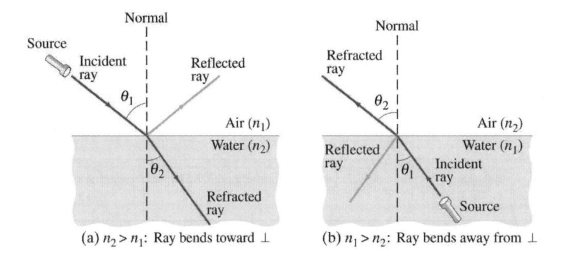

(a) $n_2 > n_1$: Ray bends toward $\perp$ (b) $n_1 > n_2$: Ray bends away from $\perp$

Mirages are produced by refraction. Hot surfaces warm up the air above them, producing air with a slightly lower index of refraction than the ambient air.

When a light ray passes through this air, it curves the light such that the observer sees an image that is a form of reflection off the ground.

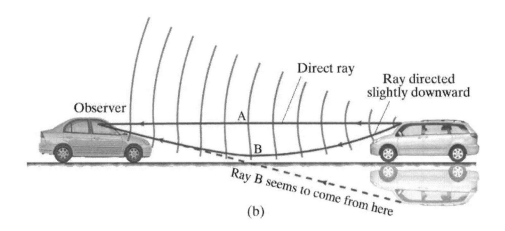

(b)

Dispersion

Dispersion is the phenomenon that separates light into its individual colors. All wavelengths of light will refract upon crossing a boundary between two different mediums, however different wavelengths of light refract at slightly different angles. Lower wavelength light refracts the most; thus, the violet light refracts at a greater angle than blue light, which refracts at a greater angle than green light, etc.

An example of dispersion is when white light passes through a prism. The diagram below shows a prism producing the visible spectrum of colors. White light is composed of the entire visible spectrum, which will all refract at slightly different angles.

If a screen is held a distance away from the prism, the visible spectrum is seen because the white light is dispersed into all the wavelengths that compose it.

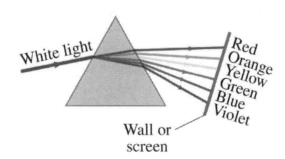

Atmospheric rainbows are created by dispersion as well.

Light passing through small raindrops or mist will refract and disperse into the visible spectrum, like a prism.

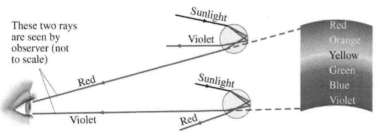

Notes

Conditions for Total Internal Reflection

The critical angle is defined as the angle of incidence for which an incident light ray will make an angle of refraction equal to 90°. The critical angle is found by using:

$$n_1 \sin (\theta_c) = n_2 \sin (90°)$$

If the angle of incidence is larger than the critical angle, then no light will be transmitted between the two mediums and the light will only be reflected back into the original medium. This is a *total internal reflection.*

The diagram below illustrates various angles of incidence and their corresponding angles of diffraction. At points, I and J, the angle of incidence are lower than the critical angle, and the light is refracted through the surface (along with a portion that is partially reflected back). At point K, the critical angle has been achieved, and the angle of refraction is exactly 90°. At point L, the angle of incidence is higher than the critical angle.

Therefore, all the light will be reflected back, resulting in total internal reflection.

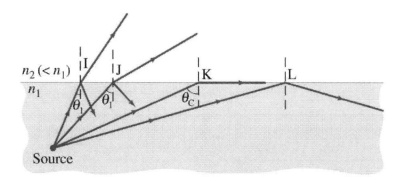

Total internal reflection is an important phenomenon because it is the principle behind the operation of fiber optics. In a fiber optic cable, light is transmitted along the fiber regardless of the loops or bends in the cable, because the indices of refraction of the cable and outer sheath are such that the light is always experiencing total internal reflection.

Notes

Mirrors

Spherical mirrors allow users to see different images than what is possible with only flat mirrors. For example, many parking garages have convex mirrors mounted near blind corners; they allow drivers to see a much wider image of what is around a corner than a flat mirror. Similarly, many beauty mirrors are slightly concave and present a magnified image to the user. Both of these examples are types of spherical mirrors, which have distinctive properties depending on the curvature of the reflective surface.

Mirror curvature, radius, focal length

Mirror curvature is concave or convex. The figure below shows a concave and a convex mirror. The *convex mirror* (diagram a) disperses light rays such that they are diverging, while the *concave mirror* (diagram b) focuses light rays such that they converge.

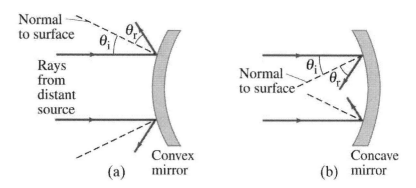

Regardless of the mirror, both convex and concave spherical mirrors have defined radii of curvature and foci. The *radius of curvature* is the radius of the curve of the mirror; in spherical mirrors, the radius of curvature is constant throughout the surface of the mirror. The *focal length* is the distance from the mirror surface to the where light rays converge (theoretically converge, in the case of a convex mirror). Concave mirrors have a positive focal length, while convex mirrors have a negative focal length. Both types have focal lengths that are equal to half the radius:

$$f = \frac{1}{2}R$$

where f is the focal length (m), and R is the radius of curvature (m).

The figure below displays the various features of a concave mirror. Point C is the *center of curvature* and is the point where the radius of curvature originates (center of a circle). Point F is the focus and demonstrates where all light rays would focus if reflected off the mirror. The distances *f* and *r* are the focal length and radius of curvature which is the distances to points F and C, respectively.

A convex mirror would have the same center of curvature, focal point, the radius of curvature and focal length; however, the light would be incident upon the outer edge of the mirror and disperse, rather than converge.

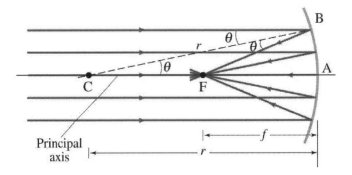

Mirror ray tracing

When looking at a mirror, it is important to know the relationship of the object held up to the mirror and the image formed by the mirror. Depending upon the object distance from the mirror, the mirror and the characteristics of the mirror, the formed image can be smaller, larger, virtual, real, erect or inverted.

The image formed by a mirror is classified by size in relation to the original object, whether the image is inverted or not and if the formed image is real or virtual. The size of the image formed by a mirror can either be equal to, larger or smaller than the size of the object held up to the mirror. Additionally, the image may be erect like the object held up to the mirror, or the image may be inverted and appear to be upside down. For example, a person's face reflected on the inside of a shiny spoon appears inverted and smaller than the face.

Finally, the formed image may be real or virtual. Real images are images that are formed when light rays converge upon a point in a real location, whereas virtual images form from light rays that diverge. A virtual image will be at the point where the light rays appear to diverge from (this point is not actually there, hence "virtual image").

Identify the image formed by a mirror is by using *ray diagrams*. Ray diagrams allow the user to visualize the image formed, depending upon object location with respect to the mirror. For ray diagrams, three rays are typically drawn:

1. A ray from the top of the object height parallel to the axis—after reflection off the mirror, it passes through the focal point.

2. A ray from the top of the object height through the focal point—after reflection, it is parallel to the axis.

3. A ray perpendicular to the mirror, which passes through the object height and the center of curvature.

For example, the figure below is of a ray diagram drawn using a concave mirror. Diagrams (a, b, c) show the paths of rays 1, 2 and 3 respectively. Notice that after the rays have been drawn in, the convergence point is the location of the image. The image height and orientation are then determined by drawing a line from the center axis to the convergence point. In this case, the image formed by the mirror is inverted, larger and real (the image is formed by the convergence of light rays on a real point).

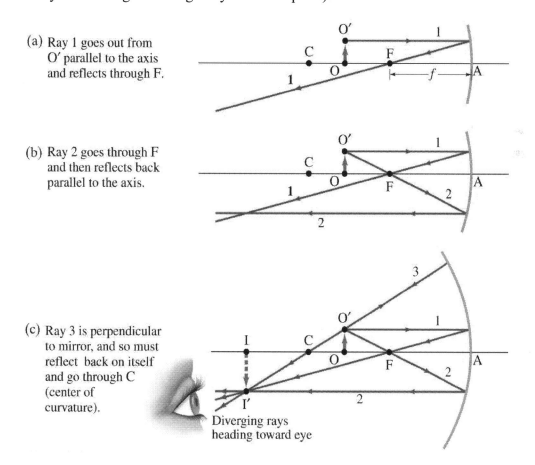

(a) Ray 1 goes out from O′ parallel to the axis and reflects through F.

(b) Ray 2 goes through F and then reflects back parallel to the axis.

(c) Ray 3 is perpendicular to mirror, and so must reflect back on itself and go through C (center of curvature).

Diverging rays heading toward eye

The location of the object determines the image.

The illustration below depicts the image formed by an object located in front of the focal point of a concave mirror. In this case, the formed image is erect, larger and virtual (the image is formed by the convergence of light rays on a virtual point)

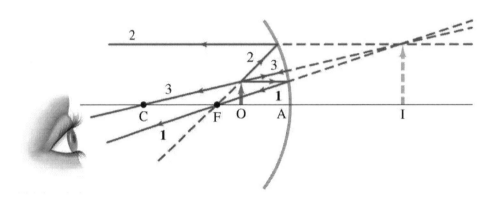

Concave mirrors can produce both real and virtual images, depending on where the object is located in relation to the mirror.

If the object is outside the radius of the sphere of the mirror, the image will be real.

If it is inside the radius, the image will be virtual.

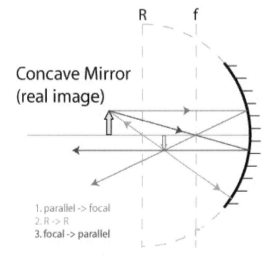

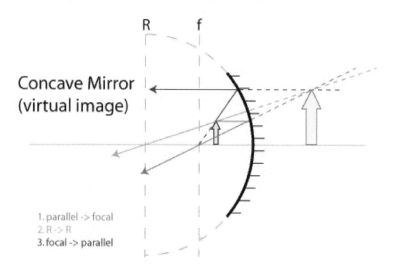

For convex mirrors, only a virtual image will be created, because the curve of the mirrors is different.

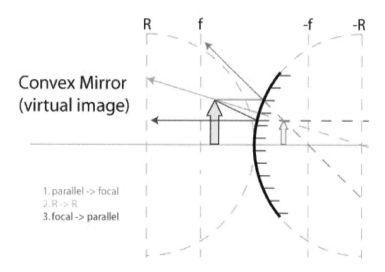

For mirrors:

1. First, draw a parallel line from the object; as it bounces off the mirror, it intersects the focal point. Now, which focal point to intersect? The left or right?

    For concave mirrors, it is going to focus the ray to the left focal point.

    For convex mirrors, which cannot focus, it is going to diverge the ray; this means extrapolation to the right focal point is needed.

2. Next, draw a line that intersects the R point on the principal axis. Which R? Left or right? The ray drawn should bounce right back its original path, and not be reflected elsewhere. By eye-balling the mirror, one can figure this out.

3. Now that two rays are drawn, an intersection is made. Use this intersection as a guide to drawing the last ray. The last ray should first intersect the focal point, then bounce off the mirror parallel to the principal axis. Which focal point to intersect? Is extrapolation necessary?

4. There is only one combination for the ray here to fit the intersection already made by the previous two rays.

   The trick to do this is to draw the parallel line first and force it to cross the intersection already made by the previous two rays.

This table gives the object-image relationship for both concave and convex mirrors:

Object Distance	Concave Mirror	Convex Mirror
Before C	inverted, smaller, real	erect, smaller, virtual
At C	inverted, equal size, real	erect, smaller, virtual
Between C and F	inverted, larger, real	erect, smaller, virtual
At F	no image	erect, smaller, virtual
Before F	erect, larger, virtual	erect, smaller, virtual

Thin Lenses

A lens is a device used to bend and focus light using the refractive properties of the lens material. For example, the lenses in a microscope bend and focus light such that objects become magnified. Eyeglasses correct vision problems by focusing the light in front of eyes so that those who wear glasses can see without blurry vision.

Regardless of the application, lenses are an important tool in many day-to-day devices and scientific instruments.

Many similarities exist between lenses and mirrors in regards to image formation; however, there are a few differences to make a note of. Primarily, a convex lens is the same as a concave mirror (both are referred to as converging) except for the following instances:

- Real images are on the opposite side of the lens as the object, because light travels through the lens and can focus on a screen behind the lens.
- Virtual images are on the same side of the lens as the object, because light cannot focus in front of a lens and be cast on a screen.
- Concave lenses are the same as convex mirrors (both are referred to as diverging) except for in the following instance:
- The virtual images formed by the lens are on the same side of the lens as the object, because light cannot focus in front of a lens and be cast on a screen.

Converging and diverging lenses, focal length

Most lens problems approximate the lens as a *thin lens*. Thin lenses are those whose thickness is small compared to their radius of curvature. They may be either converging (convex) or diverging (concave). The figure below depicts a converging lens.

Like with mirrors, the light which passes through the lens will converge on the focal point of the lens (there are two focal points, one on each side). The radius of curvature is the same as that of a spherical mirror, except that because the lens is double-sided, it has two radii of curvature (most of the time these are equal).

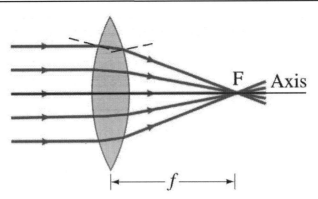

A diverging lens (concave) makes parallel light diverge; the focal point is the point where the diverging rays would converge if projected back.

Like the converging lens, the diverging lens has two radii of curvature (most of the time these are equal).

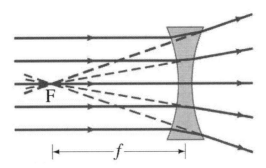

Ray tracing thin lens

Ray tracing for thin lenses is similar to that for mirrors. There are three key rays:

1. A ray from the top of the object height parallel to the axis—after transmission through the lens, it passes through the focal point.

2. A ray from the top of the object height through the focal point—after transmission, it is parallel to the axis.

3. A ray from the top of the object height through the center of the lens.

For example, the figure below demonstrates ray tracing through a converging lens. Diagrams (a, b, c) show the paths of rays 1, 2 and 3 respectively.

Notice that after the rays have been drawn in, the convergence point is the location of the image. The image height and orientation are then determined by drawing a line from the center axis to the convergence point. In this case, the image formed by the lens is inverted and real.

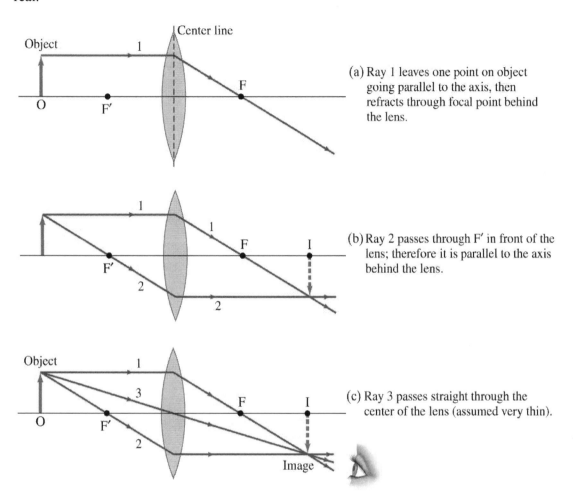

(a) Ray 1 leaves one point on object going parallel to the axis, then refracts through focal point behind the lens.

(b) Ray 2 passes through F′ in front of the lens; therefore it is parallel to the axis behind the lens.

(c) Ray 3 passes straight through the center of the lens (assumed very thin).

For a diverging lens, the same three rays can be used; the image is upright and virtual.

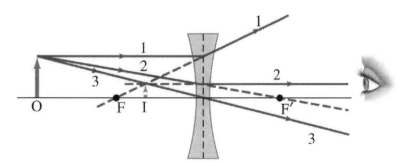

As stated previously, lenses are similar to mirrors. This means a convex lens (like a concave mirror) can create either a real or a virtual image, depending on where the real object is positioned.

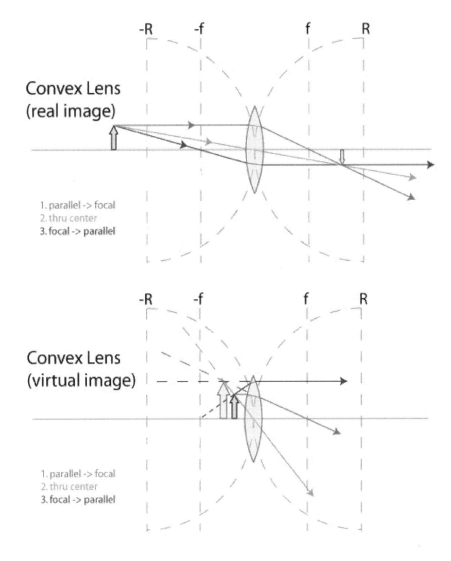

A concave lens, therefore, acts similar to a convex mirror, and only produce virtual images.

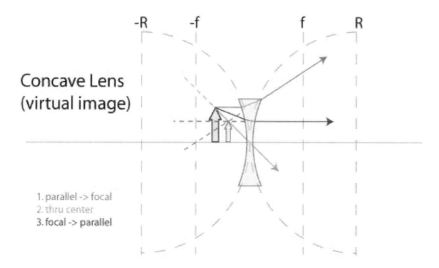

For lenses (similar to the method of drawing rays for mirrors):

1. First, draw the parallel → focal point ray. It should make sense which focal point the ray should hit/extrapolate, given the converging/diverging nature of the lens.
2. Next, draw a ray intersecting the center of the lens.
3. Lastly, using the intersection already made by the previous two rays as a guide, draw the focal point → parallel ray. Again, draw the parallel line first and force it to intersect the intersection already made by the previous two rays.

Use of formula (1/*p*) + (1/*q*) = 1/*f* with sign conventions

To determine the distance from either the mirror or lens that an image forms, the thin lens equation is used:

$$\frac{1}{d_o} + \frac{1}{d_i} = \frac{1}{f}$$

where d_o is the distance of the object away from the lens or mirror (m), d_i is the distance of the image away from the lens or mirror (m), and f is the focal length of the lens or mirror (m).

Although the thin lens equation is relatively simple, it is important that the proper sign conventions be followed for the types of mirrors and lenses. For a lens, there are several differences depending on whether the lens is converging or diverging. The focal length is written positive for converging lenses and negative for diverging. Also, the object distance is considered positive when the object is on the same side as the light entering the lens; otherwise it is negative. Finally, the image distance is positive if the image is on the opposite side from the light entering the lens; otherwise, it is negative.

For mirrors, the sign conventions are different. The focal length is written positive for concave mirrors and negative for convex mirrors. Also, the object distance is considered positive when the object is in front of the mirror, and negative if the object is behind the mirror (i.e., a virtual object, this is a rare case). Finally, the image distance is positive if the image is in front of the mirror (real image), and negative if the image is behind the mirror (virtual image).

When solving problems using the thin lens equation, be sure to perform as many steps as possible. Draw a ray diagram, and place the image where the key rays intersect. Solve for unknowns by following the sign conventions and check that the answers found are consistent with the ray diagram.

Magnification and lens power formula

The magnification of an object, in relation to image height, can be obtained for lenses and mirrors.

This is found by the *magnification equation*:

$$M = \frac{h_i}{h_0} = -\frac{d_i}{d_0}$$

where M is magnification, h_i is the height of the image (m), h_0 is the height of the object (m), d_o is the distance of the object away from the lens or mirror (m) and d_i is the distance of the image away from the lens or mirror (m).

Similar to the lens equation, the magnification equation has specific sign conventions for types of mirrors and lenses. The magnification should be expressed as positive for all types of lenses when the image is upright with respect to the object, and negative when the image is inverted.

Likewise, magnification should be expressed as positive for all types of mirrors when the image is upright with respect to the object, and negative when the image is inverted.

The power of a lens is not related to its magnification but rather is expressed as the inverse of its focal length, where lens power has units of diopters (D), which are equal to m^{-1}.

The power of a lens is positive if it is converging, and negative if it is diverging:

$$P = \frac{1}{f}$$

where P is the lens power (D).

Lensmaker's equation

The relationship between the radii of curvature of a lens and the produced focal length are related by the *Lensmaker's equation*:

$$\frac{1}{f} = (n - 1)(\frac{1}{R_1} + \frac{1}{R_2})$$

where *f* is the focal length of the lens (m), *n* is the index of refraction of the lens material, R_1 is the radius of curvature of the first lens face (m), and R_2 is the radius of curvature of the second lens face (m).

Combination of Lenses

Combinations of lenses are used to multiply the magnification of objects. This is demonstrated in light microscopes and telescopes. These devices contain multiple lenses to allow the user to magnify objects beyond what a single lens can produce.

This is possible because the real image formed by a lens can be used as the object for another lens.

The magnification by multiple lenses is the product of all of the individual magnifications and is expressed as:

$$M_{total} = M_1 M_2$$

where M_{total} is the total magnification, M_1 is the magnification of the first lens and M_2 is the magnification of the second lens.

The simplest form of a combination of lenses is when two lenses are placed in contact. In this case, the total power of the combination of lenses is the sum of the two lens's powers:

$$P_{total} = P_1 + P_2$$

or

$$\frac{1}{f_{total}} = \frac{1}{f_1} + \frac{1}{f_2}$$

If the two lenses are separated by some distance, then the total power of the combination is expressed as:

$$\frac{1}{f_{total}} = \frac{1}{f_1} + \frac{1}{f_2} - \frac{d}{f_1 f_2}$$

where d is the distance between the two lenses (m)

Notes

Lens Aberration

In real life, no lens is ideal, and the light rays will tend to converge in slightly different spots. This phenomenon is an aberration, and there are several types which can occur.

Spherical lenses and mirrors suffer from *spherical aberration*. This occurs because the curvature of the lens/mirror is large, and the rays striking the outer edges refract/reflect more and therefore bend more than the rays striking the center portion of the lens/mirror.

This is seen in the converging lens figure shown below. Spherical aberration is reduced by utilizing only the center portion of the lens or mirror.

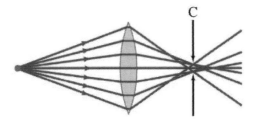

Chromatic aberration occurs in lenses and is when the light of different wavelengths focuses at different points. As stated earlier, different wavelengths of light will refract at slightly different angles in the phenomenon of dispersion. When light shines through a lens, this results in different focus points, depending upon the wavelength of light.

For instance, observe the figure below. The blue light gets refracted more than red light, so it will focus at an earlier point than the red light.

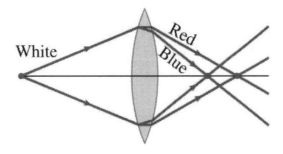

A solution for chromatic aberration is a device called an *achromatic doublet*. A second lens made of a different material is attached to the first lens.

When light passes, through the chromatic aberration will be corrected in the second lens, which focuses all wavelengths to one point.

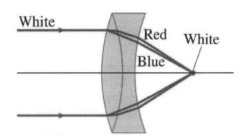

Distortion is an aberration caused when different parts of a lens have slightly different magnification factors. The two diagrams below illustrate the two types of distortion.

Diagram (a) represents *barrel distortion*, where the magnification of the image decreases with distance from the axis.

Diagram (b) represents *pincushion distortion*, where magnification increases with distance from the optical axis.

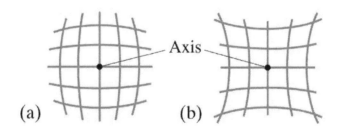

Optical Instruments

Like cameras, the human eye manipulates electromagnetic waves using an adjustable lens and an iris. The figure below shows a cross-section of an eye, with the iris and lens labeled.

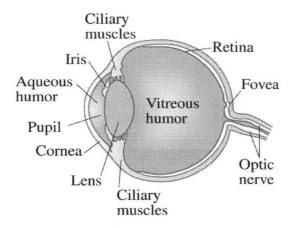

The eye works by making small adjustments of the lens shape to allow objects at different distances be focused against the retina. Most of the refraction of the light occurs at the surface of the cornea, while the lens only makes fine-tuned adjustments.

Observe the diagram below illustrating a lens adjusting to compensate for object distance. In diagram (a), the object is far away (far away objects have rays assumed to be parallel), and the lens adjusts itself such that its radius of curvature creates a focal point at the retina.

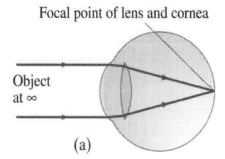

The near point is the closest distance at which the eye can focus clearly. The normal distance is about 25 cm. The far point is the farthest distance at which an object can be seen clearly. The normal distance is infinity. Nearsightedness occurs when a person's far point is too close. Conversely, farsightedness occurs when an individual's near point is too far away.

Nearsightedness (*myopia*) can be corrected with a diverging lens. In diagram (a), an eye with myopia refracts light too much and causes the focal point to be located before the retina. Diagram (b) shows the correction lens for myopia. The lens refracts the light such that the light diverges before the cornea. Consequently, the higher refraction of the eye is compensated for and the focal point occurs at the retina, producing a clear image.

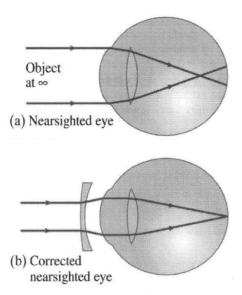

(a) Nearsighted eye

(b) Corrected
nearsighted eye

Farsightedness (*hyperopia*) is corrected with a converging lens. Hyperopia occurs when the eye refracts the incoming light too little, and the focal point occurs behind the retina, as in diagram (c). This can be corrected with a converging lens which brings the light rays to a more parallel orientation before entering the eye. The lower refractive index of the eye is accounted for, and the focal point occurs at the retina

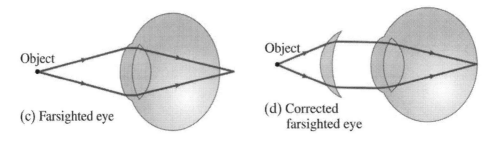

(c) Farsighted eye

(d) Corrected
farsighted eye

Magnifying glass

A magnifying glass is a converging lens. It allows the user to focus on objects closer than the near point so that they create a larger image on the retina.

The figure below demonstrates a magnifying glass in use.

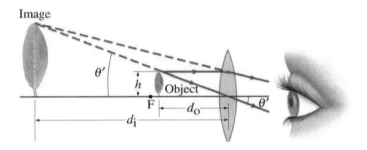

The power of a magnifying glass is described by its angular magnification:

$$M = \frac{\theta'}{\theta}$$

$$\theta \approx \frac{h}{f}$$

$$\theta' \approx \frac{25 \ cm}{h}$$

If the eye is relaxed (N is the near point distance and f the focal length), magnification is given as:

$$M = \frac{\theta'}{\theta} = \frac{h/f}{h/N} = \frac{N}{f} = \frac{25 \ cm}{f}$$

If the eye is focused at the near point, magnification is given as:

$$M = \frac{N}{f} + 1 = \frac{25 \ cm}{f} + 1$$

Refracting telescope

A refracting telescope consists of two lenses at opposite ends of a long tube.

The objective lens is closest to the object, and the eyepiece is closest to the eye.

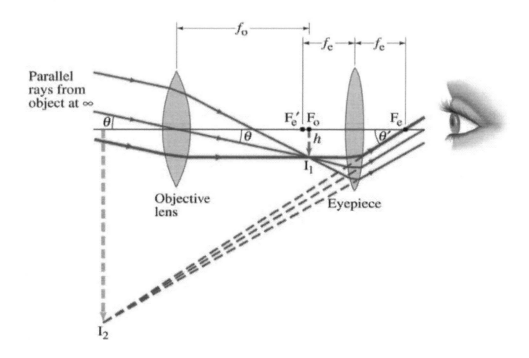

The magnification is given by:

$$M = \frac{\theta'}{\theta} = \frac{(h/f_e)}{(h/f_o)} = -\frac{f_o}{f_e}$$

Chapter Summary

Light, Refraction, and Reflection

- Light paths are rays.

- Visible spectrum of light ranges approximately from 400 nm to 750 nm.

- Two sources of light are coherent if they have the same frequency and maintain the same phase relationship.

- Index of refraction varies with wavelength, leading to dispersion.

- There are boundaries between different materials, as well as between regions of the same material that is under different conditions, such as temperature or pressure, which cause a change in the index of refraction.

- Index of refraction: $n = \dfrac{c}{v}$

- Law of Refraction (Snell's Law): $n_1 \sin (\theta_1) = n_2 \sin (\theta_2)$

- Angle of reflection equals the angle of incidence.

- Total internal reflection occurs when the angle of incidence is greater than critical angle:

$$\sin (\theta_C) = \frac{n_2}{n_1} \sin (90°) = \frac{n_2}{n_1}$$

Diffraction—Single-slit and Double-slit

- Wavelength of light in a medium with index of refraction n: $\lambda_n = \dfrac{\lambda}{n}$

- Wavelength can be measured precisely with a spectroscope.

- Young's double-slit experiment demonstrated interference:

  constructive interference occurs when: $d \sin (\theta) = m\lambda$, $m = 0,1,2,\ldots$

  and destructive interference when: $d \sin (\theta) = (m + \frac{1}{2})\lambda$, $m = 0,1,2,\ldots$

- Diffraction grating has many small slits or lines, and the same condition for constructive interference.

- Light bends around obstacles and openings in its path, producing diffraction patterns.

- Light passing through a narrow slit will produce a bright central maximum of width:

$$\sin(\theta) = \frac{\lambda}{D}$$

- Interference can occur between reflections from the front and back surfaces of a thin film.

Polarization

- Light whose electric fields are all in the same plane is plane polarized.
- The intensity of plane polarized light is reduced after it passes through another polarizer:

$$I = I_o \cos^2(\theta)$$

- Light can be polarized by reflection; it is completely polarized when the reflection angle is the polarization angle: $\tan(\theta_p) = n$

Mirrors

- Plane mirror: the image is virtual, upright and the same size as the object.
- A real image means light passes through it. A virtual image means light does not pass through it.
- A spherical mirror is concave or convex.

- The focal length of the mirror: $f = \frac{r}{2}$

- Mirror equation: $\frac{1}{d_o} + \frac{1}{d_i} = \frac{1}{f}$

- Magnification: $m = \frac{h_i}{h_o} = -\frac{d_i}{d_o}$

Lenses

- A converging lens focuses incoming parallel rays to a point, while a diverging lens spreads incoming rays so that they appear to come from a point

- Power of a lens: $P = \frac{1}{f}$

- The thin lens equation is given by: $\frac{1}{f} - \frac{1}{d_i} = \frac{1}{d_o}$ or $\frac{1}{d_o} + \frac{1}{d_i} = \frac{1}{f}$

Lens Aberrations

- Spherical aberration occurs when rays far from axis do not go through the focal point.

- Chromatic aberration occurs when different wavelengths have different focal points.

Optical Devices

- Resolution of optical devices is limited by diffraction.
- Nearsighted vision is corrected by the diverging lens, farsighted by converging.
- Simple magnifier: object at focal point

$$M = \frac{\theta'}{\theta} = \frac{h/f}{h/N} = \frac{N}{f}$$

- Magnification:

$$M = \frac{\theta'}{\theta} = \frac{(h/f_e)}{(h/f_o)} = -\frac{f_o}{f_e}$$

Notes

Practice Questions

1. Which color of the visible spectrum has photons with the most energy?

    A. Violet   **B.** Green   **C.** Orange   **D.** Red

2. An index of refraction of less than one for a medium implies that:

    A. the speed of light in the medium is less than the speed of light in a vacuum
    B. refraction is not possible
    C. the speed of light in the medium is the same as the speed of light in a vacuum
    D. the speed of light in the medium is greater than the speed of light in a vacuum

3. The colors on an oil slick are caused by reflection and:

    A. refraction   **C.** diffraction
    B. polarization   **D.** interference

4. Which of the following describes the best scenario if a person wants to start a fire using sunlight and a mirror?

    A. Use a concave mirror with the object to be ignited positioned at the center of
            the curvature of the mirror
    B. Use a concave mirror with the object to be ignited positioned halfway between the
            mirror and its center of curvature
    C. Use a plane mirror
    D. Use a convex mirror

5. A lens has a focal length of 2 m. What lens could you combine with it to get a combination with a focal length of 3 m?

    A. A lens of power 1/6 diopters   **C.** A lens of power –6 diopters
    B. A lens of power 6 diopters   **D.** A lens of power –1/6 diopters

6. An incident ray traveling in the air makes an angle of 30° with the surface of a medium with an index $n = 1.73$. What is the angle that the refracted ray makes with the surface? (Use the index of refraction for air $n = 1$)

    A. 30°   **B.** $90 \sin^{-1}(0.5)$ **C.** 60°   **D.** $\sin^{-1}(0.5)$

7. A mirage is produced because:

A. light travels faster through the air than through water

B. images of water are reflected in the sky

C. warm air has a higher index of refraction than cool air

D. warm air has a lower index of refraction than cool air

8. An object is viewed at various distances using a concave mirror with a focal length 14 m. What happens when a candle is placed at the focus?

A. Light rays end up parallel going to infinity

B. Light rays meet at the focus

C. An image is formed 7 m in front of the mirror

D. An image is formed 7 m behind the mirror

9. A material which has the ability to rotate the direction of polarization of linearly polarized light is said to be:

A. diffraction limited

B. optically active

C. circularly polarized

D. birefringent

10. When light enters a material of a higher index of refraction, its speed:

A. increases

B. stays the same

C. first increases then decreases

D. decreases

11. What is the correct order of the electromagnetic spectrum from shortest to longest wavelength?

A. Radio waves → X-rays → Ultraviolet radiation → Visible light → Infrared radiation → Microwaves → Gamma rays

B. Gamma rays → X-rays → Visible light → Ultraviolet radiation → Infrared radiation → Microwaves → Radio waves

C. Gamma rays → X-rays → Ultraviolet radiation → Visible light → Infrared radiation → Microwaves → Radio waves

D. Visible light → Infrared radiation → Microwaves → Radio waves → Gamma rays → X-rays → Ultraviolet radiation

12. The angle of incidence can vary between zero and:

A. 2π radians

B. π radians

C. $\pi/2$ radians

D. 1 radian

13. An amateur astronomer grinds a double-convex lens whose surfaces have radii of curvature of 40 cm and 60 cm. What is the focal length of this lens in air? (Use the index of refraction for glass $n = 1.54$)

    A. 44 cm   **B.** 88 cm   **C.** 132 cm   **D.** 22 cm

14. When light reflects from a stationary surface, there is a change in its:

    I. frequency   II. speed   III. wavelength

    A. I and II only   **C.** III only

    B. I and III only   **D.** none of the above

15. If a distant galaxy is moving away from the Earth at 4,300 km/s, how do the detected frequency (f_{det}) and λ of the visible light detected on Earth compare to the f and λ of the light emitted by the galaxy?

    A. The f_{det} is lower, and the λ is shifted towards the red end of the visible spectrum

    B. The f_{det} is lower, and the λ is shifted towards the blue end of the visible spectrum

    C. The f_{det} is the same, but the λ is shifted towards the red end of the visible spectrum

    D. The f_{det} is the same, but the λ is shifted towards the blue end of the visible spectrum

Solutions

1. A is correct.

Violet light has the highest frequency of the visible light colors with a range of 668 to 789 THz. Because frequency is related to photon energy by:

$$E = hf$$

Violet light is the most energetic of the visible light spectrum.

2. D is correct.

The index of refraction for a given material is expressed as the speed of light in a vacuum divided by the speed of light in that material:

$$n = c / v$$

If the index of refraction is less than one, it implies that the speed of light in the material is greater than the speed of light in vacuum. However, this is never the case because the speed of light in a vacuum can never be exceeded.

3. D is correct.

The colors observed on an oil slick pool are caused by reflection and thin film interference. This is the process by which the incoming light is reflected off the top and bottom layer of the oil slick and producing reflected waves in and out of phase. This phase change determines the interference (constructive or destructive) and colors form as a result.

4. B is correct.

$$f = \frac{1}{2}R$$

where R is the radius of curvature

5. D is correct.

The first lens has a power:

$$P_1 = 1 / f$$

$$P_1 = \frac{1}{2} \text{ D}$$

For a combination of total power:

$$P_{tot} = 1 / f_{tot}$$

$$P_{tot} = 1/3 \text{ D}$$

Thus,

$$P_2 = P_{tot} - P_1$$

$$P_2 = 1/3 \text{ D} - 1/2 \text{ D}$$

$$P_2 = -1/6 \text{ D}$$

6. A is correct.

$$n_1 \sin \theta_1 = n_1 \sin \theta_2$$

$$(1) \sin (90° - 30°) = (1.73) \sin \theta_2$$

$$\sin (60°) = 1.73 \sin \theta_2$$

$$\sin \theta_2 = \sin (60°) / 1.73$$

$$\sin \theta_2 = 0.5$$

$$\theta_2 = \sin^{-1} (0.5)$$

$$\theta_2 = 30°$$

7. D is correct.

A mirage is produced due to the higher index of refraction of cold air compared to warm air. As light from the sky goes through denser cold air and approaches the warm air (which is less dense and therefore has a lower refraction index) near the ground (generated by a hot surface of asphalt or sand), the light bends away from the warm air and the reflection of the sky is observed on the ground.

8. A is correct.

Mirror equation:

$$1/f = 1/d_o + 1/d_i$$

If the object is placed at the focus:

$$d_o = f$$
$$1/f = 1/f + 1/d_i$$
$$1/f - 1/f = 1/d_i$$
$$0 = 1/d_i$$

Only if $d_i = \infty$ this is true.

This implies that no image is formed. Thus the light rays neither converge nor diverge and travel parallel to infinity.

9. B is correct.

10. D is correct.

11. C is correct.

12. C is correct.

The angle of incidence ranges from 0° to 90°.

Convert degrees to radians:

$$0° = 0 \text{ radians}$$
$$(90° / 1) \cdot (\pi / 180°) = \pi/2 \text{ radians}$$

13. A is correct.

Double convex lens:

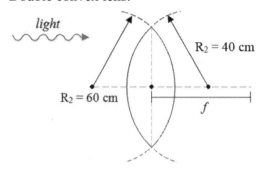

Lens maker formula:

$$1 / f = (n - 1) \cdot (1 / R_1 - 1 / R_2)$$

$$1 / f = (1.54 - 1) \cdot (1 / 40 \text{ cm} - (1 / -60 \text{ cm}))$$

$$1 / f = -0.0225 \text{ cm}^{-1}$$

$$f = 44 \text{ cm}$$

If light passes through the center of the radii of curvature (as it does to R_2) before the curve itself in the lens then that R is negative by convention.

14. D is correct.

Light does not experience a change in frequency, wavelength or speed when it reflects from a stationary surface.

15. A is correct.

The Doppler effect is qualitatively similar for both light and sound waves.

If the source and the observer move towards each other, the f_{det} is higher than the f_{source}.

If the source and the observer move away, the f_{det} is lower than the f_{source}.

Since the galaxy is moving away from the Earth, the f_{det} is lower.

The speed of light through space is constant ($c = \lambda f$).

A lower f_{det} means a longer λ_{det}, so the λ_{det} is longer than the λ_{source}.

The λ has been shifted towards the red end of the visible spectrum because red light is the visible light with the longest λ.

Chapter 7

Atomic and Nuclear Physics

- **Atomic Structure and Spectra**

- **Emission Spectrum of Hydrogen: Bohr model**

- **Atomic Energy Levels**

- **Neutrons, Protons, Isotopes**

- **Atomic Number, Atomic Weight**

- **Nuclear Forces**

- **Radioactive Decay**

- **General Nature of Fission**

- **General Nature of Fusion**

- **Mass Deficit, Energy Liberated, Binding Energy**

- **Mass Spectrometer**

Atomic Structure and Spectra

The atomic structure was discovered by John Dalton in the early 1800s. Dalton reintroduced atomic theory to explain chemical reactions.

His theory centered on five main concepts:

1. All matter is made of indivisible particles as *atoms*.

2. An *element* is made up of identical atoms.

3. Different elements have atoms with different masses.

4. Chemical compounds are made of atoms in specific integer ratios.

5. Atoms are neither created nor destroyed in chemical reactions.

The *electron* was discovered by J. J. Thomson in the late 1800s. By performing cathode ray experiments (two of which are explained below), he discovered that the electron was negatively charged.

Thomson measured the electron's charge-to-mass ratio and identified the electron as a fundamental particle.

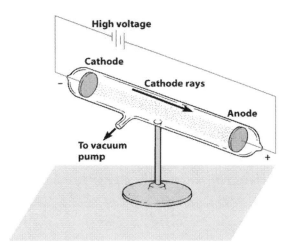

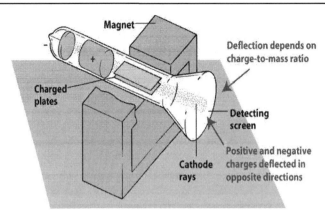

Around 1906, Robert Millikan was another scientist studying minuscule particles, specifically, charged oil droplets in an electric field. Millikan found that the charge on the oil droplets was a multiple of the electron charge. This finding, along with Thomson's results, was used to calculate the mass of the electron.

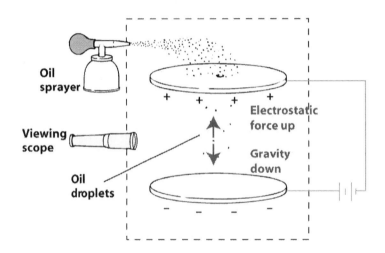

Thomson's result (charge-to-mass) was the following quantity:

$$\frac{q}{m} = 1.7584 \times 10^{11} \frac{C}{kg}$$

Millikan's result (charge) was:

$$q = 1.60 \times 10^{-19} C$$

Combined, the mass of an electron is:

$$m = \frac{q}{1.7584 \times 10^{11}} = 9.11 \times 10^{-31} kg$$

Dalton claimed that atoms were indivisible, that there were no smaller quantities involved. However, Thomson's and Millikan's experiments, along with the discovery of the electron, proved that statement false. The electron's mass is small (no measurable volume), but there needs to be a nature of an atom's positive charge. Thomson came up with what is the "plum pudding" model. Thomson thought that electrons were embedded in a blob of positively charged matter like "raisins in plum pudding."

Ernest Rutherford, in 1907, conducted an experiment which scattered alpha particles by bouncing them off gold foil.

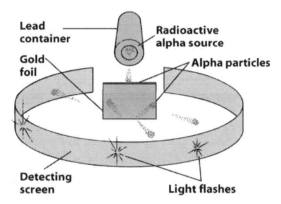

Most of the particles passed through without significant deflection, but a few scattered at large angles. Rutherford concluded that an atom's positive charge resides in a small nucleus that nonetheless contained most of the atom's mass (unlike the spread-out blob of matter containing electrons, as the plum pudding model suggested). Later, he named these positive charges protons. James Chadwick, in 1932, added the existence of neutral neutrons in the nucleus to the previous atomic theories.

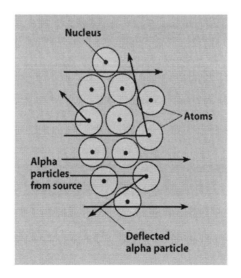

Notes

Emission Spectrum of Hydrogen; Bohr Model

The Bohr model is a depiction of the atom in which the electron orbits the nucleus in the same way that Earth orbits the Sun. Electrostatic attraction pulls the electron toward the nucleus. However, the electron orbits at high enough speeds to prevent it from crashing into the nucleus. The relationship of the electron orbit with respect to the nucleus leads to several important implications:

1. Electrons only exist in certain allowed orbits.

2. Within an orbit, the electron does not radiate.

3. Radiation is emitted or absorbed when changing orbits.

The first implication of the Bohr model is that electrons occupy different orbitals which determine their energy. These orbits are characterized by the orbital number n where n= 1 is equal to the ground state and represents the lowest energy level of the electron.

The higher the orbital number of the electron, the higher energy it will have, as well as being further away from the nucleus.

The second implication is that the electron does not radiate while orbiting the nucleus. As mentioned in earlier chapters, accelerating electric charges emit energy in the form of electromagnetic radiation. According to classical physics, the electron would, therefore, radiate away its energy (due to the energy radiated from centripetal acceleration) and crash into the nucleus. Bohr's model assumes that within the energy levels the electron does not radiate its energy and therefore stays in orbit.

The third implication of the Bohr model is that when changing energy levels, the electron must absorb or release some of its energy.

For example, in order for a ground state electron to achieve a higher orbital, it must absorb a photon (and thus absorb the photon's energy). If the electron were to drop to a lower orbital, then the electron must emit a photon equal to the energy difference between orbital levels.

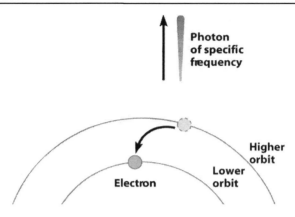

An important application of the Bohr model is in the identification of elements through their line spectrum. When an element is energized by a high potential difference, the electrons are constantly being raised to higher energy levels and then dropping back to lower energies. The photons released in the process contain specific energies which can be deduced by their frequency. These energies relate the energy differences in the different electron orbitals and allow quantization of the specific orbital energies.

For example, the figure below shows the line spectra of Hydrogen. The different series of light relates to the different orbital transitions of the Hydrogen's electrons.

Specifically, the Balmer series refers to the orbital transitions of electrons from any orbital back to n = 2.

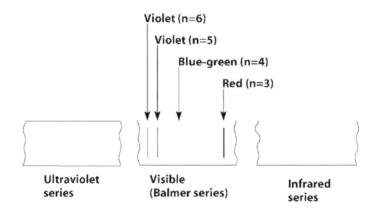

Atomic Energy Levels

The *quantum theory* of the atom declares there are a series of energy states that an electron can occupy. The lowest energy state is the "ground state," and any higher states are the "excited states." The energy of the photon emitted during a transition between energy levels equals the difference in state energies.

Below is an example of a hydrogen atom and its energy levels. The violet light represents the higher energy transitions (n = 5, 6 to n = 2) because violet has the highest energy of the visible spectrum. Red light has lower energy than violet and is the result of a lower energy transition (n = 3 to n = 2).

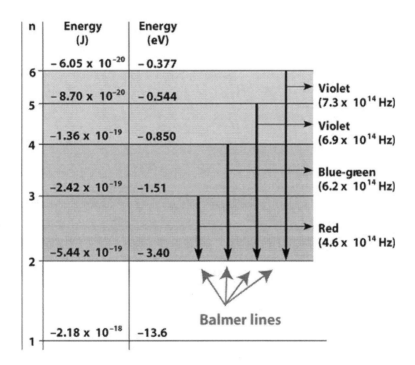

Bohr theory only holds true for the line spectrum of H, because there are only two electrons. Once more electrons are added, the theory is not able to keep up with the complications of heavier atoms. Additional experiments have established wave-particle duality of light and matter. Young's two-slit experiment, discussed previously when introducing light wave theory, produced interference patterns for both photons and electrons.

Louis de Broglie, in 1923, suggested the existence of matter waves in regards to atomic theory. The wavelength is related to momentum, and the matter waves in atoms are standing waves.

He derived the following formula for wavelength:

$$\lambda = \frac{h}{mv}$$

h = Planck's constant = 6.63×10^{-34} J·s

λ = Particle wavelength

m = mass

v = speed

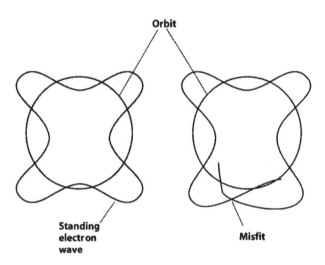

Wave mechanics was developed by Erwin Schrödinger. This method treats atoms as three-dimensional systems of waves and incorporates successful ideas of the Bohr model and much more. It describes the hydrogen atom and many electron atoms, as well as forms the fundamental understanding of chemistry.

The quantum mechanics model is a visualization of wave functions and probability distributions. Quantum numbers specify electronic quantum states, and electrons are delocalized.

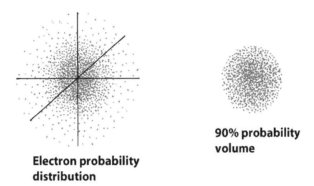

Electron probability distribution

90% probability volume

Quantum numbers are used to define and describe a certain electron in an atom.

The *principal quantum number*, given by the lowercase letter *n*, state the energy level (i.e., *shells*) in which the electron can most likely be found. It represents an average distance from the nucleus.

The second quantum number is the *angular momentum quantum number* and is given by the lowercase letter *l*. It describes the spatial distribution of the particular orbits, which are labeled *s, p, d, f, g, h*, etc.

These are *subshells*.

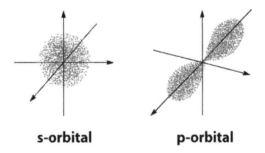

s-orbital   **p-orbital**

The third quantum number is the *magnetic quantum number*. It states the spatial orientation of the orbit within the energy (n) and the shape (l).

The magnetic quantum number (m_l) divides the subshell even more into specific orbitals that hold the electron.

The number of orbitals is given by $2l + 1$. M_l has values of $-l$ to l, with increments of one including zero ($-l$, .., *0*, ..., $+l$).

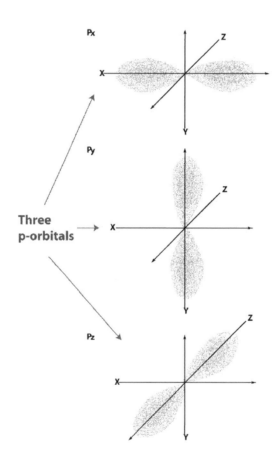

Last is the *spin quantum number*. It is either +½ or –½, and it stands for the electron spin orientation. There are only two values because an electron can only spin in one of two directions. Because of this and *Pauli's exclusion principle*, which states that no two electrons in the same atom can have the same set of quantum numbers, each orbital can only contain two electrons, and they must have opposite spins.

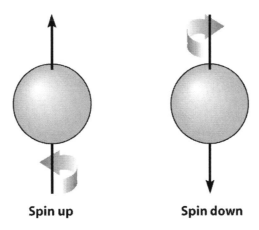

Spin up   **Spin down**

An *electron configuration* is an arrangement of electrons into atomic orbitals and specifies the atom's quantum state. The chemical properties of an atom are determined by looking at the electronic structure.

When writing electron configurations, it is imperative to follow the Pauli exclusion principle: each electron has unique quantum numbers, a maximum of two electrons per orbital, one spins up, and one spins down.

Electrons fill available orbitals in order of increasing energy (n).

Each shell can only hold so many orbitals.

Their capacities are:

$s = 2$

$p = 6$

$d = 10$

$f = 14$

Keep in mind that each orbital contains two electrons.

It is possible to fill only half an orbital, but it must be in the outer shell.

Example: strontium (38 electrons)

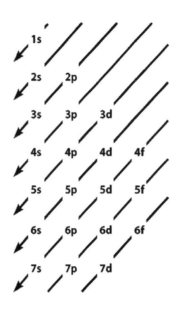

$$1s^2 2s^2 2p^6 3s^2 3p^6 4s^2 3d^{10} 4p^6 5s^2$$

The chemical properties of the elements can be understood by looking at the periodic table. Most chemical reactions follow the rules aligned with their *valence electron configuration* — electrons in the outer orbits determine chemical properties. Elements always want to have full outer shells, and will thus give their extra electrons away or take more from another element. Which of these occurs generally depends on how many valence electrons the element has.

In the periodic table, rows are *periods* and columns are *families* or *groups*. The families are:

Alkali metals (IA)

Alkaline earth (IIA)

Halogens (VIIA)

Noble gases (VIIIA)

A-group elements are the main group or the representative elements.

B-group elements are the transition elements or metals.

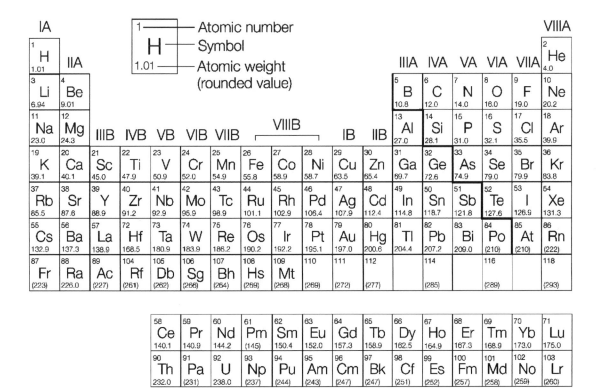

( ) represents an isotope

Noble gases (VIIIA) have completely-filled valence shells. This means they are inert or do not react easily with other elements.

Elements with 1 to 3 outer electrons will lose their valence electrons to become positive ions (such as metals).

Elements with 5 to 7 outer electrons tend to gain electrons and form negative ions (such as nonmetals).

Semiconductors are intermediate substances between metals and nonmetals.

¹H																	²He
³Li	⁴Be											⁵B	⁶C	⁷N	⁸O	⁹F	¹⁰Ne
¹¹Na	¹²Mg											¹³Al	¹⁴Si	¹⁵P	¹⁶S	¹⁷Cl	¹⁸Ar
¹⁹K	²⁰Ca	²¹Sc	²²Ti	²³V	²⁴Cr	²⁵Mn	²⁶Fe	²⁷Co	²⁸Ni	²⁹Cu	³⁰Zn	³¹Ga	³²Ge	³³As	³⁴Se	³⁵Br	³⁶Kr
³⁷Rb	³⁸Sr	³⁹Y	⁴⁰Zr	⁴¹Nb	⁴²Mo	⁴³Tc	⁴⁴Ru	⁴⁵Rh	⁴⁶Pd	⁴⁷Ag	⁴⁸Cd	⁴⁹In	⁵⁰Sn	⁵¹Sb	⁵²Te	⁵³I	⁵⁴Xe
⁵⁵Cs	⁵⁶Ba	⁵⁷La	⁷²Hf	⁷³Ta	⁷⁴W	⁷⁵Re	⁷⁶Os	⁷⁷Ir	⁷⁸Pt	⁷⁹Au	⁸⁰Hg	⁸¹Tl	⁸²Pb	⁸³Bi	⁸⁴Po	⁸⁵At	⁸⁶Rn
⁸⁷Fr	⁸⁸Ra	⁸⁹Ac	¹⁰⁴Rf	¹⁰⁵Db	¹⁰⁶Sg	¹⁰⁷Bh	¹⁰⁸Hs	¹⁰⁹Mt	¹¹⁰	¹¹¹	¹¹²		¹¹⁴		¹¹⁶		¹¹⁸

Metals · Nonmetals · Semiconductors

Quantized energy levels for electrons

In 1900, Max Planck introduced *quantized energy*. In 1905, Einstein discovered that light was made up of quantized photons. He found that higher frequency photons meant more energetic photons.

He derived the following equation:

$$E = hf$$

h = Planck's constant = 6.63×10^{-34} J·s

E = Photon energy

f = Photon frequency

The distinct lines of the emission spectrum prove that electron energy is quantized into energy levels. If electron energy is not quantized, then a continuous spectrum would be observed.

The energy of a particular level is calculated using the quantum number, and given by the equation:

$$E_n = -\frac{13.6}{n^2} \, (eV)$$

The equation is negative, so all energies are negative. Negative energies mean that energy contributes to the "stability" of the system — the electron *binding energy*. The more negative (lower) the energy, the more stable the orbit and the harder it is to knock out the electron.

The less negative (higher) the energy, the less stable the orbit and the easier it is to knock out the electron. At the highest energy, 0 eV, there is no binding energy, so the electron dissociates.

For atoms other than hydrogen, the shape of the energy level curve stays the same. However, the numerator is a constant other than 13.6 eV.

The precise relationship for atoms other than hydrogen is:

$$E = -\frac{Z^2 R_E}{n^2}$$

where Z is the atomic number.

Higher Z values give more negative binding energy (more stable) because the more charge, the more electrostatic attraction.

Calculation of energy emitted or absorbed when an electron changes energy levels

The wavelength of the emitted or absorbed radiation is governed by the *Rydberg formula*:

$$\frac{1}{\lambda} = R\left(\frac{1}{n_f^2} - \frac{1}{n_i^2}\right)$$

where λ is the wavelength, n_f is the final energy level, n_i is the initial energy level, and R is the Rydberg constant of value $1.0973 \times 10^7 \, \mathrm{m}^{-1}$.

The energy of the emitted or absorbed radiation is:

$$E = hf = h\nu = h\frac{c}{\lambda}$$

where E is energy, f and ν both mean frequency and c is the speed of light.

Energy is emitted for transitions to lower energy levels ($n_f < n_i$) and absorbed for transitions to higher energy levels ($n_f > n_i$).

The photon energy can be computed using the equation:

$$hf = E_H - E_L$$

Notes

Neutrons, Protons, Isotopes

The *nucleus* is made of protons and neutrons. *Protons* have a positive charge and a mass of:

$$m_p = 1.67262 \times 10^{-27} \text{ kg}$$

Neutrons are electrically neutral and slightly more massive than the proton:

$$m_n = 1.67493 \times 10^{-27} \text{ kg}$$

Neutrons and protons are collectively the *nucleons* (as they reside in the nucleus). The different nuclei are referred to as *nuclides*. The number of protons defines an element and refers to the neutral atom (having no charge).

If two atoms have the same number of protons, they are the same element.

An *isotope* is an atom that has the same atomic number as its counterpart on the periodic table, but which has a different number of neutrons. Isotopes often have similar chemical properties, but different stabilities. For instance, some isotopes decay and give off radiation particles, while others are stable and do not decay.

For many elements, several isotopes exist in nature. Natural abundance is the percentage of a particular element that consists of a particular isotope in nature.

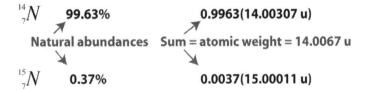

Atomic Particles			
Name	Mass (amu)	Charge	Location
Proton	1	+1	In the nucleus
Neutron	1	0	In the nucleus
Electron	0	−1	Surrounding the nucleus

Notes

Atomic Number, Atomic Weight

The number of protons is what gives an element its *atomic number* (Z). So far, we have identified 113 elements. The number of nucleons is equal to the *atomic mass* number (A). This is found by adding the number of protons and neutrons. The neutron number is given by $N = A - Z$.

The *atomic weight* is the weighted average of *atomic mass* for all isotopes of a given atom and is used for an element. The atomic mass is used for an isotope. A and Z are sufficient to specify a nuclide. Nuclides are symbolized as: $_{Z}^{A}X$

X is the chemical symbol for the element; it contains the same information as Z but in a more recognizable form.

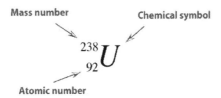

Because of wave-particle duality, the size of the nucleus is somewhat fuzzy. Measurements of high-energy electron scattering yield the radius to be:

$$r \approx (1.2 \times 10^{-15}\ m) \cdot (A^{\frac{1}{3}})$$

Masses of atoms are measured with reference to the carbon-12 atom, which is assigned a mass of exactly 12 amu. Where: $1\ u = 1.6605 \times 10^{-27}\ kg = 931.5\ MeV/c^2$

From the table, the electron is considerably less massive than a nucleon.

Rest Masses in Kilograms, Unified Atomics Mass Units, and MeV/c^2			
	Mass		
Object	**kg**	**amu**	**MeV/c^2**
Electron	9.1094×10^{-31}	0.00054858	0.51100
Proton	1.67262×10^{-27}	1.007276	938.27
$_{1}^{1}H$ atom	1.67353×10^{-27}	1.007825	938.78
Neutron	1.67493×10^{-27}	1.008665	939.57

Notes

Nuclear Forces

There are two forces are at work in the nucleus: the strong nuclear force and the electromagnetic force. The *strong nuclear force* binds the nucleons together and therefore contributes to the binding energy. The *electromagnetic force* is due to electrostatic repulsion in the group of positively charged protons in the nucleus (like-charges repel).

The nucleus stays together because the strong nuclear force is much stronger than the electromagnetic repulsion. The strong force is short-ranged, less than 10^{-15} m.

The repulsion between proton particles that it overcomes is the *proton-proton Coulomb repulsion*.

Proton-proton chain reaction

$$^1_1H + ^1_1H \rightarrow ^2_1H + ^0_1e$$

$$^2_1H + ^2_1H \rightarrow ^3_2He + ^1_0n$$

$$^3_2He + ^3_2He \rightarrow ^4_2He + 2^1_1H$$

Coulomb's Law relates the repulsion force on two charged particles depending on their charge and their distance.

The force (F) is large when the distance (r) is small.

$$F_{Coulomb} = \frac{kq_1q_2}{r^2}$$

To compare how tightly bound different nuclei are, divide the binding energy by A to get the binding energy per nucleon.

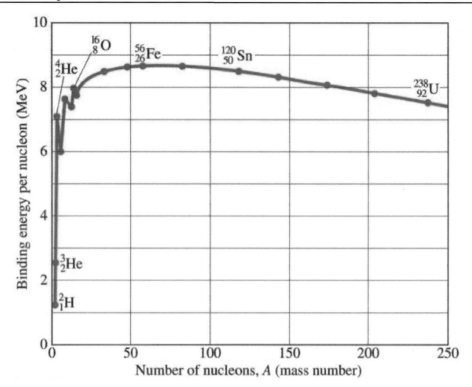

Chemical Reactions

To discuss chemical reactions, compounds and chemical change must first be explained. The atom is the smallest elemental unit. A *molecule* is the smallest particle still retaining the characteristic chemical properties of a substance; they are combinations of atoms.

Some examples of molecules are oxygen and hydrogen gas which are diatomic molecules (made of two atoms), ozone which is a triatomic oxygen molecule (made of three atoms), and the noble gases such as helium and neon, which are monatomic molecules (made of one atom, as they do not bond).

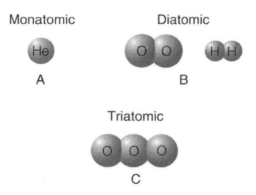

During chemical reactions, there is a formation and/or breaking of chemical bonds that form new molecules (*products*) from the starting material (*reactants*).

Chemical energy is the internal bonding potential energy, and the chemical equation is a symbolic summary of the chemical reaction.

A chemical reaction cannot be reversed. For example, firewood burned to create carbon dioxide cannot be turned back into wood.

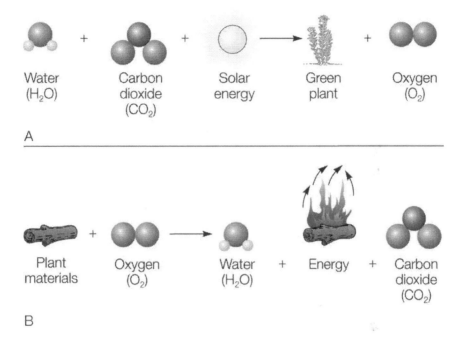

Water   Carbon   Solar   Green   Oxygen
(H_2O)   dioxide   energy   plant   (O_2)
                     (CO_2)

A

Plant   Oxygen   Water   +   Energy   +   Carbon
materials   (O_2)   (H_2O)   dioxide
                                                       (CO_2)

B

Valence electrons and ions are important when it comes to chemical reactions. The outer electrons determine the chemical properties of an atom. *Dot notation* is used to show how many electrons each element has in its outer shell.

Looking at the periodic table, this is determined by moving from left to right, with each group receiving one more electron in its outer shell than the previous.

Notice in the diagram below that the transition metals are excluded. Transition elements do not generally follow this rule. The elements shown below are the main elements used when computing dot notation reactions.

H·								He:
Li·	Be·		B ·	·C ·	·N:	·O:	:F:	:Ne:
Na·	Mg·		Al ·	·Si ·	·P:	·S:	:Cl:	:Ar:
K·	Ca·		Ga·	·Ge·	·As:	·Se:	:Br:	:Kr:
Rb·	Sr·		In ·	·Sn·	·Sb:	·Te:	: I :	:Xe:
Cs·	Ba·		Tl ·	·Pb·	·Bi:	·Po:	:At:	:Rn:
Fr·	Ra·							

Atoms attempt to acquire a full outer shell of eight electrons. Therefore, electrons can be gained, lost or shared in the process of reacting with another atom. When electrons are transferred, they must follow a few rules. The number of gained electrons must equal the number of lost electrons, and electrons are either lost or gained to form closed *octets*. This means a diatomic molecule will not be formed unless both octets are satisfied.

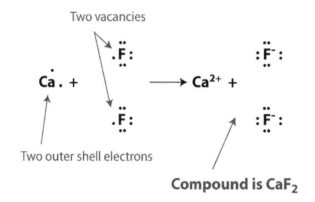

There are a few exceptions to this rule. Lithium and hydrogen are both most stable when they fill their first orbital, and therefore only have two electrons. Aluminum and boron both function well with only six valence electrons. They still want all eight, but will form stable compounds without them.

Some compounds will have more than an octet—these are mostly found in the halogen family. Another exception to the rule is noble gas compounds.

For instance, xenon reacts with six fluorine atoms to create xenon hexafluoride.

Depicted below is sodium (Na) reacting with another element and losing its one outer electron in the process. Sodium is now content because it has eight electrons in its outer shell.

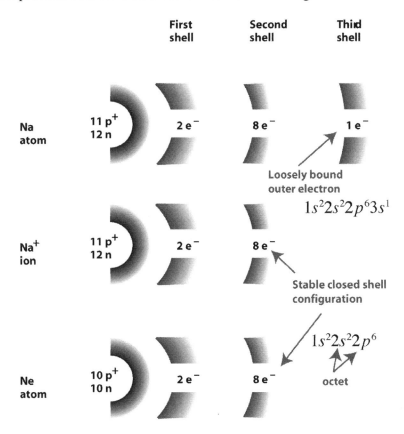

First shell **Second shell** **Third shell**

Na atom — $11 p^+$ $12 n$ — $2 e^-$ — $8 e^-$ — $1 e^-$

Loosely bound outer electron

$1s^2 2s^2 2p^6 3s^1$

Na$^+$ ion — $11 p^+$ $12 n$ — $2 e^-$ — $8 e^-$

Stable closed shell configuration

$1s^2 2s^2 2p^6$

Ne atom — $10 p^+$ $10 n$ — $2 e^-$ — $8 e^-$

octet

Chemical bonds are attractive forces that hold atoms together in compounds. They can be described in terms of molecular (delocalized) or atomic (localized) orbitals. There are three types of chemical bonds: metallic, ionic and covalent.

Metallic bonds occur between metallic elements, and the outer electrons are allowed to move freely throughout the metal. It is almost as if all of the electrons are combined to form an "electron gas" that fills in the spaces within the rigid crystalline lattice of metal atoms. This allows the efficient conduction of heat and electricity.

When these types of bonds are formed, there is not just one molecule. Rather, these bonds will create an orderly geometric structure, as depicted below in the formation of sodium chloride, or NaCl. Sodium loses an electron while chlorine gains one—both will then have eight valence electrons.

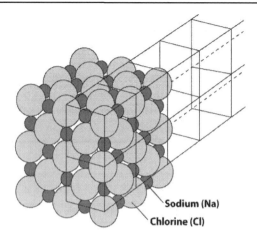

Sodium (Na)
Chlorine (Cl)

$$Na^{+1} + Cl^{-1} \rightarrow NaCl$$

A *covalent bond* is when electrons are shared between electrons, so both atoms achieve octets in their outside orbital. This overlap of shared electron clouds between nuclei yields net attraction.

Atoms within covalent compounds are electrically neutral, or nearly so.

Typically, this bonding occurs between nonmetallic elements.

A *covalent compound* is held together by covalent bonds which are represented by electron dot diagrams.

Bonding pairs are shared electrons, while lone (non-bonding) pairs are not shared.

The fluorine molecule: F₂

.F̈:+.F̈:

Lone (non-bonding) pairs

:F̈:F̈:

Bonding electron pair

Structures and compounds of nonmetallic elements combined with hydrogen:

Nonmetallic Elements	Element (E Represents Any Element of Family)	Compound
Family IVA: C, Si, Ge	·Ė·	H H:Ë:H H
Family VA: N, P, As, Sb	·Ë·	H:Ë:H H
Family VIA: O, S, Se, Te	·Ë:	H:Ë:H
Family VIIA: F, Cl, Br, I	·Ë:	H:Ë:

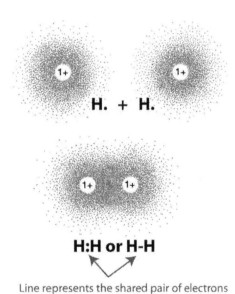

H:H or H-H

Line represents the shared pair of electrons

Some covalent bonds require the sharing of more than one electron pair. When this occurs, they are double or triple bonds.

These bonds are symbolized by a single bar, and represent two electrons.

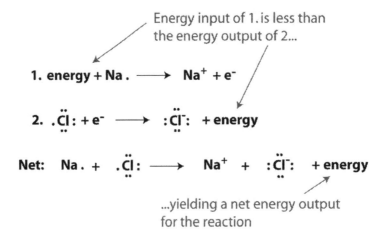

An *ionic bond* occurs when electrons are transferred between atoms. The only force involved in this bonding is the electrostatic force—this is what binds the atoms together. The reaction energy released during the reaction is equal to the heat of formation.

Each ionic reaction can be conceptually divided into half-reactions.

Ionic compounds are characterized by ionic bonds. They are commonly in the form of white, crystalline solids that are soluble in water.

Families IA and IIA lose electrons and form positive ions, whereas Families VIA and VIIA gain electrons to form negative ions.

Some ions are made up of more than one element and are *polyatomic ions*.

Common ions of some representative elements		
Element	**Symbol**	**Ion**
Lithium	Li	1+
Sodium	Na	1+
Potassium	K	1+
Magnesium	Mg	2+
Calcium	Ca	2+
Barium	Ba	2+
Aluminum	Al	3+
Oxygen	O	2-
Sulfur	S	2-
Hydrogen	H	1+ , 1–
Fluorine	F	1–
Chlorine	Cl	1–
Bromine	Br	1–
Iodine	I	1–

Common ions of some transition elements		
Single-Charge Ions		
Element	**Symbol**	**Charge**
Zinc	Zn	2+
Tungsten	W	6+
Silver	Ag	1+
Cadmium	Cd	2+
Variable-Charge Ions		
Chromium	Cr	2+ , 3+ , …
Manganese	Mn	2+ , 4+ , …
Iron	Fe	2+ , 3+
Cobalt	Co	2+ , 3+
Nickel	Ni	2+ , 3+
Copper	Cu	1+ , 2+
Tin	Sn	2+ , 4+
Gold	Au	1+ , 3+
Mercury	Hg	1+ , 2+
Lead	Pb	2+ , 4+

Some common polyatomic ions

Acetate	$(C_2H_3O_2)^-$
Ammonium	$(NH_4)^+$
Borate	$(BO_3)^{3-}$
Carbonate	$(CO_3)^{2-}$
Chlorate	$(ClO_3)^-$
Chromate	$(CrO_4)^{2-}$
Cyanide	$(CN)^-$
Dichromate	$(Cr_2O_7)^{2-}$
Hydrogen carbonate (or bicarbonate)	$(HCO_3)^-$
Hydrogen sulfate (or bisulfate)	$(HSO_4)^-$
Hydroxide	$(OH)^-$
Hypochlorite	$(ClO)^-$
Nitrate	$(NO_3)^-$
Nitrite	$(NO_2)^-$
Perchlorate	$(ClO_4)^-$
Permanganate	$(MnO_4)^-$
Phosphate	$(PO_4)^{3-}$
Phosphite	$(PO_3)^{3-}$
Sulfate	$(SO_4)^{2-}$
Sulfite	$(SO_3)^{2-}$

When writing a chemical formula for an ionic compound, list the elements in the compound and their proportions (subscripts). The proportions are decided by the amount of electron gain or loss.

Always write the symbol for a positive ion first, followed by a negative ion symbol. Then, assign subscripts to assure the compound is electrically neutral.

For example, when magnesium and chloride react, the chemical formula for the compound is $MgCl_2$. This is because magnesium has two electrons to give away (Mg^{-2}), but chlorine only wants one to fill its orbital (Cl^{+1}).

This means there must be two chlorines, and each will take one of magnesium's two extra electrons.

$$Ca \rightarrow Ca^{2+} \qquad Cl \rightarrow Cl^{-}$$

Forms +2 ion   Forms -1 ion

$$CaCl_2$$

+2+2(-1) = neutral compound

When compounds are formed, there is an unequal sharing of electrons. This is because of the difference in electronegativity in the elements involved in the reaction.

Electronegativity is the measure of an atom's ability to attract electrons.

The amount of difference reveals what type of bond is between the two atoms.

The meaning of absolute differences in electronegativity		
Absolute Difference	$\rightarrow$	**Type of Bond Expected**
1.7 or greater	means	ionic bond
between 0.5 and 1.7	means	polar covalent bond
0.5 or less	means	covalent bond

Below is a depiction of the electron cloud distribution for each kind of bond.

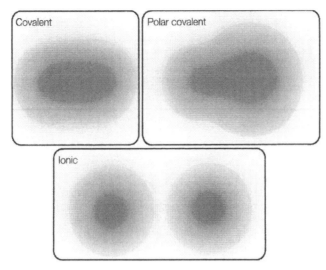

The electronegativity of each element can be found from the table:

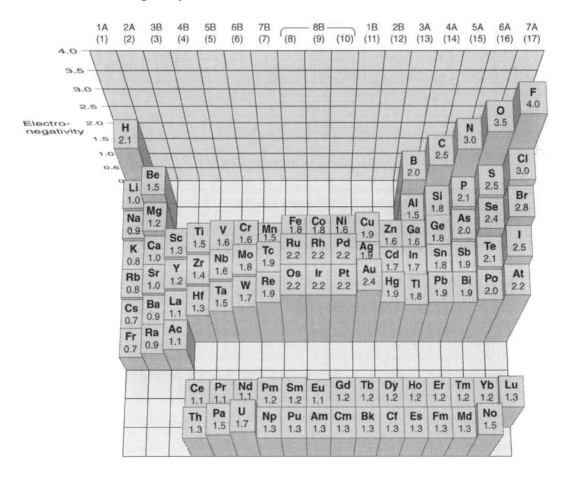

Naming Compounds

There are millions of combinations of over 90 elements. Many of these have common names related to historical usage (such as baking soda or washing soda).

However, these common names are difficult to relate to molecular composition.

The modern approach to naming compounds contains a systematic set of rules.

These rules are different for ionic vs. covalent compounds, but there is one rule: the suffix "-ide" refers to a compound that contains only two different elements.

Ionic Compounds

1. Start with the name of the metal ion (the positive one) first, then add the nonmetal ion (the negative one).

2. Use a distinguisher for elements that have more than one common ion

   – Historical suffix usage

     • "-ic" for higher of two

     • "-ous" for lower

   – Modern approach

     • English name of metal, followed by a Roman numeral indicating charge in parentheses

Modern names of some variable-charge ions	
Ion	**Name of Ion**
Fe^{2+}	Iron(II) ion
Fe^{3+}	Iron(III) ion
Cu^{+}	Copper(I) ion
Cu^{2+}	Copper(II) ion
Pb^{2+}	Lead(II) ion
Pb^{4+}	Lead(IV) ion
Sn^{2+}	Tin(II) ion
Sn^{4+}	Tin(IV) ion
Cr^{2+}	Chromium(II) ion
Cr^{3+}	Chromium(III) ion
Cr^{6+}	Chromium(VI) ion

Covalent compounds

Covalent compounds are molecular or composed of two or more nonmetals. The same elements can combine to form a number of compounds, depending on the concentration of each element involved.

When naming covalent compounds, there are two rules. Use the table below for the prefix and stem names:

1. The first element given in the formula is named first.

    −   The subscript or concentration of the element is indicated by a Greek prefix

2. Only the stem name of the second element comes next.

    −   a Greek prefix is used to indicate concentration

    −   the suffix "-ide" is added to the end

Prefixes and element stem names			
Prefix	*Meaning*	*Element*	*Stem*
Mono-	1	Hydrogen	Hydr-
Di-	2	Carbon	Carb-
Tri-	3	Nitrogen	Nitr-
Tetra-	4	Oxygen	Ox-
Penta-	5	Fluorine	Fluor-
Hexa-	6	Phosphorus	Phosph-
Hepta-	7	Sulfur	Sulf-
Octa-	8	Chlorine	Chlor-
Nona-	9	Bromine	Brom-
Deca-	10	Iodine	Iod-

Note: the a or o ending on the prefix if dropped if the stem name begins with a vowel (e.g., "tetroxide," not "tetraoxide").

Examples: carbon dioxide, carbon tetrachloride.

Radioactive Decay

Natural radioactivity is a spontaneous emission of particles or energy from an unstable nucleus. Towards the end of the 19th century, minerals were found that would darken a photographic plate even in the absence of light. This phenomenon is radioactivity.

When an atom is unstable, it will undergo *radioactive decay*. The maximum stability for a nucleon number is 2, 8, 20, 28, 50, 82 or 126. The higher the binding energy per nucleon, the more stable the nucleus. More massive nuclei require extra neutrons to overcome the Coulomb repulsion of the protons to be stable. There is a band of stability that depends on the ration of protons to neutrons that makes an atom stable. The Coulomb force is long-range; this is why extra neutrons are needed for stability in high-Z nuclei:

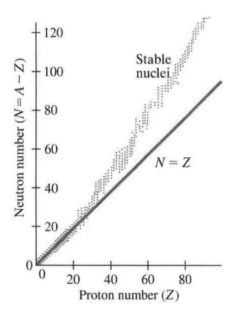

Pairs of protons and pairs of neutrons add stability to the atom. Conversely, an odd number of both protons and neutrons makes a less stable atom. For added stability, certain neutron-to-proton ratios are desired: 1:1 for isotopes with up to 20 protons and (1+1):1 for increasingly heavy isotopes. Nuclei that are unstable decay; many such decays are governed by another force, the weak nuclear force.

There are three types of decay: alpha, beta, and gamma decay. All these forms of radiation are *ionizing radiation* because they ionize material that they go through.

Alpha emission is an expulsion of a helium nucleus. It is the least penetrating and can even be stopped by a piece of paper.

Beta emission is an expulsion of an electron. This is more penetrating than alpha decay and can be stopped by 1 cm of aluminum.

Gamma decay is an emission of a high energy photon (electromagnetic radiation). This is the most penetrating, and can only be stopped by a thick, dense shield (e.g., approximately 13.5 feet of water, 6.5 feet of concrete or about 1.3 feet of lead).

Radioactive Decay			
Unstable Condition	**Type of Decay**	**Emitted**	**Product Nucleus**
More than 83 protons	Alpha emission	$^4_2\alpha$ (^4_2He)	Lost 2 protons and 2 neutrons
Neutron-to-proton ratio too large	Beta emission	$^0_{-1}\beta$ ($^0_{-1}e$)	Gained 1 proton, no mass change
Excited Nucleus	Gamma emission	$^0_0\gamma$	No change
Neutron-to-proton ratio too small	Other emission	^0_1e	Lost 1 proton, no mass change

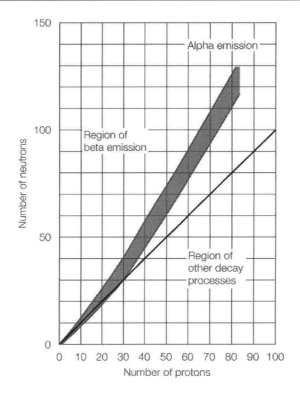

Alpha and beta rays are bent in opposite directions in a magnetic field, while gamma rays are not bent at all.

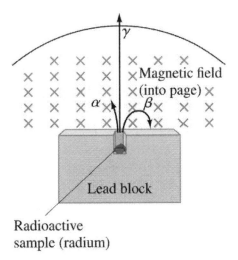

The *conservation of mass* dictates that the total atomic weight before the decay must equal the total atomic weight after. The *conservation of charge* dictates that the total atomic number before the decay must equal the total atomic number after. A new conservation law that is evident by studying radioactive decay is that the total number of nucleons cannot change. Do not get thrown off by unfamiliar particles. If they have a weight and a charge, incorporate these numbers into calculations. Test problems on identifying decay products are math work. Remember: the atomic number (the bottom number) determines the element.

Alpha Decay

An example of alpha decay is radium-227 (^{227}Ra) decaying into radon-222 (^{222}Rn):

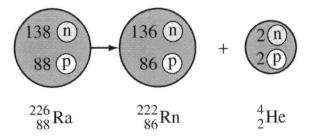

$$^{226}_{88}\text{Ra} \qquad ^{222}_{86}\text{Rn} \qquad ^{4}_{2}\text{He}$$

In general, alpha decay can be written:

$$^{A}_{Z}N \rightarrow ^{A-4}_{Z-2}N' + ^{4}_{2}He$$

Alpha decay occurs when the strong nuclear force cannot hold a large nucleus together. The mass of the parent nucleus is greater than the sum of the masses of the daughter nucleus and the alpha particle; this difference is the *disintegration energy*.

Alpha decay is much more likely than other forms of nuclear disintegration because the alpha particle itself is stable.

Some smoke detectors use alpha radiation—the presence of smoke is enough to absorb the alpha rays and keep them from striking the collector plate.

Beta Decay

Beta decay occurs when a nucleus emits an electron. An example is the decay of carbon-14 (^{14}C):

$$^{14}_{6}C \rightarrow \,^{14}_{7}N + e^- + neutrino$$

The nucleus still has 14 nucleons, but it has one more proton and one fewer neutron.

This decay is an example of an interaction that proceeds via the weak nuclear force.

The electron in beta decay is not an orbital electron; it is created in the decay.

The fundamental process is a neutron decaying to a proton, electron, and neutrino:

$$n \rightarrow p + e^- + neutrino$$

The need for a particle such as a *neutrino* was discovered through analysis of energy and momentum conservation in beta decay—it could not be a two-particle decay.

Neutrinos are difficult to detect. They interact only weakly, and direct evidence for their existence was not available for a long time.

The symbol for the neutrino is the Greek letter nu (ν); using this, the beta decay of carbon-14 is written as (the bar over the neutrino means that it is an antineutrino):

$$^{14}_{6}C \rightarrow \,^{14}_{7}N + e^- + \overline{\nu}$$

Beta decay occurs where the nucleus emits a positron rather than an electron:

$$^{19}_{10}Ne \rightarrow \, ^{19}_{9}F + e^+ + \overline{\nu}$$

And a nucleus can capture one of its inner electrons:

$$^{7}_{4}Be + e^- \rightarrow \, ^{7}_{3}Li + \nu$$

Gamma Decay

Gamma rays are high-energy photons. They are emitted when a nucleus decays from an excited state to a lower state, as photons are emitted by electrons returning to a lower state.

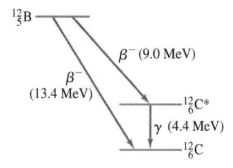

Half-life, stability, exponential decay, semi-log plots

An element's *half-life* is the amount of time required for ½ of a radioactive sample to decay.

For example, a 1 kg sample of an unstable isotope with a one-day half-life:

After 1 day - 500 g remain

After 2 days - 250 g remain

After 3 days - 125 g remain

Half-lives of some radioactive isotopes		
Isotope	**Half-Life**	**Mode of Decay**
$^{3}_{1}H$ (tritium)	12.26 years	Beta
$^{14}_{6}C$	5,730 years	Beta
$^{90}_{38}Sr$	28 years	Beta
$^{131}_{53}I$	8 days	Beta
$^{133}_{54}Xe$	5.27 days	Beta
$^{238}_{92}U$	4.51×10^9 years	Alpha
$^{242}_{94}Pu$	3.79×10^5 years	Alpha
$^{240}_{94}Pu$	6,760 years	Alpha
$^{239}_{94}Pu$	24,360 years	Alpha
$^{40}_{19}K$	1.3×10^9 years	Alpha

Half-life graphs look like the decreasing exponential:

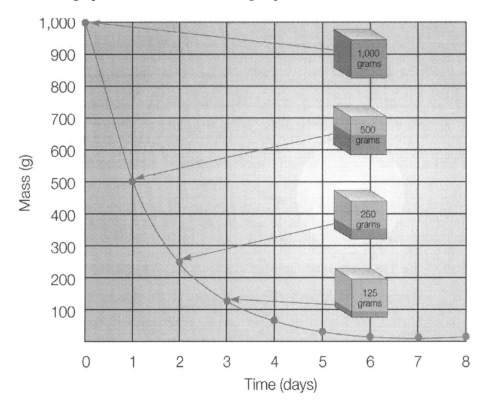

Nuclear decay is a random process; the decay of one nucleus is not influenced by the decay of any other.

Additionally, the decay rate is unaffected by temperature, pressure, volume or any other environmental factor.

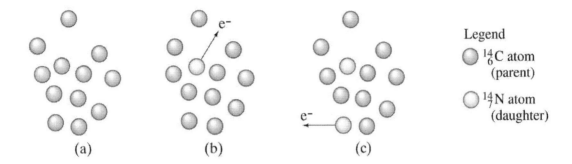

Therefore, the number of decays in a short time interval is proportional to the number of nuclei present and to the time:

$$\Delta N = -\lambda N \Delta t$$

Here, λ is a constant characteristic of that particular nuclide, the decay constant.

This equation can be solved, using calculus, for N as a function of time:

$$N = N_0 e^{-\lambda t}$$

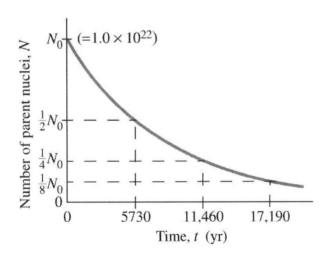

335

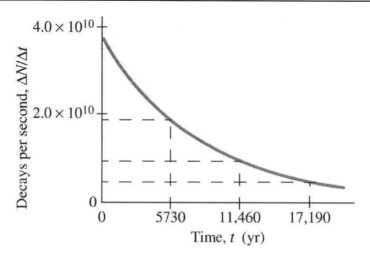

The half-life can be related to the decay constant:

$$T_{\frac{1}{2}} = \frac{\ln 2}{\lambda} = \frac{0.693}{\lambda}$$

It can be written:

$$N_t = N_{t=0} \cdot \left(\frac{1}{2}\right)^{\#half-lives} = N_{t=0} \cdot \left(\frac{1}{2}\right)^{\frac{t}{half-life}}$$

where $N_{t=0}$ is the amount the original starting material, N_t is the amount of the original material that is still left, and t is time.

Although the above is the official half-life equation, people like to multiply rather than to divide. Therefore, a more user-friendly equation is:

$$N_{t=0} = N_t \cdot 2^{\#half-lives} = N_t \cdot 2^{\frac{t}{half-life}}$$

For the purposes of the test, semi-log plots convert exponential curves into straight lines.

- Something that curves up becomes a straight line with a positive slope.
- Something that curves down becomes a straight line with a negative slope.
- For exponential decay, a semi-log plot graphs the log of amount vs. time.
- For exponential decay, a semi-log plot is a straight line with a negative slope.
- The semi-log plot intercepts the *x*-axis where the original *y*-value is 1.

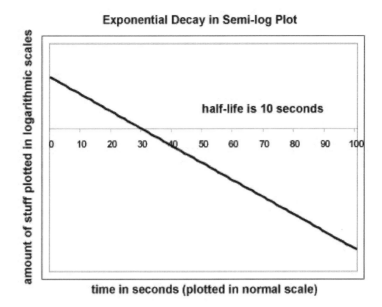

A decay series occurs when one radioactive isotope decays to another radioactive isotope, which decays to another and so on. This allows the creation of nuclei that otherwise would not exist in nature.

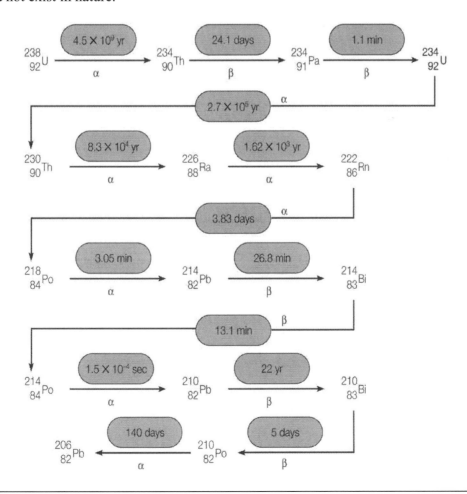

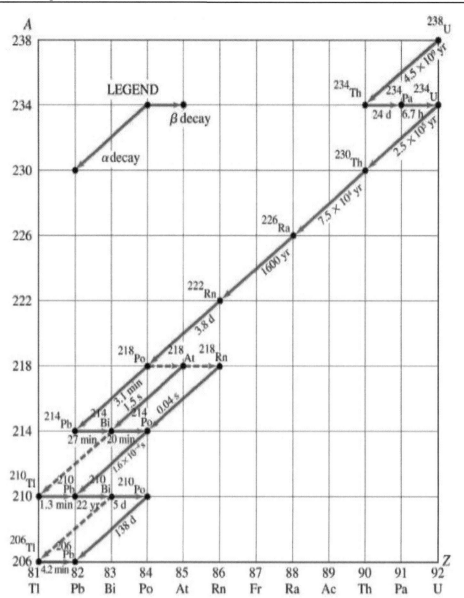

Radioactive dating can be done by analyzing the fraction of carbon in organic material that is carbon-14. The ratio of ^{14}C to ^{12}C in the atmosphere has been roughly constant over thousands of years. A living plant or tree will constantly be exchanging carbon with the atmosphere and will have the same carbon ratio in its tissue. When the plant dies, this exchange stops.

Carbon-14 has a half-life of about 5,730 years; it gradually decays away and becomes a smaller and smaller fraction of the total carbon in the plant tissue. This fraction can be measured, and the age of the tissue deduced.

Objects older than about 60,000 years cannot be dated this way—there is too little carbon-14 left. Other isotopes are useful for geologic time scale dating, Uranium-238 has a half-life of 4.5×10^9 years, and has been used to date the oldest rocks on Earth as about 4 billion years old.

When a nucleus decays through alpha emission, energy is released. Why is it that these nuclei do not decay immediately?

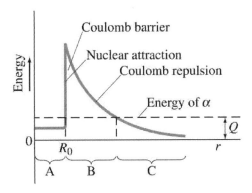

The answer is that although energy is released in the decay, there is still an energy barrier. The alpha particle can escape through a quantum mechanical phenomenon of tunneling. As stated in the *Heisenberg uncertainty principle*, energy conservation can be violated, if the violation does not last too long:

$$Q = M_p c^2 - (M_D + m_a)c^2$$

The higher the energy barrier, the less time the alpha particle has to get through it, and the less likely that is to happen. This accounts for the extremely wide variation in half-lives for alpha decay.

There are a few methods to take measurements of decay. Devices called ionization counters detect ions produced by radiation, such as a *Geiger counter*. The Geiger counter is a gas-filled tube with a wire in the center. The wire is at high voltage; the case is grounded. When a charged particle passes through, it ionizes the gas. The ions cascade onto the wire, producing a pulse.

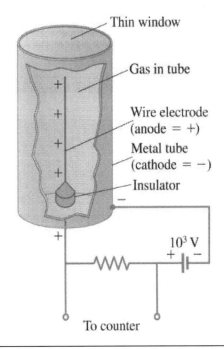

A *scintillation counter* uses a scintillator—a material that emits light when a charged particle goes through it. The scintillator is made light-tight, and the light flashes are viewed with a photomultiplier tube, which has a photocathode that emits an electron when struck by a photon, and then a series of amplifiers.

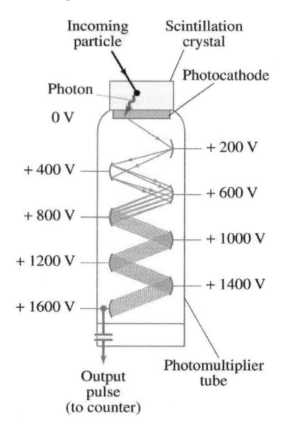

A *cloud chamber* contains a supercooled gas; when a charged particle goes through it, droplets form along its track.

Similarly, a *bubble chamber* contains a superheated liquid, which forms bubbles. In either case, the tracks can be photographed and measured.

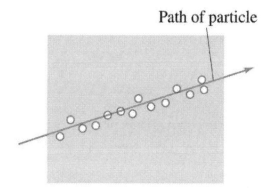

A *wire drift chamber* is somewhat similar to but vastly more sophisticated than, a Geiger counter. Many wires are present, some at high voltage and some grounded; in addition to the presence of a signal, the time it takes the pulse to arrive at the wire is measured, allowing a precise measurement of position.

Radiation can be measured at the source. The activity is the number of disintegrations per unit time.

There are many units of activity:

Names, symbols, and conversion factors for radioactivity			
Name	**Symbol**	**To Obtain**	**Multiply by**
Becquerel	Bq	Ci	2.7×10^{-11}
gray	Gy	rad	100
sievert	Sv	rem	100
curie	Ci	Bq	3.7×10^{10}
rem	rem	Sv	0.01
millirem	mrem	rem	0.001
rem	rem	millirem	1,000

Radiation is measured where it is absorbed. Human exposure is measured in rem, but the SI unit is the millisievert. Another measurement is the absorbed dose—the effect the radiation has on the absorbing material. The rad, a unit of dosage, is the amount of radiation that deposits energy at a rate of 1.00×10^{-2} J/kg in any material. The SI unit for dose is the gray, Gy. The dosage is related to effects on organisms.

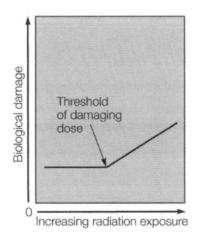
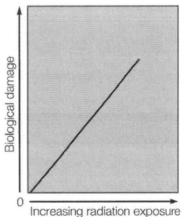

Approximate single dose, whole body effects of radiation exposure	
Level	**Comment**
0.130 rem	Average annual exposure to natural background radiation
0.500 rem	Upper limit of annual exposure to the general public
25.0 rem	Threshold for observable effects such as reduced blood cell count
100.0 rem	Fatigue and other symptoms of radiation sickness
200.0 rem	Definite radiation sickness, bone marrow damage, the possibility of developing leukemia
500.0 rem	Lethal dose for 50 percent of individuals
1,000.0 rem	Lethal dose for all

Radiation damages biological tissue, but it can be used to treat cancer and other diseases. It is important to be able to measure the amount, or dose, of radiation, received.

Relative Biological Effectiveness (RBE)	
Type	**RBE**
X- and γ rays	1
β (electrons)	1
Protons	2
Slow Neutrons	5
Fast Neutrons	≈ 10
α particles and heavy ions	≈ 20

There are different effects to tissues depending on the type of radiation. Gamma rays are the most dangerous overall because they can penetrate the whole body; however, if ingested, alpha rays being the most damaging. To get the effective dose, the dose is multiplied by the relative biological effectiveness. If the dose is measured in rad, the effective dose is in rem; if the dose is grays, the effective dose is in Sieverts (Sv).

Cancer is sometimes treated with *radiation therapy* to destroy the cancerous cells. To minimize the damage to healthy tissue, the radiation source is rotated, so it goes through different parts of the body on its way to the tumor.

Radioactive isotopes are widely used in medicine for diagnostic purposes. They can be used as non-invasive scans or tools to check for unusual concentrations that could signal a tumor or other problem. The radiation is detected with a gamma-ray detector.

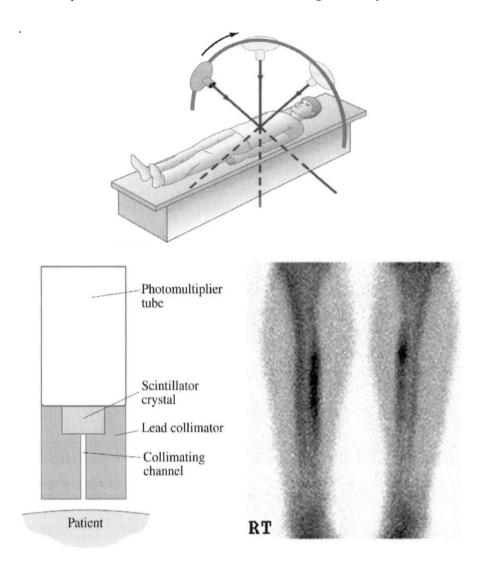

Radioactive tracers can be detected using tomographic techniques, where a three-dimensional image is gradually built up through successive scans.

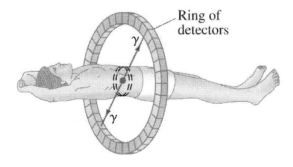

A proton in a magnetic field can have its spin either parallel or antiparallel to the field. The field splits the energy levels slightly; the energy difference is proportional to the field magnitude.

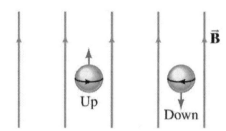

The object to be examined is placed in a static magnetic field, and radio frequency (RF) electromagnetic radiation is applied. When the radiation has the right energy to excite the spin-flip transition, many photons will be absorbed.

This is *nuclear magnetic resonance*. The value of the field depends somewhat on the local molecular neighborhood; this allows information about the structure of the molecules to be determined.

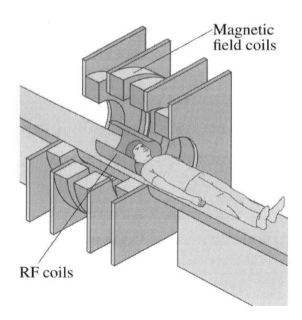

Magnetic resonance imaging works the same way; the transition is excited in hydrogen atoms, which are the most common in the human body.

Giving the field a gradient can contribute to image accuracy, as it allows determining the origin of a particular signal.

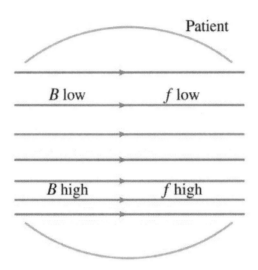

Technique	Optimal Resolution
Conventional X-ray	½ mm
CT scan, X-ray	½ mm
Nuclear medicine (tracers)	1 cm
SPECT (single photon emission)	1 cm
PET (positron emission)	2-5 mm
MRI (NMR)	½ - 1 mm
Ultrasound	0.3 - 2 mm

Notes

General Nature of Fission

There are two types of nuclear reactions: fission and fusion. Nuclear fission is the process whereby the nucleus of an atom is split into two smaller fragments. A nuclear reaction takes place when a nucleus is struck by another nucleus or particle.

For example, when the original nucleus is transformed into another, this is referred to as *transmutation*:

$$^4_2\text{He} + {}^{14}_7\text{N} \rightarrow {}^{17}_8\text{O} + {}^1_1\text{H}$$

Energy and momentum must be conserved in nuclear reactions.

$$a + X \rightarrow Y + b$$

The reaction energy, or Q-value, is the sum of the initial masses less the sum of the final masses, multiplied by c^2:

$$Q = (M_a + M_X - M_b - M_Y)c^2$$

If Q is positive, the reaction is exothermic and will occur regardless of how small the initial kinetic energy is.

If Q is negative, there is a minimum initial kinetic energy that must be available before the reaction can take place.

Neutrons are effective in nuclear reactions, as they have no charge and therefore are not repelled by the nucleus.

Neutron captured by $^{238}_{92}\text{U}$.

$^{239}_{92}\text{U}$ decays by β decay to neptunium-239.

$^{239}_{93}\text{Np}$ itself decays by β decay to produce plutonium-239.

Nuclear fission occurs when one nucleus split apart. The energy released in a fission reaction is large. Also, since smaller nuclei are stable with fewer neutrons, several neutrons emerge from each fission as well. These neutrons can be used to induce fission in other nuclei, causing a chain reaction. This occurs when Uranium undergoes fission when struck by a free neutron.

The critical mass determines if the nuclei have sufficient mass and concentration to produce a chain reaction.

The mass distribution of the fragments shows that the first two pieces are large but usually unequal in size.

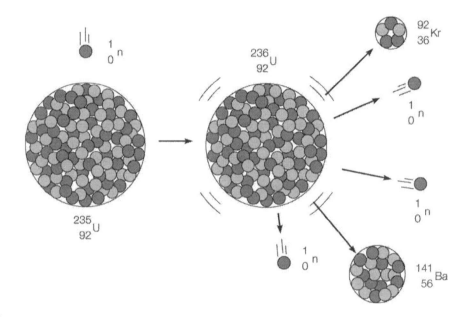

Nuclear energy is an interconversion of mass and energy. It is ultimately connected to the origins of the universe and the life cycles of the starts. The *Big Bang theory* hypothesizes that the incredibly hot, dense, primordial plasma cooled, creating protons and neutrons. Continued cooling leads to hydrogen atoms which collapsed gravitationally into 1st generation stars.

The ultimate source of nuclear energy is a gravitational attraction.

The mass deficit is the difference between the masses of reactants and products.

The binding energy is the energy required to break a nucleus into individual protons and neutrons. The ratio of binding energy to nucleon number tells you how stable a nucleus is. Iron-56 is the most stable nucleus:

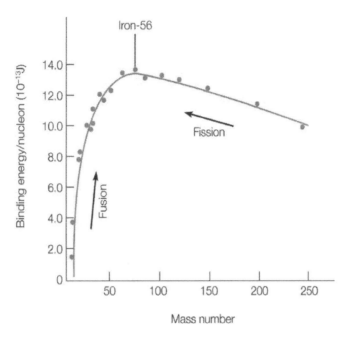

Isotope	Major Mode of Decay	Half-Life
Tritium	Beta	12.26 years
Carbon-14	Beta	5,930 years
Argon-41	Beta, gamma	1.83 hours
Iron-55	Electron capture	2.7 years
Colbalt-58	Beta, gamma	71 days
Colbalt-60	Beta, gamma	5.26 years
Nickel-63	Beta	92 years
Krypton-85	Beta, gamma	10.76 years
Strontium-89	Beta	5.4 days
Strontium-90	Beta	28 years
Yttrium-91	Beta	59 days
Isotope	Major Mode of Decay	Half-Life
Zirconium-93	Beta	9.5×10^5 years
Zirconium-95	Beta, gamma	65 days
Niobium-95	Beta, gamma	35 days
Technetium-99	Beta	2.1×10^5 years
Ruthenium-106	Beta	1 year

Iodine-129	Beta	1.6×10^7 years
Iodine-131	Beta, gamma	8 days
Xenon-133	Beta, gamma	5.27 days
Cesium-134	Beta, gamma	2.1 years
Cesium-135	Beta	2×10^6 years
Cesium-137	Beta	30 years
Cerium-141	Beta	32.5 days
Cerium-144	Beta, gamma	285 days
Promethium-147	Beta	2.6 years
Samarium-151	Beta	90 years
Europium-154	Beta, gamma	16 years
Lead-210	Beta	22 years
Radon-222	Alpha	3.8 days
Radium-226	Alpha, gamma	1,620 years
Thorium-229	Alpha	7,300 years
Thorium-230	Alpha	26,000 years
Uranium-234	Alpha	2.48×10^5 years
Uranium-235	Alpha, gamma	7.13×10^8 years
Uranium-238	Alpha	4.51×10^9 years
Neptunium-237	Alpha	2.14×10^6 years
Plutonium-238	Alpha	89 years
Plutonium-239	Alpha	24,360 years
Plutonium-240	Alpha	6,760 years
Plutonium-241	Beta	13 years
Plutonium-242	Alpha	3.79×10^5 years
Americium-241	Alpha	458 years
Americium-243	Alpha	7,650 years
Curium-242	Alpha	163 days
Curium-244	Alpha	18 years
Thorium-229	Alpha	7,300 years

To make a nuclear reactor, the chain reaction needs to be self-sustaining—it will continue indefinitely—but controlled. A *moderator* is needed to slow the neutrons; otherwise, their probability of interacting is too small. Common moderators are heavy water and graphite.

Unless the moderator is heavy water, the fraction of fissionable nuclei in natural uranium is too small to sustain a chain reaction, about 0.7%. It needs to be enriched to about 2–3%.

Neutrons that escape from the uranium do not contribute to fission.

There is a critical mass below which a chain reaction will not occur because too many neutrons escape.

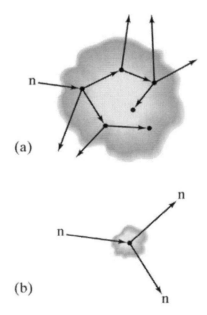

Finally, there are *control rods*, usually cadmium or boron, which absorb neutrons and can be used for fine control of the reaction, to keep it barely critical.

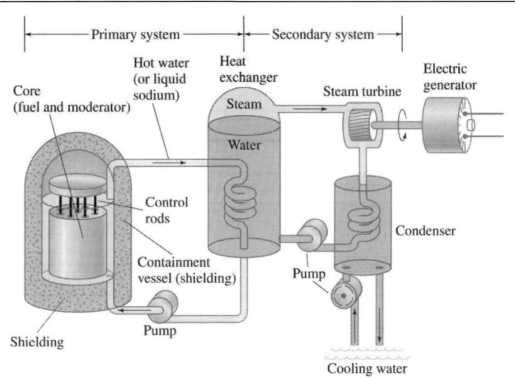

Some problems associated with nuclear reactors include the disposal of radioactive waste and the possibility of an accidental release of radiation.

An atomic bomb uses fission, but the core is deliberately designed to undergo a massive uncontrolled chain reaction when the uranium is formed into a critical mass during the detonation process.

General Nature of Fusion

Nuclear fusion occurs when less massive nuclei form more massive nuclei. Nuclear fusion is the energy source for the Sun and other stars.

Fusion requires high temperature, high density, and sufficient confinement time.

Controlled fusion is usually studied with magnetic or inertial confinement.

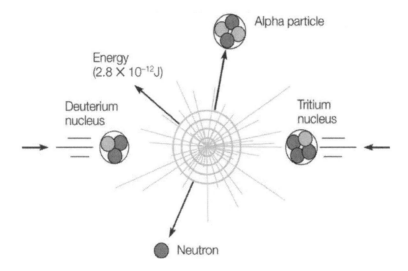

When light nuclei fuse to form heavier nuclei, they release energy in the process.

An example is the sequence of fusion processes that change hydrogen into helium in the Sun. They are listed here with the energy released in each:

$$_1^1H + {}_1^1H \rightarrow {}_1^2H + e^+ + v \qquad\qquad (0.42 \ \text{MeV})$$

$$_1^1H + {}_1^2H \rightarrow {}_2^3He + \gamma \qquad\qquad (5.49 \ \text{MeV})$$

$$_2^3He + {}_2^3He \rightarrow {}_2^4He + {}_1^1H + {}_1^1H \qquad (12.86 \ \text{MeV})$$

The net effect is to transform four protons into a helium nucleus plus two positrons, two neutrinos, and two gamma rays.

$$4\,_1^1H \rightarrow {}_2^4He + 2e^+ + 2v + 2\gamma$$

More massive stars can fuse heavier elements in their cores, all the way up to iron, the most stable nucleus.

There are three fusion reactions that are being considered for power reactors:

$$^2_1H + ^2_1H \rightarrow ^3_1H + ^1_1H \qquad (4.03 \text{ MeV})$$

$$^2_1H + ^2_1H \rightarrow ^3_2He + n \qquad (3.27 \text{ MeV})$$

$$^2_1H + ^3_1H \rightarrow ^4_2He + n \qquad (17.59 \text{ MeV})$$

These reactions use common fuels—deuterium or tritium—and release much more energy per nucleon than fission does.

A successful fusion reactor has not yet been achieved, but fusion (thermonuclear) bombs have been built.

Several geometries for the containment of the incredibly hot plasma that must exist in a fusion reactor have been developed.

Mass Deficit, Energy Liberated, Binding Energy

Nuclear reactions are presented by balanced equations. The charge is always conserved, as is the mass number.

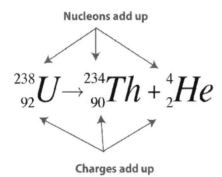

$$^{238}_{92}U \rightarrow ^{234}_{90}Th + ^{4}_{2}He$$

Names, symbols, and properties of particles in nuclear equations			
Name	Symbol	Mass Number	Charge
Proton	$^{1}_{1}H$ (or $^{1}_{1}p$)	1	1+
Electron	$^{0}_{-1}e$ (or $^{0}_{-1}\beta$)	0	1−
Neutron	$^{1}_{0}n$	1	0
Gamma Photon	$^{0}_{0}\gamma$	0	0

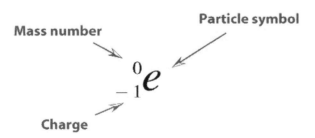

The difference in mass before and after a reaction is the mass deficit or mass defect. If the total mass before the reaction is different from the total mass after the reaction, then the difference in mass is made up for by energy.

Energy is liberated when mass is lost during a reaction because mass and energy are always conserved; the total mass and energy before a reaction is always the same as the total mass and energy after the reaction.

The energy that makes up for the mass deficit is calculated by:

Energy   Mass

$$E = mc^2$$

$$c = 3 \times 10^8 \, m/s$$

Speed of light

The mass of the nucleons will always be greater than the mass of the atom. The mass has become energy, such as radiation or kinetic energy, released during the formation of the nucleus. This difference between the total mass of the constituents and the mass of the nucleus is the total binding energy of the nucleus.

The energy liberated is equal to the binding energy. The binding energy is used when converting ΔM into its equivalent in energy (ΔMc^2).

$$M_{nucleons} = M_{atom} + \text{binding energy}/c^2$$

Binding energy commonly refers to nuclear binding energy (the energy that binds the nucleons together). Binding energy per nucleon is strongest for Iron (Fe 56), and weakest for Deuterium (the 2-nucleon isotope of hydrogen).

Less often used is the electron binding energy. Electron binding energy is commonly referred to as the ionization energy.

$$M_{nucleons} - M_{atom} = \text{mass deficit (also mass defect)} = \Delta M$$

Reactant masses

$$2(1.0078u) + 2(1.0087u) = 4.0330u$$

$$2\,{}^{1}_{1}H + 2\,{}^{1}_{0}n \rightarrow {}^{4}_{2}He$$

$$4.0026u$$

Mass defect = binding energy   **Helium mass**

$$\Delta m = 4.0330 - 4.0026 = 0.0304u = 28.3 Mev$$

Mass Spectrometer

Mass spectrometry is a chemistry technique used to identify the chemicals in a substance. A mass spectrometer is a device that measures the mass-to-charge ration of a sample, as well as the number of ions in gas-phase. This produces a mass spectrum.

Charged particles can be deflected by a magnetic field. A mass spectrometer works by turning atoms into ions, increasing their acceleration, so they all have the same kinetic energy, and deflecting them with a magnetic field. It creates ions by removing electrons from the atom—even if an atom normally forms a negative ion, a mass spectrometer usually works with positive ions. Once their paths are deflected, their mass can be calculated because the force of deflection is known, and the curve of their deflection path is used to separate the atoms.

The lighter the ion, the more it is deflected. The greater the positive charge on the ion, the more it is deflected by the magnetic field.

A mass spectrum is then produced, which looks like a bar graph.

It gives the concentration of the atom, organizing by their mass-to-charge ratio:

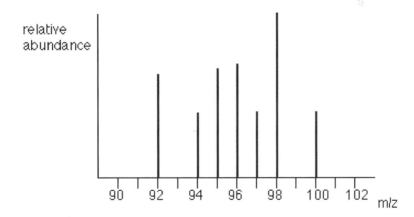

Notes

Chapter Summary

Atoms

- Nuclei contain protons and neutrons—nucleons.

- Total number of nucleons, A, is atomic mass number.

- Number of protons, Z, is atomic number.

- Isotope notation: $_{Z}^{A}X$

- Nuclear masses are measured in u; carbon-12 is defined as having a mass of 12 u.

- 1 amu $= 1.6605 \times 10^{-27}$ kg $= 931.5$ MeV/c^2

- Difference between the mass of the nucleus and the mass of its constituents is the binding energy.

Decay

- Unstable nuclei decay through alpha, beta or gamma emission.

- An alpha particle is a helium nucleus; a beta particle is an electron or positron; a gamma ray is a highly energetic photon.

- Nuclei are held together by the strong nuclear force; the weak nuclear force is responsible for beta decay.

- Electric charge, linear and angular momentum, mass-energy and nucleon number are all conserved.

- Radioactive decay is a statistical process.

- The number of decays per unit time is proportional to the number of nuclei present:
$$N = N_0 e^{-\lambda t}$$

- The half-life is the time it takes for half the nuclei to decay.

Nuclear Reactions

- The nuclear reaction occurs when nuclei collide, and different nuclei are produced.

- Reaction energy or Q-value:

$$Q = M_p c^2 - (M_D + m_a) c^2$$

- Fission is when the heavy nucleus splits into two intermediate-sized nuclei.

  - Chain reactions occurred when neutrons emitted in a fission trigger more reactions.

  - Critical mass is the minimum mass needed to sustain a chain reaction.

  - A moderator is used to slow the neutrons, so collisions are more likely.

- Fusion is when small nuclei combine to form larger ones.

  - Sun's energy comes from fusion reactions.

  - Useful fusion reactor has not yet been built.

  - Radiation damage is measured using dosimetry.

  - Effect of absorbed dose depends on the type of radiation.

Practice Questions

1. In a nuclear reaction, the mass of the products is less than the mass of the reactants. Why is this not observed in a chemical reaction?

   A. In chemical reactions, the mass is held constant by the nucleus

   B. In chemical reactions, the mass deficit is balanced by a mass surplus

   C. The mass deficit in chemical reactions is too small to be observed

   D. The mass does not convert to energy in chemical reactions

2. The isotope $^{13}_{7}\text{N}$ decays by positron emission to what isotope?

   A. $^{14}_{6}\text{C}$
      B. $^{11}_{7}\text{N}$
      C. $^{13}_{6}\text{C}$
      D. $^{12}_{6}\text{C}$

3. The radioactive gas radon is:

      I. more hazardous to smokers than nonsmokers

      II. the single greatest source of human radiation exposure

      III. a product of the radioactive decay series of uranium

   A. I only
      B. II only
      C. III only
      D. I, II and III

4. Which of the following statements best describes the strong nuclear force?

   A. The strength of the force increases with distance

   B. The force is very strong and is effective over a large range of distances

   C. The electrical force is stronger than the nuclear force

   D. The force is very strong but is effective only within a short range of distances

5. Natural line broadening can be understood in terms of the:

   A. Schrodinger wave equation
      C. de Broglie wavelength

   B. Pauli exclusion principle
      D. uncertainty principle

6. A blue photon has a:

   A. longer wavelength than a red photon and travels with a greater speed

   B. shorter wavelength than a red photon and travels with the same speed

   C. shorter wavelength than a red photon and travels with a greater speed

   D. longer wavelength than a red photon and travels with a lower speed

7. Which type of nuclear radiation is powerful light energy that is *not* deflected as it passes between electrically-charged plates?

    A. Gamma   **B.** Beta   **C.** Alpha   **D.** Nuclide

8. The main reason that there is a limit to the size of a stable nucleus is the:

    A. weakness of the electrostatic force
    B. weakness of the gravitational force
    C. short-range effect of the strong nuclear force
    D. limited range of the gravitational force

9. Elements combine in fixed mass ratios to form compounds. This requires that elements:

    A. have unambiguous atomic numbers
    B. are always chemically active
    C. are composed of continuous matter without subunits
    D. are composed of discrete subunits called atoms

10. What is a rem?

    A. A unit for measuring rapid electron motion
    B. A unit for measuring radiation exposure
    C. The number of radiation particles emitted per second
    D. The maximum exposure limit for occupational safety

11. The intensity of X-rays, gamma rays, or any other radiation is:

    A. inversely proportional to the square of the distance from the source
    B. inversely proportional to the distance from the source
    C. directly proportional to the square of the distance from the source
    D. directly proportional to the distance from the source

12. Ionizing radiation is:

    A. a neutron that has acquired a charge, resulting in the formation of an ion
    B. high-energy radiation that removes electrons from atoms or molecules
    C. radiation that only interacts with ions
    D. equivalent to a proton

13. What nucleus results when ^{55}Ni decays by positron emission?

    A. ^{55}Ca   **B.** ^{55}Ni   **C.** ^{55}Co   **D.** ^{55}Fe

14. Which of the following types of radiation has the highest energy?

A. γ rays

B. Visible light rays

C. α particles

D. β particles

15. If a star has a peak intensity at 580 nm, what is its temperature? (Use the Wien's displacement constant $b = 2.9 \times 10^{-3}$ K·m)

A. 5,000 °C   **B.** 2,000 °C   **C.** 5,000 °F   **D.** 5,000 K

Solutions

1. D is correct. Mass is conserved in a chemical reaction; no particles are created or destroyed. The atoms are rearranged to form products from reactants.

In nuclear reactions, the mass difference is due to mass converting into energy.

2. C is correct.

Positron emission occurs during β^+.

The decay equation:

$$^{13}_{7}\text{N} \rightarrow {^{13}_{6}}\text{C} + e^+ + \nu_e$$

A proton converts into a neutron, and a positron is ejected with an electron neutrino. The daughter nuclide is ^{13}C.

3. D is correct.

Radon gas is a natural decay product of uranium that accounts for the greatest source of yearly radiation exposure in humans. Radon is more hazardous to smokers due to the combined carcinogenic effects of smoking and radiation exposure.

4. D is correct. The strong nuclear force is the strongest of the four fundamental forces. However, it only acts within a small range of distance (about the diameter of the nucleus).

5. D is correct.

Natural line broadening is the extension of a spectral line over a range of frequencies. This occurs due in part to the uncertainty principle, which relates the time in which an atom is in an excited state to the energy of its emitted photon.

$$\Delta E \Delta t > \hbar / 2$$

where $\hbar$ is reduced Planck's constant

Because energy is related to frequency by:

$$E = hf$$

where h is Planck's constant

The range of frequencies observed (broadening) is due to the uncertainty in energy outlined by the uncertainty principle.

6. B is correct.

Speed is constant for all electromagnetic waves and only changes due to the transmission medium, not the frequency or wavelength of the wave.

Blue photons have higher energy and thus higher frequencies than red light due to:

$$E = hf$$

However, the frequency is inversely proportional to wavelength:

$$\lambda = c \,/\, f$$

Thus, blue photons have shorter wavelengths than red photons due to their higher frequencies.

7. A is correct.

Gamma radiation is a high energy electromagnetic wave, and as such it has no charge and will not deflect within an electric field.

8. C is correct.

Nuclei with atomic numbers over 83 are inherently unstable and thus radioactive. This limit in size is due to the fact that the strong nuclear force has a short range and as the nucleus gets larger, the strong nuclear force cannot overcome the Coulomb repulsion from the protons within the nucleus.

9. D is correct.

A mass of an element or compound can be measured by its molar mass. The molar mass relates the mass of the element or compound to a discrete number of subunits (atoms for elements, molecules for compounds).

10. B is correct.

The rem is short for the Roentgen equivalent in man and is designed to measure the biological damage of ionizing radiation. It does not measure the number of particles absorbed or emitted, nor is it the maximum occupational safety exposure limit for radiation.

11. A is correct.

The intensity of electromagnetic radiation with respect to distance from the point source:

$I = S / 4\pi r^2$

where I = intensity, S = point source strength, and r = radial distance from the point source

The intensity of the radiation from the point source is inversely proportional to the square of the distance away from the point source.

12. B is correct. Ionizing radiation can be high energy charged particles (alpha, beta) or high energy electromagnetic waves (X-rays, gamma rays).

All are termed ionizing because they possess enough energy to remove electrons from atoms or molecules and ionize them.

13. C is correct.

Nuclear reaction:

$$^{55}_{28}\text{Ni} \rightarrow \, ^{55}_{27}\text{Co} + \text{e}^+ + \nu_\text{e}$$

where Co = product, e^+ = positron and ν_e = electron neutrino

In positron emission (β^+ decay), a proton in the nucleus converts to a neutron while releasing a positron and an electron neutrino.

The atomic number decreases by one, but the mass number stays constant.

14. A is correct. Gamma rays are high energy electromagnetic waves. They have the highest energy of all radiation (e.g., alpha, beta, and electromagnetic spectrum).

15. D is correct.

Use Wien's Displacement Law:

$\lambda_{\text{max}} = b / \text{T}$

$\text{T} = (2.9 \times 10^{-3}\,\text{K·m}) / (580 \times 10^{-9}\,\text{m})$

$\text{T} = 5{,}000\,\text{K}$

Please, leave your Customer Review on Amazon

Notes

Appendix

Common Physics Formulas and Conversions

Constants and Conversion Factors

1 unified atomic mass unit	1 u (or Dalton) = 1.66×10^{-27} kg
	1 u = 931 MeV/c^2
Proton mass	$m_p = 1.67 \times 10^{-27}$ kg
Neutron mass	$m_n = 1.67 \times 10^{-27}$ kg
Electron mass	$m_e = 9.11 \times 10^{-31}$ kg
Electron charge magnitude	$e = 1.60 \times 10^{-19}$ C
Avogadro's number	$N_0 = 6.02 \times 10^{23}$ mol^{-1}
Universal gas constant	R = 8.31 J/(mol·K)
Boltzmann's constant	$k_B = 1.38 \times 10^{-23}$ J/K
Speed of light	$c = 3.00 \times 10^8$ m/s
Planck's constant	$h = 6.63 \times 10^{-34}$ J·s
	$h = 4.14 \times 10^{-15}$ eV·s
	$hc = 1.99 \times 10^{-25}$ J·m
	$hc = 1.24 \times 10^3$ eV·nm
Vacuum permittivity	$\varepsilon_0 = 8.85 \times 10^{-12}$ C^2/N·m^2
Coulomb's Law constant	$k = 1/4\pi\varepsilon_0 = 9.0 \times 10^9$ N·m^2/C^2
Vacuum permeability	$\mu_0 = 4\pi \times 10^{-7}$ (T·m)/A
Magnetic constant	$k' = \mu_0/4\pi = 10^{-7}$ (T·m)/A
Universal gravitational constant	$G = 6.67 \times 10^{-11}$ m^3/kg·s^2
Acceleration due to gravity at Earth's surface	g = 9.8 m/s^2
1 atmosphere pressure	1 atm = 1.0×10^5 N/m^2
	1 atm = 1.0×10^5 Pa
1 electron volt	1 eV = 1.60×10^{-19} J
Balmer constant	B = 3.645×10^{-7} m
Rydberg constant	R = 1.097×10^7 m^{-1}
Stefan constant	$\sigma = 5.67 \times 10^{-8}$ W/m^{2}K^4

Units			Prefixes	
Name	**Symbol**	**Factor**	**Prefix**	**Symbol**
meter	m	10^{12}	tera	T
kilogram	kg	10^{9}	giga	G
second	s	10^{6}	mega	M
ampere	A	10^{3}	kilo	k
kelvin	K	10^{-2}	centi	c
mole	mol	10^{-3}	mili	m
hertz	Hz	10^{-6}	micro	μ
newton	N	10^{-9}	nano	n
pascal	Pa	10^{-12}	pico	p
joule	J			
watt	W			
coulomb	C			
volt	V			
ohm	Ω			
henry	H			
farad	F			
tesla	T			
degree Celsius	°C			
electronvolt	eV			

Values of Trigonometric Functions for Common Angles

θ	$\sin \theta$	$\cos \theta$	$\tan \theta$
0°	0	1	0
30°	1/2	$\sqrt{3}/2$	$\sqrt{3}/3$
37°	3/5	4/5	3/4
45°	$\sqrt{2}/2$	$\sqrt{2}/2$	1
53°	4/5	3/5	4/3
60°	$\sqrt{3}/2$	1/2	$\sqrt{3}$
90°	1	0	∞

Electricity and Magnetism

		$A = area$
Electric Field	$\vec{E} = \dfrac{\vec{F}_E}{q}$	$B = magnetic\ field$
		$C = capacitance$
Electric Field Strength	$\|\vec{E}\| = \dfrac{1}{4\pi\varepsilon_0}\dfrac{\|q\|}{r^2}$	$d = distance$
		$E = electric\ field$
Electric Field Strength	$\|\vec{E}\| = \dfrac{\|\Delta V\|}{\|\Delta r\|}$	$\epsilon = emf$
		$F = force$
Electrostatic Force Between Charged Particles	$\|\vec{F}_E\| = \dfrac{1}{4\pi\varepsilon_0}\dfrac{\|q_1 q_2\|}{r^2}$	$I = current$
		$l = length$
Electric Potential Energy	$\Delta U_E = q\Delta V$	$P = power$
		$Q = charge$
Electrostatic Potential due to a Charge	$V = \dfrac{1}{4\pi\varepsilon_0}\dfrac{q}{r}$	$q = point\ charge$
		$R = resistance$
Capacitor Voltage	$V = \dfrac{Q}{C}$	$r = separation$
		$t = time$
Capacitance of a Parallel Plate Capacitor	$C = \kappa\varepsilon_0\dfrac{A}{d}$	$U = potential\ energy$
		$V = electric\ potential$
Electric Field Inside a Parallel Plate Capacitor	$E = \dfrac{Q}{\varepsilon_0 A}$	$v = speed$
		$\kappa = dielectric\ constant$
Capacitor Potential Energy	$U_C = \frac{1}{2}Q\Delta V = \frac{1}{2}C(\Delta V)^2$	$\rho = resistivity$
		$\theta = angle$
Current	$I = \dfrac{\Delta Q}{\Delta t}$	$\Phi = flux$
Resistance	$R = \dfrac{\rho l}{A}$	

Power	$P = I\Delta V$
Current	$I = \dfrac{\Delta V}{R}$
Resistors in Series	$R_s = \sum_i R_i$
Resistors in Parallel	$\dfrac{1}{R_p} = \sum_i \dfrac{1}{R_i}$
Capacitors in Parallel	$C_p = \sum_i C_i$
Capacitors in Series	$\dfrac{1}{C_s} = \sum_i \dfrac{1}{C_i}$
Magnetic Field Strength	$B = \dfrac{\mu_0 I}{2\pi r}$
Magnetic Force	$\vec{F}_M = q\vec{v} \times \vec{B}$
	$\vec{F}_M = |q\vec{v}||\sin\theta||\vec{B}|$
	$\vec{F}_M = I\vec{l} \times \vec{B}$
	$\vec{F}_M = |I\vec{l}||\sin\theta||\vec{B}|$
Magnetic Flux	$\Phi_B = \vec{B} \cdot \vec{A}$
	$\Phi_B = |\vec{B}|\cos\theta\,|\vec{A}|$
Electromagnetic Induction	$\epsilon = \dfrac{-\Delta\Phi_B}{\Delta t}$
	$\epsilon = Blv$

Fluid Mechanics and Thermal Physics

Density	$$\rho = \frac{m}{V}$$	A = area
		c = specific heat
Pressure	$$P = \frac{F}{A}$$	d = thickness
		e = emissivity
Absolute Pressure	$P = P_0 + \rho g h$	F = force
Buoyant Force	$F_b = \rho V g$	h = depth
Fluid Continuity Equation	$A_1 v_1 = A_2 v_2$	k = thermal conductivity
		K = kinetic energy
Bernoulli's Equation	$P_1 + \rho g y_1 + \frac{1}{2}\rho v_1^2 = P_2 + \rho g y_2 + \frac{1}{2}\rho v_2^2$	l = length
		L = latent heat
Heat Conduction	$$\frac{Q}{\Delta t} = \frac{kA\Delta T}{d}$$	m = mass
		n = number of moles
		n_c = efficiency
Thermal Radiation	$P = e\sigma A(T^4 - T_C^4)$	N = number of molecules
Ideal Gas Law	$PV = nRT = Nk_B T$	P = pressure or power
		Q = energy transferred to
Average Energy	$$K = \frac{3}{2}k_B T$$	a system by heating
		T = temperature
Work	$W = -P\Delta V$	t = time
Conservation of Energy	$\Delta E = Q + W$	E = internal energy
Linear Expansion	$\Delta l = \alpha l_o \Delta T$	V = volume
Heat Engine Efficiency	$n_c = |W/Q_H|$	v = speed
		W = work done on a
Carnot Heat Engine Efficiency	$$n_c = \frac{T_H - T_C}{T_H}$$	system
		y = height
		σ = Stefan constant
Energy of Temperature Change	$Q = mc\Delta T$	α = coefficient of linear expansion
Energy of Phase Change	$Q = mL$	ρ = density

Optics

		d = separation
Wavelength to Frequency	$\lambda = \dfrac{v}{f}$	f = frequency or focal length
		h = height
Index of Refraction	$n = \dfrac{c}{v}$	L = distance
		M = magnification
Snell's Law	$n_1 \sin\theta_1 = n_2 \sin\theta_2$	m = an integer
Thin Lens Equation	$\dfrac{1}{s_i} + \dfrac{1}{s_0} = \dfrac{1}{f}$	n = index of refraction
		R = radius of curvature
Magnification Equation	$\lvert M \rvert = \left\lvert \dfrac{h_i}{h_o} \right\rvert = \left\lvert \dfrac{s_i}{s_o} \right\rvert$	s = distance
		v = speed
Double Slit Diffraction	$d \sin\theta = m\lambda$	x = position
	$\Delta L = m\lambda$	λ = wavelength
		θ = angle
Critical Angle	$\sin\theta_c = \dfrac{n_2}{n_1}$	
Focal Length of Spherical Mirror	$f = \dfrac{R}{2}$	

Modern Physics

Photon Energy	$E = hf$	B = Balmer constant
		c = speed of light
Photoelectric Electron Energy	$K_{max} = hf - \phi$	E = energy
		f = frequency
Electron Wavelength	$\lambda = \dfrac{h}{p}$	K = kinetic energy
		m = mass
Energy Mass Relationship	$E = mc^2$	p = momentum
Rydberg Formula	$\dfrac{1}{\lambda} = R\left(\dfrac{1}{n_f^2} - \dfrac{1}{n_i^2}\right)$	R = Rydberg constant
		v = velocity
Balmer Formula	$\lambda = B\left(\dfrac{n^2}{n^2 - 2^2}\right)$	λ = wavelength
		ϕ = work function
Lorentz Factor	$\gamma = \dfrac{1}{\sqrt{1 - \dfrac{v^2}{c^2}}}$	γ = Lorentz factor

Geometry and Trigonometry

Rectangle	$A = bh$	$A = area$
		$C = circumference$
Triangle	$A = \dfrac{1}{2}bh$	$V = volume$
		$S = surface\ area$
Circle	$A = \pi r^2$	$b = base$
	$C = 2\pi r$	$h = height$
Rectangular Solid	$V = lwh$	$l = length$
		$w = width$
Cylinder	$V = \pi r^2 l$	$r = radius$
	$S = 2\pi rl + 2\pi r^2$	$\theta = angle$
Sphere	$V = \dfrac{4}{3}\pi r^3$ $S = 4\pi r^2$	
Right Triangle	$a^2 + b^2 = c^2$ $\sin\theta = \dfrac{a}{c}$ $\cos\theta = \dfrac{b}{c}$ $\tan\theta = \dfrac{a}{b}$	

Physics Glossary

A

Absolute humidity (or saturation value) – the maximum amount of water vapor that could be present in 1 m³ of the air at any given temperature.

Absolute magnitude – a classification scheme which compensates for the differences in the distance to stars; calculates the brightness that stars would appear to have if they were all at a defined, standard distance of 10 parsecs.

Absolute scale – temperature scale set so that zero is the theoretical lowest temperature possible (this would occur when all random motion of molecules has ceased).

Absolute zero – the theoretical lowest temperature possible, at which the molecular motion ceases to exist; –273.16 or 0 K.

Absorptance – the ratio of the total absorbed radiation to the total incident radiation.

Acceleration – the rate of change of velocity of a moving object with respect to time; the SI units are m/s²; by definition, this change in velocity can result from a change in speed, a change in direction or a combination of changes in both speed and direction.

Acceleration due to gravity – the acceleration produced in a body due to the Earth's attraction; denoted by the letter g (SI unit – m/s²); on the surface of the Earth, its average value is 9.8 m/s²; increases when going towards the poles from the equator; decreases with altitude and with depth inside the Earth; the value of g at the center of the Earth is zero.

Achromatic – capable of transmitting light without decomposing it into its constituent colors.

Acoustics – the science of the production, transmission, and effects of sound.

Acoustic shielding – a sound barrier that prevents the transmission of acoustic energy.

Adiabatic – any change in which there is no gain or loss of heat.

Adiabatic cooling – the decrease in temperature of an expanding gas that involves no additional heat flowing out of the gas; the cooling from the energy lost by expansion.

Adiabatic heating – the increase in temperature of the compressed gas that involves no additional heat flowing into the gas; the heating from the energy gained by compression.

Afocal lens – a lens of zero convergent power whose focal points are infinitely distant.

Air mass − a large, more or less uniform body of air with nearly the same temperature and moisture conditions throughout.

Albedo − the fraction of the total light incident on a reflecting surface, especially a celestial body, which is reflected back in all directions.

Allotropic forms − elements that can have several structures with different physical properties (e.g., graphite and diamond).

Alpha (α) particle – the nucleus of a helium atom (two protons and two neutrons) emitted as radiation from a decaying heavy nucleus (α-decay).

Alternating current − an electric current that first moves in one direction, then in the opposite direction with a regular frequency.

Amorphous – term that describes solids that have neither definite form nor structure.

Amp − unit of electric current; equivalent to coulomb/second.

Ampere – the full name of the unit amp; the SI unit of electric current; one ampere is the flow of one coulomb of charge per second.

Amplitude − the maximum absolute value attained by the disturbance of a wave or by any quantity that varies periodically.

Amplitude (of an oscillation) − the maximum displacement of a body from its mean position during an oscillatory motion.

Amplitude (of waves) − the maximum displacement of particles of the medium from their mean positions during the propagation of a wave.

Angle of contact − the angle between tangents to the liquid surface and the solid surface inside the liquid; both the tangents are drawn at the point of contact.

Angle of incidence – the angle of an incident (arriving) ray or particle to a surface; measured from a line perpendicular to the surface (the normal).

Angle of reflection – the angle of a reflected ray or particle from a surface; measured from a line perpendicular to the surface (the normal).

Angle of refraction − the angle between the refracted ray and the normal.

Angle of repose − the angle of inclination of a plane with the horizontal such that a body placed on the plane is on the verge of sliding but does not.

Angstrom − a unit of length; $1 = 10^{-10}$ m.

Angular acceleration − the rate of change of angular velocity of a body moving along a circular path; denoted by a.

Angular displacement − the angle described at the center of the circle by a moving body along a circular path. It is measured in radians.

Angular momentum − also a moment of momentum; the cross-product of position vector and momentum.

Angular momentum quantum number − from quantum mechanics model of the atom, one of four descriptions of the energy state of an electron wave; describes the energy sublevels of electrons within the main energy levels of an atom.

Angular velocity − the rate of change of angular displacement per unit of time.

Annihilation − a process in which a particle and an antiparticle combine and release their rest energies in other particles.

Antineutrino − the antiparticle of neutrino; has zero mass and spin ½.

Archimedes principle − a body immersed in a fluid experiences an apparent loss of weight which is equal to the weight of the fluid displaced by the body.

Astronomical unit − the radius of the Earth's orbit is defined as one astronomical unit (A.U.).

Atom − the smallest unit of an element that can exist alone or in combination with other elements.

Atomic mass unit − relative mass unit (amu) of an isotope based on the standard of the ^{12}C isotope; one atomic mass unit (1 amu) = 1/12 the mass of a Carbon–12 atom = 1.66×10^{-27} Kg.

Atomic number − the number of protons in the nucleus of an atom.

Atomic weight − weighted average of the masses of stable isotopes of an element as they occur in nature; based on the abundance of each isotope of the element and the atomic mass of the isotope compared to carbon-12.

Avogadro's number − the number of carbon-12 atoms in exactly 12.00 g of C that is 6.02×10^{23} atoms or other chemical units; the number of chemical units in one mole of a substance.

Avogadro's Law − under the same conditions of temperature and pressure, equal volumes of all gases contain an equal number of molecules.

Axis − the imaginary line about which a planet or other object rotates.

B

Background radiation − ionizing radiation (e.g., alpha, beta, gamma rays) from natural sources.

Balanced forces − when a number of forces act on a body and the resultant force is zero; see *Resultant forces*.

Balmer lines − lines in the spectrum of the hydrogen atom in the visible range; produced by the transition between n 2 and n = 2, with n being the principal quantum number.

Balmer series − a set of four line spectra; narrow lines of color emitted by hydrogen atom electrons as they drop from excited states to the ground state.

Bar – a unit of pressure; equal to 10^5 Pascals.

Barometer − an instrument that measures atmospheric pressure; used in weather forecasting and determining elevation above sea level.

Baryon − subatomic particle composed of three quarks.

Beat − a phenomenon of the periodic variation in the intensity of sound due to the superposition of waves differing slightly in frequency; rhythmic increases and decreases of volume from constructive and destructive interference between two sound waves of slightly different frequencies.

Bernoulli's theorem – states that the total energy per unit volume of a non-viscous, incompressible fluid in a streamline flow will remain constant.

Beta (β) particle − high-energy electron emitted as ionizing radiation from a decaying nucleus (β-decay); also a beta ray.

Big bang theory − current model of galactic evolution in which the universe is assumed to have been created by an intense and brilliant explosion from a primeval fireball.

Binding energy – the net energy required to break a nucleus into its constituent protons and neutrons; also the energy equivalent released when a nucleus is formed.

Black body − an ideal body which would absorb all incident radiation and reflect none.

Black body radiation − electromagnetic radiation emitted by an ideal material (the black body) that perfectly absorbs and perfectly emits radiation.

Black hole − the remaining theoretical core of a supernova that is so dense that even light cannot escape.

Bohr model − the structure of the atom that attempted to correct the deficiencies of the solar system model and account for the Balmer series.

Boiling point – the temperature at which a phase change of liquid to gas takes place through boiling; the same temperature as the condensation point.

Boundary – the division between two regions of differing physical properties.

Boyle's Law – for a given mass of a gas at constant temperature, the volume of the gas is inversely proportional to the pressure.

Brewster's Law – states that the refractive index of a material is equal to the tangent of the polarizing angle for the material.

British thermal unit (Btu) – the amount of energy or heat needed to increase the temperature of one pound of water one degree Fahrenheit.

Brownian motion – the continuous random motion of solid microscopic particles when suspended in a fluid medium due to their ongoing bombardment by atoms and molecules.

Bulk's modulus of elasticity – the ratio of normal stress to the volumetric strain produced in a body.

Buoyant force – the upward force on an object immersed in a fluid.

C

Calorie – a unit of heat; 1 Calorie = 4.186 joule.

Candela – the SI unit of luminous intensity defined as the luminous intensity in a given direction of a source that emits monochromatic photons of frequency 540×10^{12} Hz and has a radiant intensity in that direction of 1/683 W/sr.

Capacitance – the ratio of charge stored per increase in potential difference.

Capacitor – electrical device used to store charge and energy in the electrical field.

Capillarity – the rise or fall of a liquid in a tube of very fine bore.

Carnot's theorem – no engine operating between two temperatures can be more efficient than a reversible engine working between the same two temperatures.

Cathode rays – negatively charged particles (electrons) that are emitted from a negative terminal in an evacuated glass tube.

Celsius scale of temperature – the ice-point is taken as the lower fixed point (0 °C), and the steam-point is taken as the upper fixed point (100 °C); the interval between the ice-point and the steam-point is divided into 100 equal divisions; the unit division on this scale is 1 °C; previously called the centigrade scale; the temperatures on the Celsius scale and the Fahrenheit scale are related by the relationship, C/100 = (F – 32) / 180; the temperature of a healthy person is 37 °C or 98.6 °F.

Centrifugal force − an apparent outward force on an object in circular motion; a consequence of the Third Law of Motion.

Centripetal force − the radial force required to keep an object moving in a circular path.

Chain reaction − a self-sustaining reaction where some of the products are able to produce more reactions of the same kind (e.g., in a nuclear chain reaction, neutrons are the products that produce more nuclear reactions in a self-sustaining series).

Charles' Law − for a given mass of a gas at constant pressure, the volume is directly proportional to the temperature.

Chromatic aberration − an optical lens defect causing color fringes due to the lens bringing different colors of light to focus at different points.

Circular motion − the motion of a body along a circular path.

Closed system − the system which cannot exchange heat or matter with the surroundings.

Coefficient of areal expansion − the fractional change in surface area per degree of temperature change; see *Coefficient of thermal expansion.*

Coefficient of linear expansion − the fractional change in length per degree of temperature change; see *Coefficient of thermal expansion.*

Coefficient of thermal expansion − the fractional change in the size of an object per degree of change in temperature at a constant pressure; the SI unit is K^{-1}.

Coefficient of volumetric expansion − the fractional change in volume per degree of temperature change; see *Coefficient of thermal expansion.*

Coherent source − a source in which there is a constant phase difference between waves emitted from different parts of the source.

Compression − a part of a longitudinal wave in which the density of the particles of the medium is higher than the normal density.

Compressive stress − a force that tends to compress the surface as the Earth's plates move into each other.

Condensation (sound) − a compression of gas molecules; a pulse of increased density and pressure that moves through the air at the speed of sound.

Condensation (water vapor) − where more vapor or gas molecules are returning to the liquid state than are evaporating.

Condensation nuclei – tiny particles such as tiny dust, smoke, soot or salt crystals suspended in the air on which water condenses.

Condensation point – the temperature at which a gas or vapor changes back to liquid; see *Boiling point*.

Conduction – the transfer of heat from a region of higher temperature to a region of lower temperature by increased kinetic energy moving from molecule to molecule.

Constructive interference – the condition in which two waves arriving at the same place at the same time and in phase add amplitudes to create a new wave.

Control rods – rods inserted between fuel rods in a nuclear reactor to absorb neutrons and control the rate of the nuclear chain reaction.

Convection – transfer of heat from a region of higher temperature to a region of lower temperature by the displacement of high-energy molecules (e.g., the displacement of warmer, less dense air (higher kinetic energy) by cooler, denser air (lower kinetic energy)).

Conventional current – the opposite of electron current; considers an electric current to consist of a drift of positive charges that flow from the positive terminal to the negative terminal of a battery.

Coulomb – unit used to measure the quantity of electric charge; equivalent to the charge resulting from the transfer of 6.24 billion particles such as the electron.

Coulomb's Law – relationship between charge, distance, and magnitude of the electrical force between two bodies; the force between any two charges is directly proportional to the product of charges and inversely proportional to the square of the distance between the charges.

Covalent bond – a chemical bond formed by the sharing of a pair of electrons.

Covalent compound – chemical compound held together by a covalent bond or bonds.

Crest – the point of maximum positive displacement on a transverse wave.

Critical angle – the limit to the angle of incidence when all light rays are reflected internally.

Critical mass – the mass of fissionable material needed to sustain a chain reaction.

Curvilinear motion – the motion of a body along a curved path.

Cycle – a complete vibration.

Cyclotron – a device used to accelerate the charged particles.

D

De-acceleration − negative acceleration when the velocity of a body decreases with time.

Decibel − unit of the sound level; if P1 & P2 are two amounts of power, the first is said to be n decibels greater, where n = 10 log10 (P1 / P2).

Decibel scale − a nonlinear scale of loudness based on the ratio of the intensity level of a sound to the intensity at the threshold of hearing.

Density − the mass of a substance per unit volume.

Destructive interference − the condition in which two waves arriving at the same point at the same time out of phase add amplitudes that cancel to create zero total disturbance; see *Constructive interference*.

Dewpoint temperature − the temperature at which condensation begins.

Dew − condensation of water vapor into droplets of liquid on surfaces.

Diffraction − the bending of light around the edge of an opaque object.

Diffuse reflection − light rays reflected in many random directions, as opposed to the parallel rays reflected from a perfectly smooth surface such as a mirror.

Diopter − unit of measure of the refractive power of a lens.

Direct current − an electrical current which always flows in one direction.

Direct proportion − when two variables increase or decrease together in the same ratio (at the same rate).

Dispersion − the splitting of white light into its component colors of the spectrum.

Displacement – a vector quantity for the change in the position of an object as it moves in a particular direction; also the shortest distance between the initial position and the final position of a moving body.

Distance − a scalar quantity for the length of the path traveled by a body irrespective of the direction it goes in.

Doppler effect − an apparent change in the frequency of sound or light due to the relative motion between the source of the sound or light and the observer.

E

Echo – a reflected sound that can be distinguished from the original sound, usually arriving 0.1 s or more after the original sound.

Einstein mass-energy relation – $E = mc^2$; E is the energy released, m is the mass defect and c is the speed of light.

Elastic potential energy – the potential energy of a body by virtue of its configuration (i.e., shape).

Elastic strain – an adjustment to stress in which materials recover their original shape after stress is released.

Electric circuit – consists of a voltage source that maintains an electrical potential, a continuous conducting path for a current to follow and a device where work is done by the electrical potential; a switch in the circuit is used to complete or interrupt the conducting path.

Electric current – the flow of electric charge; the electric force field produced by an electrical charge.

Electric field line – an imaginary curve tangent to which at any given point gives the direction of the electric field at that point.

Electric field lines – a map of an electric field representing the direction of the force that a test charge would experience; the direction of an electric field shown by lines of force.

Electric generator – a mechanical device that uses wire loops rotating in a magnetic field to produce electromagnetic induction to generate electricity.

Electric potential energy – potential energy due to the position of a charge near other charges.

Electrical conductors – materials that have electrons that are free to move throughout the material (e.g., metals); allows electric current to flow through the material.

Electrical energy – a form of energy from electromagnetic interactions.

Electric force – a fundamental force that results from the interaction of electrical charges; it is the most powerful force in the universe.

Electrical insulators – electrical nonconductors, or materials that obstruct the flow of electric current.

Electrical nonconductors – materials that have electrons that do not move easily within the material (e.g., rubber); also electrical insulators.

Electrical resistance – the property of opposing or reducing electric current.

Electrolyte – water solution of ionic substances that will conduct an electric current.

Electromagnet − a magnet formed by a solenoid that can be turned on and off by turning the current on and off.

Electromagnetic force − one of four fundamental forces; the force of attraction or repulsion between two charged particles.

Electromagnetic induction − the process in which current is induced in a coil whenever there is a change in the magnetic flux linked with the coil.

Electromagnetic waves − the waves which are due to oscillating electrical and magnetic fields and do not need any material medium for their propagation; can travel through a material medium (e.g., light waves and radio waves); travel in a vacuum with a speed of 3×10 8 m/s.

Electron − subatomic particle that has the smallest negative charge possible; usually found in an orbital of an atom but is gained or lost when atoms become ions.

Electron configuration − the arrangement of electrons in orbits and sub-orbits about the nucleus of an atom.

Electron current – the opposite of conventional current; considers electric current to consist of a drift of negative charges that flows from the negative terminal to the positive terminal of a battery.

Electron pair − a pair of electrons with different spin quantum numbers that may occupy an orbital.

Electron volt − the energy gained by an electron moving across a potential difference of one volt; equal to 1.60×10^{-19} Joules.

Electronegativity − the comparative ability of atoms of an element to attract bonding electrons.

Electrostatic charge − an accumulated electric charge on an object from a surplus of electrons or a deficiency of electrons.

Element − a pure chemical substance that cannot be broken down into anything simpler by chemical or physical means; there are over 100 known elements, the fundamental materials of which all matter is made.

Endothermic process − the process in which heat is absorbed.

Energy − the capacity of a body to do work; a scalar quantity; the SI unit is the Joule; there are five forms: mechanical, chemical, radiant, electrical and nuclear.

Escape velocity − the minimum velocity with which an object must be thrown upward to overcome the gravitational pull and escape into space; the escape velocity depends on the mass and radius of the planet/star, but not on the mass of the body being thrown upward.

Evaporation − process of more molecules leaving a liquid for the gaseous state than returning from the gas to the liquid; can occur at any given temperature from the surface of a liquid; takes place only from the surface of the liquid; causes cooling; faster if the surface of the liquid is large, the temperature is higher, and the surrounding atmosphere does not contain a large amount of vapor of the liquid.

Exothermic process − the process in which heat is evolved.

F

Fahrenheit scale of temperature − the ice-point (lower fixed point) is taken as 32 °F, and the steam-point (upper fixed point) is taken as 212 °F; the interval between these two points is divided into 180 equal divisions; the unit division on the Fahrenheit scale is 1 °F; the temperatures on the Celsius scale and the Fahrenheit scale are related by the relationship, $C/100 = (F − 32) / 180$; the temperature of a healthy person is 37 °C or 98.6 °F.

Farad − the SI unit of capacitance; the capacitance of a capacitor that, if charged to 1 C, has a potential difference of 1 V.

Faraday − the electric charge required to liberate a gram equivalent of a substance; 1 Faraday = 96,485 coulomb/mole.

Fermat's principle − an electromagnetic wave takes a path that involves the least time when propagating between two points.

First Law of Motion – every object remains at rest or in a state of uniform straight-line motion unless acted on by an unbalanced force.

Fluid − matter that has the ability to flow or be poured; the individual molecules of a fluid are able to move, rolling over or by one another.

Focus − the point to which rays that are initially parallel to the axis of a lens or mirror converge or from which they appear to diverge.

Force − a push or pull which tends to change the state of rest or of uniform motion, the direction of motion or the shape and size of a body; a vector quantity; the SI unit is a Newton, denoted by N; one N is the force which when acting on a body of mass 1 kg produces an acceleration of 1 m/s².

Force of gravitation − the force with which two objects attract by their masses; acts even if the two objects are not connected; an action-at-a-distance force.

Fracture strain − an adjustment to stress in which materials crack or break as a result of the stress.

Fraunhofer lines − the dark lines in the spectrum of the sun or a star.

Freefall − the motion of a body falling to Earth with no other force except the force of gravity acting on it; all free-falling bodies are weightless.

Freezing point − the temperature at which a phase change of liquid to solid takes place; the same temperature as the melting point for a given substance.

Frequency − the number of oscillations completed in 1 second by an oscillating body.

Frequency (of oscillations) − the number of oscillations made by an oscillating body per second.

Frequency (of waves) − the number of waves produced per second.

Friction − the force that resists the motion of one surface relative to another with which it is in contact; caused by the humps and crests of surfaces, even those on a microscopic scale; the area of contact is small, and the consequent high pressure leads to local pressure welding of the surface; in motion the welds are broken and remade continually.

Fuel rod − long zirconium alloy tubes containing fissionable material for use in a nuclear reactor.

Fundamental charge – the smallest common charge known; the magnitude of the charge of an electron and a proton, which is 1.60×10^{-19} coulomb.

Fundamental frequency − the lowest frequency (longest wavelength) at which a system vibrates freely and can set up standing waves in an air column or on a string.

Fundamental properties − a property that cannot be defined in simpler terms other than to describe how it is measured; the fundamental properties are length, mass, time and charge.

G

g − symbol representing the acceleration of an object in free fall due to the force of gravity; its magnitude is 9.80 m/s^2.

Gamma (γ) ray − a high energy photon of short wavelength electromagnetic radiation emitted by decaying nuclei (γ-decay).

Gases – a phase of matter composed of molecules that are relatively far apart moving freely in constant, random motion and have weak cohesive forces acting between them, resulting in the characteristic indefinite shape and indefinite volume of a gas.

Graham's Law of Diffusion – the rate of diffusion of a gas is inversely proportional to the square root of its density.

Gram-atomic weight – the mass in grams of one mole of an element that is numerically equal to its atomic weight.

Gram-formula weight – the mass in grams of one mole of a compound that is numerically equal to its formula weight.

Gram-molecular weight – the gram-formula weight of a molecular compound.

Gravitational constant G – appears in the equation for Newton's Law of Gravitation; numerically, it is equal to the force of gravitation, which acts between two bodies with a mass of 1 kg each separated by a distance of 1 m; the value of G is 6.67×10^{-11} Nm²/kg².

Gravitational potential at a point – the amount of work done against the gravitational forces to move a particle of unit mass from infinity to that point.

Gravitational potential energy – the potential energy possessed by a body by virtue of its height from the ground; equals *mgh*.

Gravity – the gravitational attraction at the surface of a planet or other celestial body.

Greenhouse effect – the process of increasing the temperature of the lower parts of the atmosphere through redirecting energy back toward the surface; the absorption and re-emission of infrared radiation by carbon dioxide, water vapor, and a few other gases in the atmosphere.

Ground state – the energy state of an atom with its electrons at the lowest energy state possible for that atom.

H

Half-life – the time required for one-half of the unstable nuclei in a radioactive substance to decay into a new element.

Heat – a form of energy that makes a body hot or cold; measured by the temperature-effect, it produces in any material body; the SI unit is the Joule (J).

Heisenberg uncertainty principle – states that there is a fundamental limit to the precision with which certain pairs of physical properties of a particle (i.e., **complementary variables**) can be known simultaneously (e.g., one cannot measure both the exact momentum and the exact position of a subatomic particle at the same time – the more one is certain of one, the less certain one can be of the other).

Hertz – unit of frequency (Hz); equivalent to one cycle per second.

Hooke's Law – within the elastic limit, stress is directly proportional to strain.

Horsepower – unit of power; 1 hp = 746 Watts.

Humidity – the ratio of water vapor in a sample of air to the volume of the sample.

Huygens' principle – each point on a light wavefront can be regarded as a source of secondary waves, the envelope of these secondary waves determining the position of the wavefront at a later time.

Hypothesis – a tentative explanation of a phenomenon that is compatible with the data and provides a framework for understanding and describing that phenomenon.

I

Ice-point – the melting point of ice under 1 atm pressure; equal to 0 °C or 32 °F.

Ideal gas equation – $PV = nRT$.

Impulse – equal to the product of the force acting on a body and the time for which it acts; if the force is variable, the impulse is the integral of Fd_t from t_0 to t_1; the impulse of a force acting for a given time interval is equal to change in momentum produced over that interval; $J = m(v - u)$, assuming that the mass m remains constant while the velocity changes from v to u; the SI units are kg m/s.

Impulsive force – the force which acts on a body for a short time but produces a large change in the momentum of the body.

Incandescent – matter emitting visible light as a result of high temperature (e.g., a light bulb, a flame from any burning source, the Sun).

Incident ray – line representing the direction of motion of incoming light approaching a boundary.

Index of refraction – the ratio of the speed of light in a vacuum to the speed of light in a material.

Inertia − the property of matter that causes it to resist any change in its state of rest or of uniform motion; there are three kinds of inertia: the inertia of rest, the inertia of motion and the inertia of direction; the mass of a body is a measure of its inertia.

Infrasonic − sound waves at a frequency below the range of human hearing (less than 20 Hz).

Insulators − materials that are poor conductors of heat or electricity (e.g., wood or glass); materials with air pockets slow down the movement of heat because the air molecules are far apart.

Intensity − a measure of the energy carried by a wave.

Interference − the redistribution of energy due to the superposition of waves with a phase difference from coherent sources, resulting in alternate light and dark bands.

Intermolecular forces − forces of interaction between molecules.

Internal energy – the sum of the kinetic energy and potential energy of all molecules of an object.

Inverse proportion − the relationship in which the value of one variable increases while the value of a second variable decreases at the same rate (in the same ratio).

Ionization − process of forming ions from molecules.

Ionized − an atom or a particle that has a net charge because it has gained or lost electrons.

Isobaric process − in which pressure remains constant.

Isochoric process − in which volume remains constant.

Isostasy − a balance or equilibrium between adjacent blocks of Earth's crust.

Isothermal process − in which temperature remains constant.

Isotope − atoms of the same element with the same atomic number (i.e., number of protons) but with a different mass number (i.e., number of neutrons).

J

Joule − the unit used to measure work and energy; can also be used to measure heat; $1 \text{ J} = 1 \text{N·m}$.

Joule's Law of Heating – states that the heat produced when a current (I) flows through a resistor (R) for a given time (t) is given by $Q = I^2 R t$.

K

Kelvin scale of temperature − the ice-point (the lower fixed point) is taken as 273.15 K, and the steam-point (the upper fixed point) is taken as 373.15 K; the interval between these two points is divided into 100 equal parts; each division is equal to 1K.

Kelvin's statement of Second Law of Thermodynamics − it is impossible that, at the end of a cycle of changes, heat has been extracted from a reservoir and an equal amount of work has been produced without producing some other effect.

Kepler's Laws of Planetary Motion − the three laws describing the motion of the planets.

Kepler's First Law – in planetary motion, each planet moves in an elliptical orbit, with the Sun located at one focus.

Kepler's Second Law – a radius vector between the Sun and a planet moves over equal areas of the ellipse during equal time intervals.

Kepler's Third Law – the square of the period of an orbit is directly proportional to the cube of the radius of the major axis of the orbit.

Kilocalorie − the amount of energy required to raise the temperature of 1 kg of water by 1 °C; 1 Kcal = 1,000 calorie.

Kilogram − the fundamental unit of mass in the metric system of measurement.

Kinetic energy − energy possessed by a body due to its motion; $KE = \frac{1}{2}mv^2$, where m is mass and v is velocity.

L

Laser − a device that produces a coherent stream of light through stimulated emission of radiation.

Latent heat − energy released or absorbed by a body during a constant-temperature phase change.

Latent heat of vaporization − the heat absorbed when one gram of a substance changes from the liquid phase to the gaseous phase; also, the heat released when one gram of gas changes from the gaseous phase to the liquid phase.

Latent heat of fusion − the quantity of heat required to convert one-unit mass of a substance from a solid state to a liquid state at its melting point without any change in its temperature; the SI unit is J kg^{-1}.

Latent heat of sublimation − the quantity of heat required to convert one unit of mass of a substance from a solid state to a gaseous state without any change in its temperature.

Law of Conservation of Energy – states that energy can neither be created nor destroyed, but can be transformed from one form to another.

Law of Conservation of Mass – states that mass (including single atoms) can neither be created nor destroyed in a chemical reaction.

Law of Conservation of Matter – states that matter can neither be created nor destroyed in a chemical reaction.

Law of Conservation of Momentum – states that the total momentum of a group of interacting objects remains constant in the absence of external forces.

Lenz's Law – states that the induced current always flows in such a direction that it opposes the cause producing it.

Light-year – the distance that light travels in a vacuum in one year (365.25 days); approximately 9.46×10^{15} m.

Line spectrum – an emission (of light, sound or other radiation) spectrum consisting of separate isolated lines (discrete frequencies or energies); can be used to identify the elements in a matter of unknown composition.

Lines of force – lines drawn to make an electric field strength map, with each line originating on a positive charge and ending on a negative charge; each line represents a path on which a charge would experience a constant force; having the lines closer indicates a stronger electric field.

Liquids – a phase of matter composed of molecules that have interactions stronger than those found in gas but not strong enough to keep the molecules near the equilibrium positions of a solid, resulting in the characteristic definite volume but the indefinite shape of a liquid.

Liter – a metric system unit of volume; usually used for liquids.

Longitudinal strain – the ratio of change in the length of a body to its initial length.

Longitudinal waves – the wave in which the particles of the medium oscillate along the direction of propagation of a wave (e.g., sound waves).

Loudness – a subjective interpretation of a sound that is related to the energy of the vibrating source, related to the condition of the transmitting medium and the distance involved.

Luminosity – the total amount of energy radiated into space each second from the surface of a star.

Luminous – an object or objects that produce visible light (e.g., the Sun, stars, light bulbs, burning materials).

Lyman series – a group of lines in the ultraviolet region in the spectrum of hydrogen.

M

Magnetic domain − tiny physical regions in permanent magnets, approximately 0.01 to 1 mm, that have magnetically aligned atoms, giving the domain an overall polarity.

Magnetic field − the region around a magnet where its magnetic force is experienced by other magnetic objects; a model used to describe how magnetic forces on moving charges act at a distance.

Magnetic poles − the ends, or sides, of a magnet about which the force of magnetic attraction seems to be concentrated.

Magnetic quantum number − from quantum mechanics model of the atom, one of four descriptions of the energy state of an electron wave; describes the energy of an electron orbital as the orbital is oriented in space by an external magnetic field, a kind of energy sub-sublevel.

Magnetic reversal − the changing of polarity of the Earth's magnetic field as the north magnetic pole and the south magnetic pole exchange positions.

Magnetic wave − the spread of magnetization from a small portion of a substance where an abrupt change in the magnetic field has taken place.

Magnification − the ratio of the size of the image to the size of the object.

Magnitude − the size of a measurement of a vector; scalar quantities that consist of a number and unit only.

Malus Law – states that the intensity of the light transmitted from the analyzer varies directly as the square of the cosine of the angle between the plane of transmission of the analyzer and the polarizer.

Maser − microwave amplification by stimulated emission of radiation.

Mass − the quantity of matter contained in a body; the SI unit is the kg; remains the same everywhere; a measure of inertia, which means resistance to a change of motion.

Mass defect − the difference between the sum of the masses of the individual nucleons forming a nucleus and the mass of that nucleus.

Mass number − the sum of the number of protons and neutrons in a nucleus; used to identify isotopes (e.g., Uranium^{238}).

Matter − anything that occupies space and has mass.

Mean life − the average time during which a system, such as an atom or a nucleus, exists in a specified form.

Mechanical energy − the sum of the potential energy and the kinetic energy of a body; energy associated with the position of a body.

Mechanical wave − those waves that need a material medium for their propagation (e.g., sound waves and water waves); also elastic waves.

Megahertz − unit of frequency; equal to 106 Hertz.

Melting point − the temperature at which a phase change of solid to liquid takes place.

Metal − matter having the physical properties of conductivity, malleability, ductility, and luster.

Meter − the fundamental metric unit of length.

MeV − unit of energy; equal to 1.6×10^{-13} joules.

Millibar − a measure of atmospheric pressure equivalent to 1,000 dynes per cm^2.

Miscible fluids − fluids that can mix in any proportion.

Mixture − matter made of unlike parts that have a variable composition and can be separated into their component parts by physical means.

Model − a mental or physical representation of something that cannot be observed directly; usually used as an aid to understanding.

Modulus of elasticity − the ratio of stress to the strain produced in a body.

Modulus of rigidity − the ratio of tangential stress to the shear strain produced in a body.

Mole − the amount of a substance that contains Avogadro's number of atoms, ions, molecules or any other chemical unit; 6.02×10^{23} atoms, ions or other chemical units.

Momentum − a measure of the quantity of motion in a body; the product of the mass and the velocity of a body; SI units are kg·m /s.

Monochromatic light − consisting of a single wavelength.

N

Natural frequency − the frequency of oscillation of an elastic object in the absence of external forces; depends on the size, composition, and shape of the object.

Negative electric charge − one of the two types of electric charge; repels other negative charges and attracts positive charges.

Negative ion − atom or particle that has a surplus or imbalance of electrons and a negative charge.

Net force − the resulting force after all vector forces have been added; if a net force is zero, all the vector forces have canceled, and there is not an unbalanced force.

Newton (N) − a unit of force defined as kg·m/s^2; 1 Newton is needed to accelerate a 1 kg mass by 1 m/s^2.

Newton's First Law of Motion − a body continues in a state of rest or of uniform motion in a straight line unless it is acted upon by an external (unbalanced) force.

Newton's Law of Gravitation − the gravitational force of attraction acting between any two particles is directly proportional to the product of their masses and inversely proportional to the square of the distance between them; the force of attraction acts along the line joining the two particles; real bodies having spherical symmetry act as point masses with their mass assumed to be concentrated at their center of mass.

Newton's Second Law of Motion − the rate of change of momentum is equal to the force applied; the force acting on a body is directly proportional to the product of its mass and acceleration produced by force in the body.

Newton's Third Law of Motion − states that to every action there is an equal and opposite reaction; the action and the reaction act on two different bodies simultaneously.

Noise − sounds made up of groups of waves of random frequency and intensity.

Non-uniform acceleration − when the velocity of a body increases by unequal amounts in equal intervals of time.

Non-uniform speed − when a body travels unequal distances in equal intervals of time.

Non-uniform velocity − when a body covers unequal distances in equal intervals of time in a particular direction, or when it covers equal distances in equal intervals but changes its direction.

Normal − a line perpendicular to the surface of a boundary.

Nuclear energy − the form of energy from reactions involving the nucleus.

Nuclear fission − the splitting of a heavy nucleus into more stable, lighter nuclei with an accompanying release of energy.

Nuclear force − one of four fundamental forces; a strong force of attraction that operates over short distances between subatomic particles; overcomes the electric repulsion of protons in a nucleus and binds the nucleus together.

Nuclear fusion − nuclear reaction of low mass nuclei fusing together to form a more stable and more massive nucleus with an accompanying release of energy.

Nuclear reactor – a steel vessel in which a controlled chain reaction of fissionable materials releases energy.

Nucleons – a collective name for protons and neutrons in the nucleus of an atom.

Nucleus – the central, positively charged, dense portion of an atom; contains protons and neutrons.

O

Ohm – unit of resistance; 1 ohm = 1 volt/ampere.

Ohm's Law – states that the current flowing through a conductor is directly proportional to the potential difference across the ends of the conductor.

Open system – a system across whose boundaries both matter and energy can pass.

Optical fiber – a long, thin thread of fused silica; used to transmit light; based on total internal reflection.

Orbital – the region of space around the nucleus of an atom where an electron is likely to be found.

Origin – the only point on a graph where the x and the y variables both have a value of zero at the same time.

Oscillatory motion – the to and fro motion (periodic in nature) of a body about its mean position; also vibratory motion.

P

Pascal – a unit of pressure, equal to the pressure resulting from a force of 1 Newton acting uniformly over an area of 1 m^2.

Pascal's Law – states that the pressure exerted on a liquid is transmitted equally in all directions.

Paschen series – a group of lines in the infrared region in the spectrum of hydrogen.

Pauli exclusion principle – no two electrons in an atom can have the same four quantum numbers; a maximum of two electrons can occupy a given orbital.

Peltier effect – the evolution or absorption of heat at the junction of two dissimilar metals carrying current.

Period (of a wave) − the time taken by a wave to travel through a distance equal to its wavelength; denoted by T; time period of a wave = 1/frequency of the wave.

Period (of an oscillation) − the time taken to complete one oscillation; does not depend upon the mass of the bob and amplitude of oscillation; directly proportional to the square root of the length and inversely proportional to the square root of the acceleration due to gravity.

Periodic wave − a wave in which the particles of the medium oscillate continuously about their mean positions regularly at fixed intervals of time.

Periodic motion − a motion which repeats itself at regular intervals of time.

Permeability − the ability to transmit fluids through openings, small passageways or gaps.

Phase – when the particles in a wave are in the same state of vibration (i.e., in the same position and in the same direction of motion).

Phase change − the action of a substance changing from one state of matter to another; always absorbs or releases internal potential energy that is not associated with a temperature change.

Photons − quanta of energy in the light wave; the particle associated with light.

Photoelectric effect − the emission of electrons in some materials when the light of a suitable frequency falls on them.

Physical change − a change of the state of a substance but not in the identity of the substance.

Planck's constant − proportionality constant in the ratio of the energy of vibrating molecules to their frequency of vibration; a value of 6.63×10^{-34} J·s.

Plasma − a phase of matter; a very hot highly ionized gas consisting of electrons and atoms that have been stripped of their electrons because of high kinetic energies.

Plasticity − the property of a solid whereby it undergoes a permanent change in shape or size when subjected to a stress.

Plastic strain − an adjustment to stress in which materials become molded or bent out of shape under stress and do not return to their original shape after the stress is released.

Polarized Light − light whose constituent transverse waves are all vibrating in the same plane.

Polaroid − a film that transmits only polarized light.

Polaroid or polarizer − a device that produces polarized light.

Positive electric charge − one of the two types of electric charge; repels other positive charges and attracts negative charges.

Positive ion − atom or particle that has a net positive charge due to an electron or electrons being torn away.

Positron − an elementary particle having the same mass as that of an electron but equal and positive charge.

Potential Energy − energy possessed by a body by virtue of its position or configuration; see *Gravitational potential energy* and *Elastic potential energy*.

Power − scalar quantity for the rate of doing work; the SI unit is Watt; 1 W = 1 J/s.

Pressure – **a** measure of force per unit area (e.g., kilograms per square meter (kg/m^2).

Primary coil − part of a transformer; a coil of wire connected to a source of alternating current.

Primary colors − three colors (red, yellow and blue) which can be combined in various proportions to produce any other color.

Principal quantum number − from quantum mechanics model of the atom, one of four descriptions of the energy state of an electron wave; describes the main energy level of an electron in terms of its most probable distance from the nucleus.

Principle of calorimetry – states that if two bodies of different temperature are in thermal contact, and no heat is allowed to go out or enter into the system, then heat lost by the body with higher temperature is equal to the heat gained by the body of lower temperature (i.e., heat lost = heat gained).

Progressive wave − a wave which transfers energy from one part of a medium to another.

Projectile − an object thrown into space either horizontally or at an acute angle and under the action of gravity; the path followed by a projectile is its trajectory; the horizontal distance traveled by a projectile is its range; the time is taken from the moment it is thrown until the moment it hits the ground is its time of flight.

Proof − a measure of ethanol concentration of an alcoholic beverage; double the concentration by volume (e.g., 50% by volume is 100 proof).

Properties − qualities or attributes that, taken together, are usually unique to an object (e.g., color, texture, and size).

Proportionality constant − a constant applied to a proportionality statement that transforms the statement into an equation.

Pulse – a wave of short duration confined to a small portion of the medium at any given time; also a wave pulse.

Q

Quanta – fixed amounts; usually referring to fixed amounts of energy absorbed or emitted by matter.

Quantum limit – the shortest wavelength; present in a continuous x-ray spectrum.

Quantum mechanics – model of the atom based on the wave nature of subatomic particles and the mechanics of electron waves; also wave mechanics.

Quantum numbers – numbers that describe the energy states of an electron; in the Bohr model of the atom, the orbit quantum numbers could be any whole number (e.g., 1, 2, 3, etc.); in the quantum mechanics model of the atom, four quantum numbers are used to describe the energy state of an electron wave (*n, m, l,* and *s*).

Quark – one of the hypothetical basic particles; has a charge with magnitudes of one-third or two-thirds of the charge on an electron.

R

Rad – a measure of radiation received by a material (radiation-absorbed dose).

Radiant energy – the form of energy that can travel through space (e.g., visible light and other parts of the electromagnetic spectrum).

Radiation – the emission and propagation of waves transmitting energy through space or through some medium.

Radioactive decay – the natural, spontaneous disintegration or decomposition of a nucleus.

Radioactive decay constant – a specific constant for a particular isotope that is the ratio of the rate of nuclear disintegration per unit of time to the total number of radioactive nuclei.

Radioactive decay series – series of decay reactions that begins with one radioactive nucleus that decays to a second nucleus that decays to a third nucleus and so on, until a stable nucleus is reached.

Radioactive decay law – the rate of disintegration of a radioactive substance is directly proportional to the number of undecayed nuclei.

Radioactivity – spontaneous emission of particles or energy from an atomic nucleus as it disintegrates.

Rarefaction – a part of a longitudinal wave in which the density of the particles of the medium is less than the normal density.

Real image − an image generated by a lens or mirror that can be projected onto a screen.

Rectilinear motion − the motion of a body in a straight line.

Reflected ray − a line representing the direction of motion of light reflected from a boundary.

Refraction − the bending of a light wave, a sound wave or another wave from its straight-line path as it travels from one medium to another.

Refractive index − the ratio of the speed of light in a vacuum to that in the medium.

Relative density – (also referred to as *specific gravity*) is the ratio of the density (mass of a unit volume) of a substance to the density of given reference material. *Specific gravity* usually means relative density with respect to water. The term *relative density* is more common in modern scientific usage.

Relative humidity − the percentage of the amount of water vapor present in a certain volume of the air to the amount of water vapor needed to saturate it.

Resolving power − a quantitative measure of the ability of an optical instrument to produce separable images of different points of an object.

Resonance − when the frequency of an external force matches the natural frequency of the body.

Restoring force − the force which tends to bring an oscillating body back to its mean position whenever it is displaced from the mean position.

Resultant force − a single force, which acts on a body to produce the same effect on it as done by all other forces collectively; see *Balanced forces*.

Reverberation − apparent increase in the volume of sound caused by reflections from the boundary surfaces, usually arriving within 0.1 seconds after the original sound.

Rigid body − an idealized extended body whose size and shape is fixed and remains unaltered when forces are applied.

S

Saturated air − air in which an equilibrium exists between evaporation and condensation; the relative humidity will be 100 percent.

Saturated solution − the apparent limit to dissolving a given solid in a specified amount of water at a given temperature; a state of equilibrium that exists between dissolving solute and solute coming out of solution.

Scalar quantity − a physical quantity described completely by its magnitude.

Scientific law − a relationship between quantities; usually described by an equation in the physical sciences; describes a wider range of phenomena and is more important than a scientific principle.

Scientific principle − a relationship between quantities concerned with a specific or narrow range of observations and behavior.

Second − the standard unit of time in both the metric and English systems of measurement.

Second Law of Motion − the acceleration of an object is directly proportional to the net force acting on that object and inversely proportional to the mass of the object.

Secondary coil − part of a transformer; a coil of wire in which the voltage of the original alternating current in the primary coil can be stepped up or down by way of electromagnetic induction.

Second's pendulum − a simple pendulum whose time period on the surface of the Earth is 2 seconds.

Semiconductors − elements whose electrical conductivity is intermediate between that of a conductor and an insulator.

Shear strain − the ratio of the relative displacements of one plane to its distance from the fixed plane.

Shear stress − the restoring force developed per unit area when deforming force acts tangentially to the surface of a body, producing a change in the shape of the body without any change in volume.

Siemens − the derived SI unit of electrical conductance; equal to the conductance of an element that has a resistance of 1 ohm; also written as ohm^{-1}.

Simple harmonic motion − the vibratory motion that occurs when the restoring force is proportional to the displacement from the mean position and is directed opposite to the displacement.

Simple pendulum − a heavy point mass (actually a small metallic ball), suspended by a light inextensible string from the frictionless rigid support; a simple machine based on the effect of gravity.

Snell's Law − states that the ratio of sin i to sin r is a constant and is equal to the refractive index of the second medium with respect to the first.

Solenoid − a cylindrical coil of wire that becomes electromagnetic when a current is run through it.

Solids − a phase of matter with molecules that remain close to fixed equilibrium positions due to strong interactions between the molecules, resulting in the characteristic definite shape and definite volume of a solid.

Sonic boom – sound waves that pile up into a shock wave when a source is traveling at or faster than the speed of sound.

Specific gravity – see *Relative density*.

Specific heat – the amount of heat energy required to increase the temperature of 1 g of a substance by 1 °C; each substance has its specific heat value.

Speed – a scalar quantity for the distance traveled by a body per unit of time; if a body covers the distance in time, then its speed is given by distance/time; SI units are m/s.

Spin quantum number – from quantum mechanics model of the atom, one of four descriptions of the energy state of an electron wave; describes the spin orientation of an electron relative to an external magnetic field.

Standing waves – the condition where two waves of equal frequency traveling in opposite directions meet and form stationary regions of maximum displacement due to constructive interference and stationary regions of zero displacement due to destructive interference.

State of motion – when a body changes its position with respect to a fixed point in its surroundings; the states of rest and motion are relative to the frame of reference.

State of rest – when a body does not change its position with respect to a fixed point in its surrounding; the states of rest and motion are relative to the frame of reference.

Steam-point – the temperature of steam over pure boiling water under 1 atm pressure; taken as the upper fixed point (100 °C or 212 °F) for temperature scales.

Stefan-Boltzmann Law – the amount of energy radiated per second per unit area of a perfectly black body, is directly proportional to the fourth power of the absolute temperature of the surface of the body.

Superconductors – some materials in which, under certain conditions, the electrical resistance approaches zero.

Super-cooled – water in the liquid phase when the temperature is below the freezing point.

Supersaturated – containing more than the normal saturation amount of a solute at a given temperature.

Surface tension – the property of a liquid due to which its surface behaves like a stretched membrane.

T

Temperature – a numerical measure of the hotness or coldness of a body; according to the molecular model, it is a measure of the average kinetic energy of the molecules of the body; heat flows from a body at higher temperature to a body at a lower temperature.

Tensional stress – the opposite of compressional stress; occurs when one part of a plate moves away from another part that does not move.

Tesla – the SI unit of magnetic flux density; the magnetic flux density of a magnetic flux of 1 Wb through an area of 1 m^2.

Thermal Capacity – the quantity of heat required to raise the temperature of the whole body by one degree (1 K or 1 °C).

Thermal equilibrium – when two bodies in contact are at the same temperature, and there is no flow of heat between them; also, the common temperature of the bodies in thermal equilibrium.

Thermal expansion – the increase in the size of an object when heated.

Thermometer – a device used for the numerical measurement of temperature; the mercury thermometer is commonly used.

Third Law of Motion – whenever two objects interact, the force exerted on one object is equal in size and opposite in direction to the force exerted on the other object; forces always occur in matched pairs that are equal and opposite.

Total internal reflection – condition where all light is reflected back from a boundary between materials; occurs when light travels from a denser to a rarer medium, and the angle of incidence is greater than the critical angle.

Transformation of energy – the conversion of one form of energy into another (e.g., when a body falls, its potential energy is converted to kinetic energy).

Transverse wave – a wave in which the particles of the medium oscillate in a direction perpendicular of the direction of propagation of the wave (e.g., water waves, light waves, radio waves).

Trough – the point of maximum negative displacement on a transverse wave.

U

Ultrasonic − sound waves too high in frequency (above 20,000 Hz) to be heard by the human ear.

Unbalanced forces − when a number of forces act on a body and the resultant force is not zero.

Uniform acceleration − when the velocity of a body increases by equal amounts in equal intervals of time.

Uniform circular motion − the motion of an object in a circular path with uniform speed; accelerated motion.

Uniform speed − when a body travels equal distances in equal intervals of time.

Uniform velocity − when a body travels along a straight line in a particular direction and covers equal distances in equal intervals of time.

Universal Law of Gravitation − every object in the universe is attracted to every other object with force directly proportional to the product of their masses and inversely proportional to the square of the distance between the centers of the two masses.

Unpolarized light − light consisting of transverse waves vibrating in all possible random directions.

V

Van der Waals force − general term for weak attractive intermolecular forces.

Vapor − the gaseous state of a substance that is normally in a liquid state.

Vector quantity − a quantity which needs both magnitude and direction to describe it.

Velocity − distance traveled by a body in a particular direction per unit time; the displacement of the body per unit time; a vector quantity; the SI units are m/s.

Vibration − a back and forth motion that repeats itself.

Virtual image − an image formed when the reflected or refracted light rays appear to meet; this image cannot be projected on a screen.

Volt − unit of potential difference equivalent to joules/coulomb.

Voltage drop − the difference in electric potential across a resistor or other part of a circuit that consumes power.

W

Watt − SI unit for power; equivalent to joule/s.

Wave − a disturbance or oscillation that moves through a medium.

Wavelength − the distance between the two nearest points on a wave which are in the same phase; the distance between two adjacent crests or two adjacent troughs.

Wave (mechanical) − a periodic disturbance produced in a material medium due to the vibratory motion of the particles of the medium.

Wave mechanics − alternate name for quantum mechanics derived from the wavelike properties of subatomic particles.

Wave motion − the movement of a disturbance from one part of a medium to another involving the transfer of energy but not the transfer of matter.

Wave period − the time required for two successive crests or other successive parts of the wave to pass a given point.

Wave velocity − the distance traveled by a wave in one second; it depends on the nature of the medium through which it passes.

Weight − the force with which a body is attracted towards the center of the Earth; the SI unit is N; the gravitational units are kg·wt and g·wt; the weight of a body is given by *mg*.

Weightlessness − the state when the apparent weight of a body becomes zero; all objects while falling freely under the action of gravity are seemingly weightless.

Wien's Displacement Law − states that for a black body, the product of the wavelength corresponding to its maximum radiance and its absolute temperature is constant.

Work − work is done when a force acting on a body displaces it; Work = Force × Displacement in the direction of the force; work is a scalar quantity; the SI unit is Joule.

Y

Young's modulus of elasticity − the ratio of normal stress to the longitudinal strain produced in a body.

Z

Zeeman effect − the splitting of the spectral lines in a spectrum when the source is exposed to a magnetic field.

Zeroth Law of Thermodynamics – states that if body A is in thermal equilibrium with body B, and B is also in thermal equilibrium with C, then A is necessarily in thermal equilibrium with C.

We want to hear from you

Your feedback is important to us because we strive to provide the highest quality prep materials. Email us if you have any questions, comments or suggestions, so we can incorporate your feedback into future editions.

Customer Satisfaction Guarantee

If you have any concerns about this book, including printing issues, contact us and we will resolve any issues to your satisfaction.

info@sterling-prep.com

We reply to all emails – please check your spam folder

Thank you for choosing our products to achieve your educational goals!

To access online AP tests at a special pricing visit:
http://ap.sterling-prep.com/bookowner.htm

Please, leave your Customer Review on Amazon

Made in the USA
Middletown, DE
23 August 2019